URBAN SLUMS AND POVERTY

URBAN SLUMS
AND
POVERTY

Edited by

Dr. (Mrs.) D. Sai Sujatha

Post-Graduate

Associate Professor

Deptt. of Population Studies and Social Work

Sri Venkateshwara University

Tirupati (Andhra Pradesh)

(INDIA)

DISCOVERY PUBLISHING HOUSE PVT. LTD.

NEW DELHI-110 002

Published by:
Tilak Wasan

DISCOVERY PUBLISHING HOUSE PVT. LTD.
4383/4B, Ansari Road, Darya Ganj
New Delhi-110 002 (India)
Phone : +91-11-23279245, 43596064-65
Fax : +91-11-23253475
E-mail : parul.wasan@gmail.com
discoverypublishinghouse@gmail.com
web : www.discoverypublishinggroup.com

First Edition: **2012**
ISBN: 978-93-5056-127-0

Urban Slums and Poverty

Printed at:
Shree Balaji Art Press
Delhi

Preface

Ugly, Chaotic and unhygienic, slums are seen as the bane of Indian cities. They are, however, an important part of the urbanization process and cannot be wished away. The solution lies in recognizing them as rapidly evolving ecosystems that play an important role in naturalizing rural migrants into the urban land scape. All developed countries have had to deal with slums at some stage. This means we should anticipate slums and design for them rather than dream about "slum-free" cities. Indian politicians, policy-makers and intellectuals like to talk about "development', uttering pious words about investment in agriculture. However, the process of development essentially requires the shifting of people from subsistence farming to othr forms of livelihood. Urbanization is the spatial mirror of this process. This is why every developed country is urbanized and they have all seen an urban explosion at some point in their past.

In the next 30 years, 350 million people have to be accommodated in our cities and towns as well as brand new urban spaces. More poor migrants are moving into the cities in particular to slums. The poor do not need charity. They need a property ladder that they can climb. There are many ways to create this ladder. The government should not see its intervention as a subsidy scheme. Instead, it should invest in the commons even as it encourages a functioning real estate market for the poor.

The present book contains articles on various issues of urban slums and poverty, on their living conditions, urban poverty, poverty alleviation, housing situation, and impact on housing along with a focuss on disabled, child labour and street children. These articles can provide an insight on the overall view about the various aspects of urbal slums and its problems due to growing urbanization.

This book is a backdrop of the National Seminar on "Growing Urbanization: Basic Amenities Challenges and Strategies" with special focuss on urban slums and the academicians of different universities and organizations examined the various challenges, to provide the strategies for improving the living conditions of the urban poor. It provides a wealth of information and analysis that will benefit the policy-makers, implementing agencies, civil societies, academicians, students and above all, the slum dwellers to get a better understanding of living conditions in slums and its associated problems.

I am grateful to Andhra Pradesh State Council of Higher Education, Hyderabad, and the Indian Council of Social Science Research, New Delhi, for their financial support to organize the seminar. I convey my profound gratitude to all the contributors for their contribution to this volume. I am highly thankful to all those who helped me directly and indirectly in bringing out this volume.

Dr. (Mrs.) D. Sai Sujatha

Contents

List of Contributors

Dr. Venkateswarlu, Professor, Department of Sociology, S.V. University, Tirupat 517 502.

Mrs. P. Sobha, Research Scholar, Department of Sociology, S.V. University, Tirupati 517 502.

Dr. D. Sai Sujatha, Associate Professor, Department of Population Studies and Social Work, S.V. University, Tirupati 517 502.

Mr. P. Rasidulla, Research Scholar, Department of Population Studies and Social Work, S.V. University, Tirupati 517 502.

Dr. K. Hymavathi, Senior Project Personnel, Young Lives (International) Project (DFID), SPMVV, Tirupati 517 502.

Dr. R. Srinivas, Assistant Professor, Department of Social Work, Acharya Nagarjuna University, Ongole Campus, Ongole 523 001.

Mr. T. Mallikarjuna, Research Scholar, Department of Sociology, S.V. University, Tirupati.

Dr. Janaki Ramaiah, Associate Professor, Department of Sociology, S.V. University, Tirupati.

Prof. V. Reddeppa Naidu, Professor, Department of Sociology, S.V. University, Tirupati.

Dr. **Saraswati Raju Iyer**, Assistant Professor, Department of Sociology and Social Work, Acharya Nagarjuna University, Nagarjuna Nagar, Guntur 522501.

Mrs. A. Jyotsna, Young Professional, Young Professionalist (CAPART), Counsil for Social Devolopment, Hyderabad.

Mr. B. Venkata Subba Reddy, Academic Consultant, Department of Social Work Vikrama Simhapuri University, Nellore.

Mrs. V. Usha Reddy, Assistant Professor, Department of EEE, SVU College of Engineering, Tirupati.

Ms. N. Anitha, Final Year B.Tech Student, S.V. University College of Engineering, Tirupati.

Dr. T. Ramashri, Associate Professor, Department of EEE, SVU College of Engineering, Tirupati.

Mr. P. Murali Dhar, Research Scholar, Department of Geography, Sri Venkateswara University, Tirupati.

Mrs.V. Nirmala, Academic Consultant, Department, of Human Rights, Sri Venkateswara University, Tirupati.

Dr. Marri Padmaja, Assistant Professor, Centre for South East Asia Pacific Studies, S.V. University, Tirupati.

Ms. Khim Kumari Kausila, Master in Disability Rehabilitation Administration, Management Trainee, National Institute for the Mentally Handicapped (NIMH), Manovikas Nagar, Secunderabad, Andhra Pradesh 500 009.

Ms. V. Prakasini, Research Scholar, Department, of Sociology and Social Work, Acharya Nagarjuna University, Nagarjuna Nagar, Guntur 522501.

Dr. R. K. Anuradha, Associate Professor, Department of Home Science, S.V. University, Tirupati.

Mrs. K. Tirumala, Research Scholar, Department of Home Science, S.V. University, Tirupati.

Mr. G. Sudhakar, Research Scholar, Department of Home Science, S.V. University, Tirupati.

Mrs. R. Hemalatha, Research Scholar, Department of Home Science, S.V. University, Tirupati.

Dr. P. Subbarama Raju, Assistant Professor, Department of Social Work, Vikrama Simhapuri University, Nellore 524 003.

Mr. M. Mallesh Naik, MSW Student, Department of Social Work, Vikrama Simhapuri University, Nellore 524 003.

Mr. V. Hari Babu, MSW Student, Department of Social Work, Vikrama Simhapuri University, Nellore 524 003.

Ms. M.V. Chandini, III Btech Student, SITS, Puttur.

Dr. K. Rajasekhar, Associate Professor, Department of Population Studies and Social Work, S.V. University, Tirupati.

Dr. V. Sunitha, Department of Social Work, Sri Padmavathi Mahila Viswa Vidyalayam, Tirupati.

Dr. K. Suneetha, Asst, Professor, Department of Social Work, Vikrama Simhapuri University, Nellore 524 003.

Prof. K. Surekha Rao, Former Professor, Department of Social Work, Sri Padmavathi Mahila Viswa Vidyalayam, Tirupati 517 502.

Mr. D. Mahammad Rafi, MSW Student, Department. of Population Studies and Social Work, S.V. University, Tirupati 517 502.

Dr. P. Subramanyachary, Assistant Professor, Department of MBA, SIET, Puttur, Chittoor District.

Dr. C. Sheela Reddy, Assistant Professor, Department of Political Science and Public Administration, S.V. University, Tirupati.

Dr. V. Satish Reddy, Department, of Political Science and Public Administration, S.V. University, Tirupati.

Mrs. S. Vidyalatha, Research Scholar Department of Population Studies and Social Work, S.V. University, Tirupati.

Mrs. K. Sujatha, Head, Department, of Population Studies, S.P.W. College, Tirupati.

Dr. M. Reddi Ramu, Assistant Professor, Siddartha Institute of Engineering and Technology, Narayanavanam Road, Puttur, Chittoor (District).

Mr. P. Subramanyam, Research Assistant, Centre for Gandhian Studies, S.V. University, Tirupati.

Mrs. P. Tavitamma, Assistant Professor, Department of Social Work, Sri Padmavathi Mahila University,Tirupati.

Mrs. K. Srilakshmi, Academic Consultant, Department of Social Work, Sri Padmavathi Mahila University, Tirupati.

Tirupati City with Many Slums

Dr. Venkateswarlu
P. Sobha

INTRODUCTION

The ancient and sacred temple of Sri Venkateswara is located on the seventh peak, Venkatachala (Venkata Hill) of Sri Venkateswara Swamy against the backdrop of the Golden Vimanam the Tirupati Hill, and lies on the southern banks of Sri Swami Pushkarini.

It is by the Lord's presidency over Venkatachala, that He has received the appellation, Venkateswara (Lord of the Venkata Hill). He is also called the Lord of the Seven Hills.

The temple of Sri Venkateswara has acquired unique sanctity in Indian religious lore. The *Sastras, Puranas, Sthala Mahatyams* and *Alwa*r hymns unequivocally declare that, in the *Kali Yuga*, one can attain *mukti*, only by worshipping Venkata Nayaka or Sri Venkateswara.

The benefits acquired by a pilgrimage to Venkatachala are mentioned in the *Rig Veda* and *Asthadasa Puranas*. In these epics, Sri Venkateswara is described as the great bestower of boons. There are several legends associated with the manifestation of the Lord at Tirumala.

The temple has its origins in *Vaishnavism*, an ancient sect which advocates the principles of equality and love, and prohibits animal sacrifice.

The *sanctum sanctorum* which houses the awe-inspiring idol of the Lord of the Seven Hills is situated in the main temple complex of Tirumala.

TIRUPATI

Tirupati is a Vibrant Pilgrim town located in Chittoor District of Andhra Pradesh, dramatically sited at the foot of bluff red sand stone that marks the Tirumala Hills.

It has closed link to two metros i.e., Chennai and Bangaluru at a distance of 150 km and 258 km, respectively.

Tirupati town itself is focused on the Govindaraja Swamy temple (16-17th Century) with the streets of town laid on the East-West axis, with the temple at the centre and surrounded by Sri Padmavathi Temple, Tiruchanoor, Sri Kodanda Ramaswamy Temple and Rama Chandra Koneru, Kapilatheeratham, Agastheeswara Temple at Thondavada (Mukkoti), Srinivasa Mangapuram.

Tirupati, foothill town of Tirumala hills and the abode of Lord Venkateswara, a pilgrim place is visited by over 180 lakh devotees annually.

Municipal Corporation spread over an area of 24.00 sq.km with 20 Revenue Wards and 50 election wards with 42 poor slums.

ESTABLISHMENT OF TIRUPATI MUNICIPALITY

The most important among the administrative institutions so far as the town is concerned, is the city Municipality. One of the reasons for the formation of Tirupati Municipality was the desire of the Government to improve the sanitation of the place and to provide basic health facilities to the pilgrims.

Tirupati was constituted in to a third grade Municipality by the Government of Madras on 1st April, 1886, even though its population was less than 10,000. It was the biggest town in Chittoor District in 1901 through it was a class V town. It was upgraded into class III town in 1911. Later on it was upgraded into Second grade during 1962 and into First grade during 1970. Again it was upgraded into special grade during 1978. In 1981, it become class I city. Tirupati was constituted into a Municipality on the 1st April, 1986. This is the only Municipality in the district which completed 100 years of service by 1986.

The jurisdiction of the Municipality is confined to the urban limits to Tirupati covering a geographical area of 16.21 Sq. km.

The Municipality is looking after the construction, taxation, execution of productive and non-productive works of the municipality, repair of roads within the municipal limits, lighting, sanitation, public health, conservancy, primary and secondary education, slum clearance, town planning, water supply for the entire city, apart form the municipal administration.

ESTABLISHMENT OF TIRUPATI URBAN DEVELOPMENT AUTHORITY

In order to solve the problem of urbanization of Tirupati town, the Government of Andhra Pradesh has constituted the Tirupati Urban Development Authority (TUDA) in 1982. The areas covered by Tirupati Municipality and the panchayats of Renigunta, Chandragiri and other nearby areas brought under the purview of TUDA, with the hope that it will solve the two important problem of Tirupati, viz., housing and supply.

Tirupati is well-connected with other parts of the country by rail, and road. In 1887 a railway line connecting Tirupati, with Gudur on the main line of Channai towards North was laid down. Further the line was extended towards the West to Pakala to provide access to the Southern districts. Direct trains to South Central Railway which is about 10 km from Tirupati, on Madras–Bombay broad gauge line.

Tirupati is connected by air with Hyderabad, Vijayawada, Madras, Bangaluru and Mysore. Indian Airlines and Vayudoot operate daily flights to these places.

Tirupati is also well-connected by road with all the major towns and cities of South India. Regular bus services to Tirupati in the radius of 700 km are operated daily by Andhra Pradesh Road Transport Corporation (APRTC) and others.

The phenomenon of rapid urbanization in conjunction with industrialization has resulted in the growth of slums. The sprouting of slums occur due to many factors, such as the shortage of developed land for housing, the high prices of land beyond the reach of urban poor, and a large influx of rural migrants to the cities in search of jobs etc. The existence of 'urban slums' is one of the major problems faced by almost all the metropolitan cities throughout the world and Indian cities are no exception. These slums are known by different names in different regions of India such as *'Katras'* or *'Jhuggi-Jhonpari'* in Delhi, *'Jhopadpatti'* or *'Chawls'* in Mumbai, *'Bustees'* in Kolkata, *'Cheris'* in Chennai and *'Keris'* in Bangaluru. The basic characteristics of these slums essentially remain the same. As the authors live in Tirupati, an important piligrim centre, their experience in the city motivated then to do research on slums in Tirupati.

The Eco City Project in Tirupati covers the core area of the town, which attracts tourists and pilgrims, including Govindaraja Swamy Temple of 12th Century AD, railway station, bus terminus, old residential area, hotels and schools. The core area, at the start of the Eco City Project, had a number of problems related to environmental quality, traffic and transportation, sewerage and drainage and solid waste management.

The main results expected to be achieved under the Eco-City Project are:

- Revival of Koneru and its surroundings.
- Improved sanitary conditions including efficient solid waste management and drainage system.
- Improved environmental quality.
- Improved traffic and transportation system including pilgrim/tourist friendly routes.
- Organized informal sector.
- Availability of trained manpower in the Tirupati Municipal Council on the issues related to urban management including waste management, waste water management.

An "Eco-City Development Plan" has been prepared to identified project area through the GTZ Consultants (School of Planning and Architecture, JNTU, Hyderabad). A number of project interventions, such as the following, are proposed for implementation:

- Replenishment of water in Koneru with improved surroundings.
- Improved sanitation including storm water drainage and solid waste management.
- Improving traffic and transportation system including pedestrian zones, parking facilities, signage etc.
- Providing public toilets and drinking water facilities.
- Development of ornamental landscaping.

The above projects are at various stages of planning, designing and implementation.

Objectives of the Present Study

1. To identify the number of slums in Tirupati city.
2. To know the city area and its population size.
3. To collect population information of the different slums in Tirupati.
4. To identify the denser slums.

MATERIALS AND METHODS

The present investigation is based on both secondary and primary data. The secondary data pertaining to slums, land-use and population have been collected from the Tirupati Municipal Authority office and Tirupati Urban Development Authority office. The secondary data were also collected from the census handbooks of Chittoor district (1971, 1981 1991 and 2001).

The primary data relating to the structure, pattern and growth of slums and socio-economic aspects of slum dwellers have been collected with the help of schedules. In the present study statistical techniques are applied to describe the significance of slums in Tirupati.

LOCATION AND TOPOGRAPHY

Tirupati is a sacred place of pilgrimage and is situated in the latitudes of 13º40′N and longitudes of 79º27E and at a height of 500 feet above the mean sea level in Chittoor district of Andhra Pradesh. Tirupati rests in the midst of an amphitheatre encircled by a range of Eastern Ghats. The Tirumala hills form the northern part of this chain and the city is about two kilometres to the south of the hills.

Tirupati city is easily accessible by train and road. Renigunta Junction on the way to Tirupati is on the way of Mumbai-Raychur-Chennai broad gauge line. Tirupati city, in the name of Tirupati east railway station, is connected to Renigunta Junction. It is also connected to the three State capitals of the southern States by road and it is about 580 km from Hyderabad; 137 km from Chennai and 248 km from Bangaluru. The district headquarters Chittoor is about 69 km southwest of Tirupati.

Tirupati city is not a district headquarters but a *mandal* headquarters. It is the seat of the administration of Tirumala-Tirupati Devasthnams' management as several of its offices are located here. It derives its importance and growth mainly due to its location as a pilgrim centre. It has also grown up as an important centre of education with the location of Sri Venkateswara University, Sri Padmavathi Mahila University, N.G. Ranga Agriculture University, Veterinary, Medical and several engineering and educational colleges and also famous hospitals such as SVIMS, BIIRD etc. The data related to slums in Tirupati were presented in the form of tables.

RESULTS

Table 1.1: Tirupati in a Glance

Tirupati	:	An Important Pilgrim Centre in India
Total Area	:	16.28 sq.km
Total Population	:	3.2 lakhs
Total No. of Slums	:	42
Floating Population	:	50,000 per day

The data collected from the above methods were analyzed for further study of Tirupati City with special reference to slums in Table 1.2.

Table 1.2: Slums in Tirupati as per 2001 Census

S. No.	Name of the Slum	Ward No.	Population per hec	Area in hec	Population Density
1	2	3	4	5	6
1.	Sapthagiri Nagar	2	3520	4.80	733
2.	Suraiah Katta	2	1121	0.20	5605
3.	Sivajyothi Nagar	3	4586	2.40	1910
4.	Yerramitta	3	3691	2.00	1845
5.	Korlagunta, Maruthi Nagar	4	8444	4.40	1919
6.	Sanjay Gandhi Colony	4	6422	1.20	5351
7.	Chandrasekhar Reddy Colony	5	527	2.40	219
8.	Kothapalli	5	551	0.80	688
9.	Yerukula Colony	5	97	0.80	121
10.	Ashok Nagar	6	5377	1.20	4480

(Contd...)

1	2	3	4	5	6
11.	Scavengers City	7	314	2.00	157
12.	Murikineela Gunta	8	2382	6.00	397
13.	Yosodha Nagar	9	4094	1.20	3411
14.	Tataiah Gunta	13	3879	1.20	3232
15.	Mallaiahgunta Katta	14	1023	1.21	845
16.	Chinatalachenu	17	704	1.20	845
17.	Uppanki Harijanwada	17	869	2.40	362
18.	Laxmipuram	18	1178	1.16	1015
19.	Gandhipuram	18	430	0.30	1433
20.	Dasarimatam	18	2158	1.51	1429
21.	New Indira Nagar	19	3173	0.48	6610
22.	Pedda Harijanawada	20	5742	1.00	5742
23.	S.T.V. Nagar	20	4164	4.04	1030
24.	Bhagat Singh Colony	21	552	0.50	1104
25.	Pachigunta	26	171	0.24	712
26.	Chenna Reddy Ciolony	27	5620	2.96	1898
27.	Ambedkar Colony	27	215	1.45	148
28.	Haridwar Colony	27	60	0.20	300
29.	Singalagunta	28	1922	2.97	647
30.	Sanjeevaiah Colony beside Maty. Hospital	28	337	0.58	851
31.	Giripuram	29	1172	1.50	781
32.	Sanjeevaiah Colony Opp. to Medical College	29	1222	0.60	2036
33.	Nehru Nagar	31	7367	7.28	1011
34.	Bommagunta	32	943	1.40	673
35.	Ramakrishna Puram	32	165	0.89	185
36.	Poola Thota	34	1568	0.12	13066
37.	Kummarathopu	35	3164	0.28	11300
38.	Indira Nagar	36	3173	3.69	859
39.	Parvathipuram	17	1504	0.56	2685
40.	Lenin Nagar	17	246	0.35	702
41.	Ambedkar Society Colony	27	66	1.00	66
42.	Chinnagunta	32	144	0.94	153

Discussion

The slums are characterized by dilapidated and infirm housing structures, poor ventilation, acute over-crowding, faulty alignment of streets, inadequate lighting, paucity of safe drinking water, water-logging during rains, absence of toilet facilities and non-availability of basic physical and social services. The living conditions in slums are usually unhygienic and contrary to all norms of planned urban growth and are an important factor in accelerating transmission of various air and water borne diseases.

Table 1.3: Over Crowded Slums in Tirupati

S. No.	Name of the Slum	Papulation Density	Poor Water Supply	Water, Air, Soil Pollution
1.	Poolathota	13066	T	T
2.	Kummarathopu	11300	T	T
3.	New Indira Nagar	6610	-	T
4.	Pedda Hrijanada	5742	T	T
5.	Suraiah Katta	5605	T	T
6.	Sanjay Gandhi Colony	5351	-	T
7.	Ashok Nagar	4480	T	T

Under these circumstances in the important pilgrim centre Tirupati, there are 42 slums identified within the municipal limits of Tirupati city (Fig.1/ Table 1.1). Korlagunta slum is the biggest one in terms of population (8444), while Haridwar Colony is in the lowest population size with 60 persons. The fourth ward [korlagunta (8444) and Sanjay Gandhi Colony (6422)] (14866) is having the highest number of slum population while the 27th ward (Ambedkar Society Colony) is having the lowest number of slum population with 66 persons. These slums have originated due to rural-urban migrations and the unplanned mushroom growth of slums are a threat to the pilgrim centre.

The total number of slums identified were 42 in a small important area. The total area of the city is 16.28 sq.km and its population is 3.2 lakhs according to the 2001 census (Table 1.2). Among 42 slums, the over crowded slums are Poolathota, Kummarathopu, New Indira Nagar, Pedda Harijanawada, Suraiah Katta, Sanjay Gandhi Colony and Ashok Nagar as shown in the Table 1.3. In these slums poor water supply and unhygenic environments of water, air and soil are also observed. Since it is an important pilgrim centre and educational centre with 50,000 floating population per day, the town is elevated to a special grade municipality. In these slums the socio-economic conditions and quality of life are also very poor. The poor piligrims coming to the city generally stay in the slum areas, where certain people dwelling in slums give lodging and board to the pilgrims, e.g. Nehru Nagar, Parasala Veedi etc.

SUMMARY AND CONCLUSIONS

The area of the Tirupati city is 16.28 sq. km. In this small area there are 42 slums. Moreover, it is an important pilgrim centre in the country. Its population is 3.2 lakh according to 2001 census and floating population is 50,000 per day. Korlagunta slum is the biggest one in terms of population (8444). Poolathota, Kummarathopu, New Indira Nagar, Pedda Harijanawada, Suraiah Katta and Ashok Nagar are identified the denser slums. These slums are causing an ill-health environment to the town in terms of over crowding, unclean environment, drainage water stagnation, presence of mosquitoes, disease-proneness and favorable conditions to the spread of diseases etc. If the situation continues, unknown diseases come with the strangers and go with the strangers if they stay in the unhygienic conditions of the slums. It is more a danger for the city and for the pilgrims. If these slums are not developed in a planned way, it becomes a disease spreading centre instead of pilgrim centre causing people to be afraid to come to Tirupati, and it loses its sanctity and importance.

Suggestions

1. Apartment type of colonies must be developed with high ventilation in the places of slums.
2. Roads and streets must be spaciously widened.
3. Hygienic awareness must be created in the slum dwellings.
4. Underground drainage system, toilets must be constructed.

REFERENCES

Eswaramma, P. (2000) M. Phil Thesis on "Urban Growth in Tirupati City with Special Reference to Slums".

Maurya, S.D. (1988), *Urban Environment Management*, Chugh Publications Allahabad.

Singh, Anupam (1997), *Adolescent Girls in Slum Problems and Prospects*, Anmol Publications Pvt. Ltd., New Delhi.

Urban Slums Implications for Food Security

Dr. D. Sai Sujatha
P. Rasidulla

INTRODUCTION

Today, the most important issues inter-related with urban environment are the challenge of slums, along with pollution and waste management. Slums can be seen both as cause and effect of environmental degradation and pollution in cities. Slums are supposed to be potential target for the habitation of displaced people. Environmental displacement has already become intense in geographically and environmentally vulnerable areas in India. Thus, climate induced migration to big cities or nearby places is getting spontaneous over the past few decades. For instance, frequent exposure to natural disasters makes coastal people often bound to migrate in search of secure lives and livelihoods. Therefore, increased slum settlements indicate physical manifestation of growing urban poverty.

Urban poverty will increase if environmentally displaced people keep moving to city, while slum is their potential target for habitation. Such people create pressure on limited natural resources like land, water. Also, the poor are often compelled to live in environmentally hazardous area like low lying flood prone area occupying swamps, natural lakes. Crucial in this context is water and sanitation.

Migration to urban areas is a regular phenomenon and the growing number of people rush to city's slums creates urban crisis. But urban slums located mostly in low lying environmentally hazardous area coupled with inadequate facilities such as food, shelter, sanitation, health care make their life even worse. Growing number of people in urban slums over the past creates extra pressure on existing systems leading to food shortage and challenge to government development activities like slum development and poverty reduction strategy.

Poor living conditions and insanitary environment have been substantiated in the elements of food security. In National Food Policy, 2006, food security has been defined as availability of and access to sufficient, safe and nutritious food that meets their dietary needs. The other essential element of food security is biological utilization of food emphasizing environmental sanitation, clean water, and adequate diet. Availability does not ensure food security at specific level like household or individual level. Household or individual's access to food and more specifically, to absorb diet properly lead to food security.

According to the 2002 National Sample Survey (NSS), an estimated 8.23 million households in urban areas of the country were living in slums. However, unlike household surveys, where household information is collected from a responsible household member, these surveys collect information from knowledgeable persons in the community on households and their living conditions and on socio-economic characteristics.

According to the 2001 Census, 42.6 million people lived in slums in 8.2 million households and 640 towns spread across 26 States and Union Territories in India. The slum estimates did not include towns below 50,000 population, as well as a few towns and cities with a population of 50,000 or more where local bodies did not recognize any slum area (136 towns in all, including such large cities as Lucknow) and a few northeastern states that did not have any urban centre with 50,000 or more population or that did not have any slum act (Office of the Registrar General and Census Commissioner, 2005).

As per the Ministry of Housing and Urban Poverty Alleviation (MOHUPA), the number of people living in slums more than doubled from 27.9 million in 1981 to 61.8 million in 2001. When the provisional census results on slums were released by the Registrar General of India, the Ministry of Housing and Urban Poverty Alleviation (MOHUPA) said that the census estimates were too low. As per the Ministry of Housing and Urban Poverty Alleviation (MOHUPA), the number of people living in slums more than doubled from 27.9 million in 1981 to 61.8 million in 2001. According to UN-HABITAT, the slum population in India was approximately 169 million in 2005 and it is projected to increase to 202 million by 2020 (UN-HABITAT, 2006).

SLUMS AND URBAN POVERTY

As elsewhere in the world, the increasing concentration of population in slums in urban areas in India is seen as an indication of increasing urban poverty. The data on the level and trend of poverty in India show that although there has been a decline in rural poverty at the national level, the urban poverty level has increased. In 1999-2000, about one-quarter of the population in rural areas (27%) and urban areas (24%) were living below the poverty line. According to the Planning Commission's estimates for 2004-05,

26 per cent of the population in urban areas fell below the poverty line (Planning Commission, 2007). Therefore, poverty is no longer a rural phenomenon.

It is undoubtedly simplistic to assume that most of the urban poor live in slums or that slum dwellers in urban areas are necessarily poor. In cities such as Delhi and Mumbai, most slum-dwellers are likely to have income levels that put them way above the poverty line (*Business Standard*, 2001). A survey of nine slums in Howrah in West Bengal revealed that almost two thirds of the people living in slums were above the poverty line (Sengupta, 1999). It has alsobeen observed that poverty in urban areas is qualitatively very different from rural poverty and that it is multidimensional. Urban poverty presents some issues that are distinct from those addressed in the typical analysis of poverty, such as commoditization, environmental hazard, and social fragmentation (Baker and Schuler, 2004). A recent study based on the analysis of NSSO data also concluded that contrary to popular perception, not all slum dwellers are poor. Non-slum residents are not unequivocally better off than slum residents. The study also suggests that the poorest non-slum residents are worse off than the poorest slum dwellers. Even in big cities, the poorest people do not all live in slums (Chandrasekhar and Mukhopadhyay, 2008).

The MOHUPA 2009 report accepts the NSSO estimate that over 80 million poor people live in the cities and towns in India. The size of the urban poor population in India is almost twice the size of the slum population estimated in the 2001 Census (42.6 million). Even if we include all the houseless urban population in India (around 780,000 as per the 2001 Census) in the category of urban poor, the estimates of the urban poor are much higher than the estimates of the slum and houseless population. Thus, urban poverty is not indicated by the place of residence of a person (slum/non-slum), although slums remain the most visible manifestation of poverty.

Assessment of Food Security

Measurement of food security is an integration of many factors such as agro-ecological, environmental, socio-economic, political and biological factors. The concept is generalized into three main aspects like (WFP, 2002):

- Availability of food.
- Access to food.
- Utilization of food.

Availability of food is examined through sufficient supply of food to satisfy domestic need. Food availability is determined by supply and demand oriented approach while supply of food is integrated with domestic production, imports (public, private, food aid) and changes in national stock. But the issue of food aid in food availability is often being questioned. Also, it is found that availability of food cannot often measure what people actually obtained. In this case access to food depicts people's purchasing power to buy food. Poverty is one of the main obstacles affecting people's purchasing power. Access to food is not only enough in food security, while utilization of food guarantees one's capacity to absorb and utilize nutrients in food consumed. Utilization of food is determined through caring practices, eating habits, hygiene, access to health and sanitary facilities (WFP, 2002).

This study particularly depicts living condition and its implications for food security of urban poor slum-dwellers Assessment of food security is a complex phenomenon as it is interrelated with many factors. This study investigates second and third elements of food security in terms of living conditions of slum-dwellers through field survey. A set of indicators is used to analyze living conditions and the situation of food security of urban poor living in slums. Socio-economic factors including income, expenditure and education influence food habit and knowledge about hygiene. Socio-economic factors entail individual's ability to have adequate and nutritious food as well as water treatment practice for safe drinking water. Environmental sanitation is characterized by household's latrine type and waste disposal system, while children are easy victim of unhygienic environment. Following figure (Fig. 2.1) depicts conceptual framework of assessing food security integrating inter-related factors. Children's health status measured by water-borne disease occurrence well depicts their exposure to sanitation. Children's health status is a good indication of food security as it is said that healthy children can recover diarrhea quickly.

METHODOLOGY

The study is based on both primary and secondary data. Living conditions of slum-dwellers is depicted using primary data. Asifnagar (Karwan) slum which is oldest and one of the largest slums in Hyderabad city has been selected for sample survey. The survey questionnaire includes household's socio-economic, physical environment, health behaviour and health outcome. For this study, total 100 samples using purposive sampling to investigate household's food security by collecting information on selected factors. The target group of questionnaire survey is mothers of the children who are supposed to be well-informed about children's food intake and health status. Socio-economic factors characterizing living conditions, physical environment (mode of wasted is disposal), households' health behavior particularly dietary practice and health outcome (disease occurrence) have been analyzed by applying statistical technique, frequency distribution.

FACTORS INFLUENCING CHILDREN'S FOOD SECURITY IN SLUMS

Children's food habit and health status are directed by household's socio-economic condition. Also, children are susceptible to environmental sanitation while they are found most of the time playing around or spending outside environment which is very unhygienic. Socio-economic factors such as income, expenditure and education are analyzed to depict households' ability and knowledge about dietary practice and prevalence of disease occurrence among children.

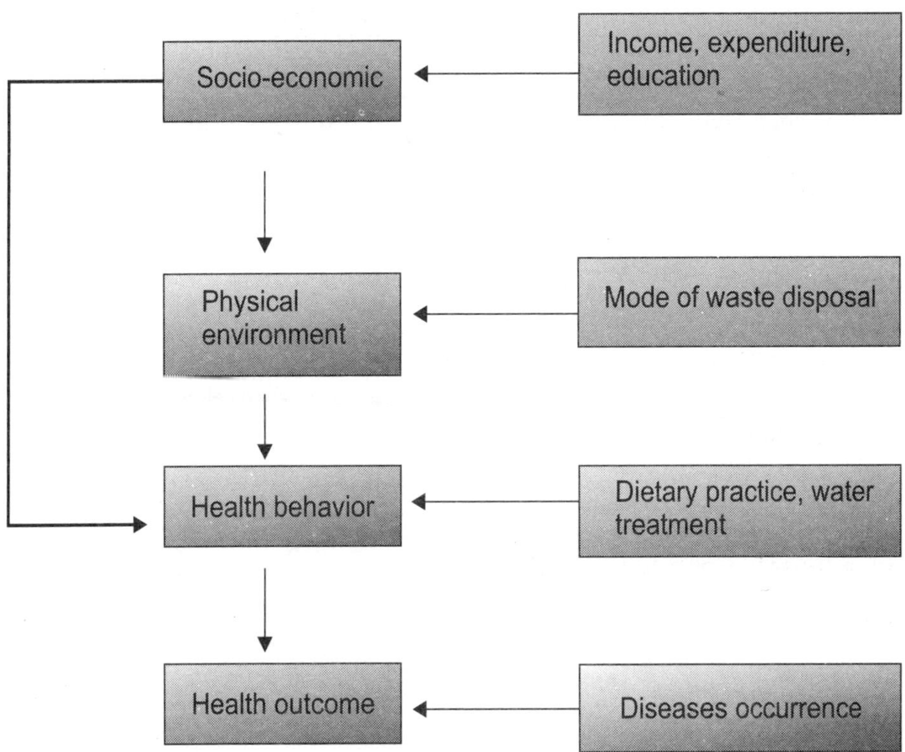

Figure 2.1: Conceptual Framework (Adapted from Cohen *et al.*, 2003)

Table: 2.1: Age wise Distribution of the Slum-Dwellers **N= 100**

Particulars	Category	Frequency	%
Young aged	Up to 30	37	37%
Medium	31-40	51	51%
Old aged	Above 40	12	12%

More than 37 per cent of the respondents came under the category of the young aged of age below 30 years. While about 51 per cent of the respondents were of the medium aged of age between 21 and 40 years of age. It was observed that about 12 per cent of the respondents were of old aged of age above 40 years (Table 2.1).

Table 2.2: Educational Status of the Slum-Dwellers **N = 100**

Particulars	Category	Frequency	%
Illiterate	—	45	45%
Primary	Up to 5th	31	31%
High School	Up to 10th	13	13%
Junior College	Up to 12th	8	8%
Degree/PG	—	3	3%

It is seen that 45 per cent of the total migrants are illiterate, 31 per cent are from Primary school education, 13 per cent of them are of High school standard, 8 per cent are educated up to Junior College level and about 3 per cent are degree/PG education (Table 2.2).

Income

According to survey data, 61 per cent of households have income less than Rs. 5,000 and 39 per cent have income Rs. 5,000-10,000. The sampled populations in survey area represent lower income group according to income group categorized in urban area.

Expenditure

A major portion of households' income is spent on food items following expenditure on non-food items and house rent. Survey data reveal that a major share of their income is spent on food (average monthly expenditure Rs. 3232) followed by house rent (Rs. 933 on average) and non-food items (Rs. 872 on average) respectively.

Consumption Pattern

According to respondents, children are provided with three meals in a day. But in adequate quality and lack of diversity of food are matters of concern in food habit. Consumption pattern of slum-dwellers depict that rice, potato, vegetable and edible oil are consumed on daily basis. Food composition sometimes is only rice with potato or fish which are cheap to them. But access to protein rich animal product (milk and milk product, meat or poultry, eggs) is very low among the poor. They can consume them mainly on monthly basis or sometimes on special occasion like Eid festival. According to households these are expensive food item and most of them cannot afford it. Though, a large number of households can manage fish in weekly basis, but the quality of fish is relatively low. Also, most of them replied eating fruits on weekly basis. In this case, they can afford mainly banana which is relatively cheaper than other seasonal fruits (Table 2.3).

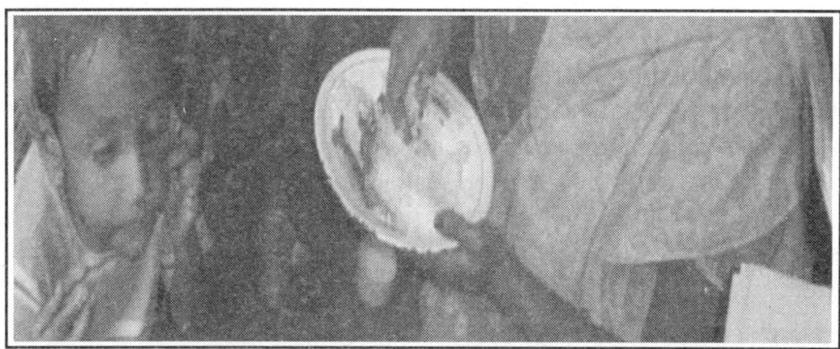

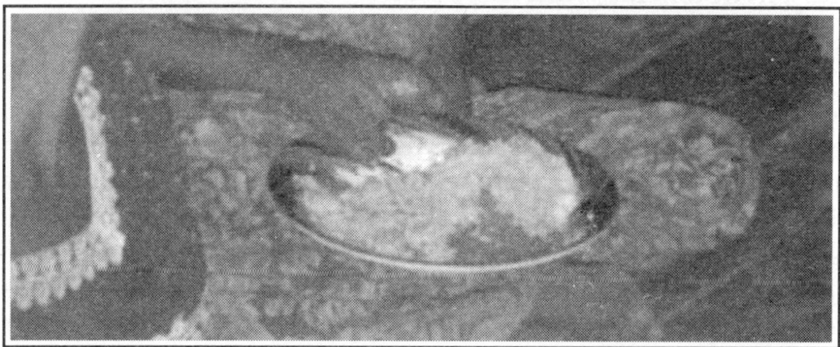

Lack of Diversity in Food Items

Protein energy intake is widely low in urban slums. Protein deficiency hinders physical growth of children and their brain development.

Table 2.3: Consumption Pattern of Households Living in Slums

Food Consumed	Number of Households					
	Daily	Weekly	Monthly	Special Occasion	Never	Others
Rice	95	–	–	–	–	5
Bread	60	10	4	3	15	8
Cereal	4	3	16	7	67	3
Vegetables	88	2	1	–	–	9
Edible oil	96	–	–	–	–	4
Potato	96	2	–	–	–	2
Fish	2	18	62	8	4	6
Egg	1	21	61	4	4	9
Milk and milk powder	4	14	19	61	–	2
Meat/poultry	–	8	51	31	9	1
Fruit	3	38	27	22	8	2

Water Treatment

There are limited water treatment practices which are applied at household level for safe drinking water. In this case, a large group of respondents (87%) answered, no treatment practices are taken, while only 13 per cent households do treat water before drinking. The most common water treatment practices applied by households are boiling and filtering. On the other hand, the reasons of not treating water before drinking are lack of affordability in buying fuel for boiling water and in some cases, lack of knowledge.

Physical Environment: Waste Disposal

According to the households in study area, there is no fixed place for waste disposal. Generally wastes are disposed wherever they live like on the ground or above the water body. Therefore, scattered wastes are found visible in open place. It indicates that adequate facilities of waste disposal as well as collection are almost non-existent in slum area. From the sample data, it has been found that a large number of households (67%) dispose wastes into the water body, while 31 per cent of households dispose on the ground, mainly on the street. Though, only two per cent of households have been found to dispose wastes in dustbin. Exposure to such dirty environment is very risky for children as they spend most of their time playing outside.

Scattered Disposal of Wastes

Health Status: Disease Occurrence

Almost half of total 178 children are reported sick due to different types of water-borne diseases. Sixty one per cent of affected children have been reported as suffering from diarwcrhea. The higher prevalence of disease among children reveals inadequate education or lack of consciousness among parents to give proper care to the children. Most of the time mothers are busy with household works; therefore children are not given enough care by them. Also unhealthy environment and mother's lack of knowledge about hygiene and dietary practice make children more vulnerable. Even though parents have some kind of primary education but lack of affordability to consume healthy food indicates poor dietary practice among children living in slums. It is said that nutritious food prevents chronic disease as it helps children to recover disease quickly like diarrhea. But majority of households cannot afford healthy food items like protein food, not even in weekly basis.

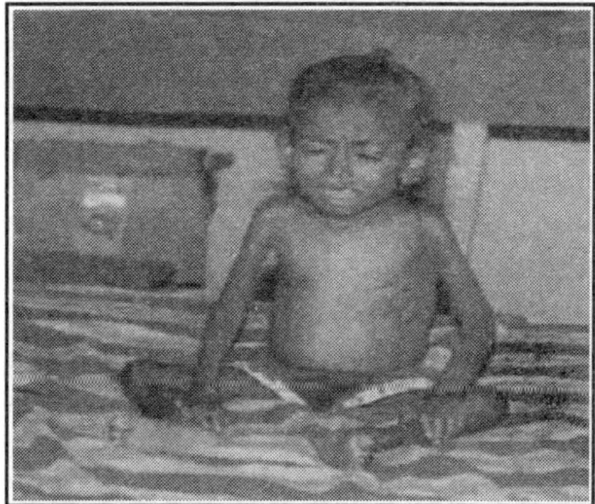

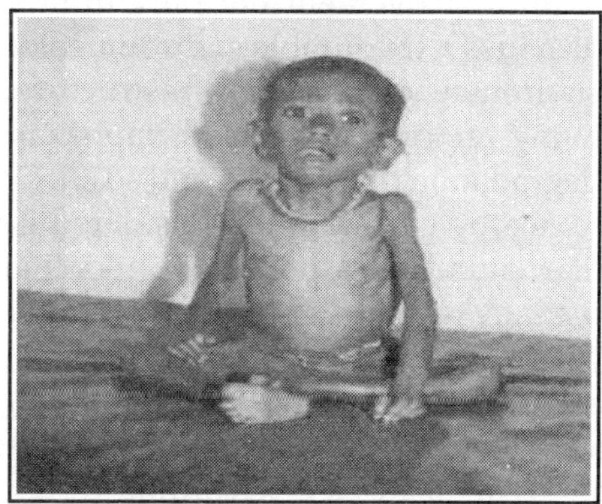

Diarrhoea in Children

SOLUTIONS

Over the past four decades, the Government of India has adopted many explicit population distribution policies and programmes to decongest urban areas and facilitate a more balanced spatial development. The closed city programmes were aimed at reducing migration to metropolitan regions through such instruments as tax incentives, limitations on investments and demolition of squatter settlements. The Government also promoted intermediate–size cities and regions by extending support services to them, improving their infrastructure, and strengthening linkages between intermediate–size and large cities.

Moreover, land colonization programmes were introduced by the Government to re-settle residence from overpopulated rural areas to frontier regions are underutilized areas. The policy instruments commonly employed for this purpose were the transfer of land titles and provision of credit and other facilities to increase the productivity and income of settlers. Apart from this, the Government should take effective steps to implement the rural development programmes like Small Farmers development Agency/Marginal Farmers and Agricultural Labourers projects, Rural Landless Employment Guarantee Programme, Whole Village Development Programme, Integrated Rural Development Programme and so on to reduce the rural-urban migrants.

CONCLUSIONS

Living conditions of urban poor is observed to be poor according to the survey findings. Socio-economic status of slum dwellers can be characterized as mainly low income group with inadequate education (for both parents and children). Also, poor physical environment with non-existent solid waste disposal system is very common phenomenon in slum areas. Therefore, high prevalence of disease (water-borne) among children living in slums indicates leading unhealthy environment. In such circumstance, to ensure food security of urban poor is a challenge if their socio-economic condition remains bleak. Slum improvement not only uplifts living quality of urban poor but also provides a favourable environmental conditions for survival. Design of built environment including infrastructure, sanitation facilities will advance healthy living removing effects of haphazard growth and effects of environmental degradation due to rains and so on. Decentralization of some slum settlements to nearby cities can be considered if located elevated above the water body like natural lakes, ponds.The poor living in slums contribute to urban economy in many ways. To secure their living standard socio-economically, their income (daily or monthly) should be stable. According to survey data, most of them are daily laborer like rickshaw puller, brick breaker. Thus, their income is very much susceptible to some natural or man-made events like water logging in Hyderabad city. According to respondents, they often stay hunger until they earn something to eat. Sufferings of such people considering recent and future urban hazards need to be integrated during policy preparation.

Education can play vital role in influencing parent's knowledge about nutrition, hygiene and health. Sometimes respondents are found to be conscious about food habit but can't afford healthy food which is expensive to them. As slum dwellers do not own any land and stay in public and private land, so they cannot grow food in their own land. Consequently, they are mostly dependent on market price of food. However, market price fluctuates without considering their ability to buy. So this state of price fluctuations has to be given priority in case of household level to make them food secure. Moreover, integration of personal sanitation should be part of comprehensive food security. Thus this effort will reduce disease burden facilitating healthy and productive life.

REFERENCES

Baker, J. and N. Schuler, 2004, *Analyzing Urban Poverty: A Summary of Methods and Approaches, World Bank Policy Research Working Paper 3399*, Washington, D.C.: World Bank.

Business Standard, 2001, Number Crunchers and Slum, December 10.

Chandrasekhar, S. and A. Mukhopadhyay, 2008, *Multidimensions of Urban Poverty: Evidence from India, 2007-08, Indira Gandhi Institute of Development ResearchWorking Paper*, Mumbai: Indira Gandhi Institute of Development Research.

Cohen, D. A., Mason, K., Bedimo, A., Scribner, R., Basolo, V., & Farley, T. A. 2003, Neighborhood Physical Conditions and Health, *American Journal of Public Health*, 93 (3): 467-471.

Government of India, 2002, *National Health Policy*, New Delhi: Government of India.

Ministry of Housing and Urban Poverty Alleviation (Mohupa) and UNDP, 2009, *Poverty in India*, New Delhi: Mohupa and UNDP.

Office of the Registrar General and Census Commissioner. 2005, *Slum Population, India, Series-I, Census of India 2001*, New Delhi: Office of the Registrar General and Census Commissioner.

Office of the Registrar General and Census Commissioner, 2001, *Final Population Totals*, New Delhi: Office of the Registrar General and Census Commissioner.

Planning Commission, 2007, Poverty Estimates for 2004-05. Planning Commission, Government of India, March, 2007.

Sengupta, C., 1999, Dynamics of Community Environmental Management in Howrah Slums, *Economic and Political Weekly* 22: 1290-96.

UN-HABITAT., 2006, *State of the World's Cities 2006/7: The Millennium Development Goals and Urban Sustainability*, London: Earthscan Publications Ltd.

World Food Programme (WFP), 2002, *Food Security Assessment in Bangladesh, Issues and Implications for Mapping Food Insecurity and Vulnerability*, Analysis and Mapping, Bangladesh.

3

Problems of Poor in Urban Slums

Dr. K. Hymavathi

INTRODUCTION

Urbanization is a universal phenomenon, which is part and parcel of economic development. The positive role of urbanization is often over shadowed by the evident deterioration in the physical environment and quality of life in the urban areas caused by the widening gap between demand and supply of essential services and infrastructure. Asia has been witnessing the triple dynamics of growth, rapid urbanization and growing poverty. Many Asian countries witnessed higher economic growth, the growth pattern brought about enormous disparities across and within nations. India has shared the growth pattern and rapid urbanization with some of the fastest growing regions in Asia. In India, cities contribute over 55 per cent to country's GDP and urbanization has been recognized as an important component of economic growth on one side of the coin and on the other side of the coin life of the poor people is very worse and coupled with number of problems. The present paper mainly focuses the Urbanization of Poverty, Key issues/problems of the urban poor, Some initiatives of government, Methodology, Major Findings and discussion, Challenges for controlling the urban poverty, Approaches for reducing urban poverty, Suggestions and Conclusion. The next section of this chapter high light about the urbanization of poverty its characteristics, scope, trends of urban poverty in India and AP in addition to changing factors.

URBANIZATION OF POVERTY

Poverty is not only a lack of income. Amartya Sen (2000) defines poverty as a lack of basic capabilities to lead the kind of life one values. Poverty should therefore not be seen merely in financial terms. Poverty has three dimensions: poverty of income and productive assets, poverty of access to essential services, and poverty of power, participation and respect. Deprived of these essential attributes, people will not be able to realize their full capabilities, and therefore will not be able to benefit from, contribute to and have an influence on development.

CHARACTERSTICS OF URBAN POVERTY

The multi-dimensional nature of poverty in urban areas is usually characterized by:

- Inadequate household income.
- Limited asset base.
- Inadequate protection by the law.
- Inadequate provision of 'public' infrastructure and services.
- Socio-cultural heterogeneity.
- Voiceless ness and powerlessness within the political system.
- Exploitation and discrimination.

These factors can automatically push the people into poverty and ill-being and causes inequality in all aspects.

THE SCOPE OF URBAN POVERTY

Measuring urban poverty is not an easy task. There are numerous debates around the topic of poverty measurement related to the use of money metric approaches given the multi-dimensional nature of poverty, where to set poverty lines, and how to account for the higher cost of living in urban areas in national level poverty estimates. There are also debates on the definition of 'urban' which affects estimates of urban poverty.

Urban Poverty in India

As per 2001 Census report the slum population of India was 42.6 million, which constitute 15 per cent of the total urban population of the country. Only 12.7 per cent of total Indian towns have reported slum. As per the data 11.2 million of the total slum population of the country is in Maharashtra followed by Andhra Pradesh 5.2, Uttar Pradesh 4.4 and West Bengal 4.1 million (Census of India 2001). The reasons behind urban poverty are as follows:

- Improper training/lack of vocational education/training.
- Growing population/rapid increase in population.
- Slower job growth/limited job opportunities of employment in the cities.
- Migration of rural youth towards cities.

- Lack of housing facilities.
- No proper implementation of public distribution system (PDS)/failure of PDS system.

If we look into the changing aspect of poverty line we can understand the reality nature of poverty trend over a period of time.

TRENDS OF URBAN POVERTY

During the period of 1993-2002, the incidence of urban poverty has not changed much globally using the $1/day line, and has shown a decline for the $2/day line following the trends of overall declines in poverty. Overall, the urbanization process has played an important role in poverty reduction by providing new opportunities for migrants and through the second-round impact on those who stay in rural areas. The pace in urban poverty reduction has been slower than the reductions in rural poverty reduction, reflecting an overall urbanization of poverty. Of the total decline in the poverty rate for the $2/day line (8.7%), 4.8 per cent is attributed to rural poverty reduction, 2.3 per cent to urban, and 1.6 per cent to the population shift effect (Ravallion, et al., 2007).

POVERTY SITUATION IN ANDHRA PRADESH

According to the Planning Commission in Andhra Pradesh poverty level is higher in urban areas than in rural areas. The rate of decline in urban poverty was slower [in the State up to 1993-94] but the pace of decline subsequently increased, especially between 1993-94 and 2004-05. While rural poverty declined significantly from about 27 per cent in 1983 to 11 per cent in 2004-05, urban poverty declined from 37 per cent to 28 per cent during the same period which was still high and higher than the all-India figure. This indicates that urban areas contribute about half of the total poor in Andhra Pradesh [Human Development Report–Andhra Pradesh, 2007].

The coming part of this chapter visualizes the problem scenario and type of problems that urban poor had in slums and general in urban areas.

KAY ISSUES/PROBLEMS OF THE POOR IN URBAN SLUMS

The urban poor are quite diverse across regions, countries and even within cities, they tend to face a number of common deprivations which affect their day-to-day life. The main issues are:

(i) Limited access to income and employment.

(ii) Inadequate and insecure living conditions.

(iii) Poor infrastructure and services.

(iv) Vulnerability to risks such as natural disasters, environmental hazards and health risks particularly associated with living in slums.

(*v*) Spatial issues which inhibit mobility and transport

(*vi*) Inequality closely linked to problems of exclusion.

These issues are described below:

Rural-Urban Migration

There are many types of migration. People migrate not only from rural to urban areas; there is also rural-rural migration, urban-urban migration and urban-rural migration. Some migrants move permanently; others move temporarily (i.e. for a season, for a few years) and then return to their place of origin. Some migrants move alone, either because they are not yet married or because they prefer to leave their family behind. In some migration streams, male migrants dominate; in others women are the main migrants. It is important to distinguish different types of migrants and migration, because they have different housing needs.

People have a wide Range of Reasons to Migrate

People migrate either because they are "pushed" out of their place of origin or because they are "pulled" to their migration destination. Generally, people move because of a combination of both "push" factors and "pull" factors. Some are "pushed" out of their present place of residence because they cannot earn sufficient income to sustain themselves or their families. Others may be forced out of their place, either temporarily or permanently, because of a natural disaster such as floods, drought or earthquake or sustained ecological change such as desertification or soil erosion. People are "pulled" to their migration destination by better economic prospects, better education and health facilities, or more freedom from restrictive social and cultural norms for themselves and for their children.

Rural-Urban Migration is Often Part of the Survival Strategy of Rural Families

In order to spread economic risks, families may split into several groups that locate themselves in different places: rural areas, small towns, and big cities, while some family members may even move abroad. In this way, the family's sources of income are diversified and do not depend on an economic downturn in a particular place. This arrangement also allows small children and the elderly to remain in the rural areas where the cost of living is low, while income earners and school-aged children move to the most suitable places.

The Prospects of an Adequate Livelihood in Agriculture for Most are Not Bright

Most people in the rural areas work in the agricultural sector, but agriculture is highly dependent on weather conditions, rural land is limited and its fertility is sometimes low or declining, land holdings are small, and many families have always been or have become landless. As a result, rural incomes tend to be low. In order to increase income, small farmers need to increase their productivity, but they are often too poor to buy the necessary technology, whether it is equipment, high-yield seeds or fertilizer. Increasingly, farmers and others in rural areas supplement their income from agriculture with non-farm income, in the rural areas where possible, or in the urban areas through temporary migration.

The Urban Informal Sector a Visible Manifestation of Rapid Urbanization is the Growth of Informal Settlements

Most people refer to such neighbourhoods as "slums". In fact, it is important to distinguish between "slums" and "squatter settlements". Slums can be defined as legally constructed permanent buildings where the housing conditions are substandard due to age, neglect, subdivision and consequent overcrowding.

The urban poor live in unsafe and over-crowded housing, which lacks access to safe water, or to excreta disposal. They are much more likely than the wealthy to be exposed to pollution (both indoors and outdoors), traffic, industry (associated with both the formal and informal sector), and other risks at home, work, and in their communities. They are more likely to consume insufficient food, or food of poor quality, making them even more vulnerable to the ill-health effects from environmental exposures. Poor children are particularly affected by adverse environmental conditions. Not only are they more exposed to health threats in the environment, they are also more vulnerable to the ill-health effects stemming from problems such as a lack of clean air and water. The next section of this paper highlights the interventions of government for tackling the problems of poor in urban areas and for the general pubic.

SOME NATIONAL INITIATIVES FOR PROMOTING THE WELL-BEING OF POOR IN URBAN SLUMS

Urban poverty poses the problems of housing and shelter, water, sanitation, health, education, social security and livelihoods along with special needs of vulnerable groups such as women, children and aged people. Poor people live in slums which are over-crowded, often polluted and lack basic civic amenities like clean drinking water, sanitation and health facilities. Most of them are involved in informal sector activities where there is constant threat of eviction, removal, confiscation of goods and almost non-existent social security cover. Such type of situations creates lot of inconvenience and leads to vulnerability.

In order to over come from the above mentioned problems of the urban poor and to reduce the severity of those issues on the growth and development of poor with regard to urban areas, the government of India has came forward since independence with certain schemes and programmes particularly for the wellbeing of urban population specifically to meet the basic needs of the urban poor as major agenda in the form of i.e., National Slum Policy (2001).

The objective of the National Slum Policy was to integrate slum settlements and the communities residing within them into the urban area and to strengthen the legal and policy framework to facilitate the process of slum development and improvement on a sustainable basis. Slum improvement has broadly been done through the following channels:

- Central government policies for slum improvement and poverty alleviation.
- Slum improvement in selected cities through international and bilateral aid.
- Slum improvement and tenure regularization through state legislation/ state government programs.
- Slum improvement/redevelopment projects with private sector participation.
- City specific initiatives.

The details of those programmes were given below which were aimed at the urban poor and these can be categorized as three types:

- Those aimed at improving living conditions mainly through slum upgrading but also through public housing schemes, sites and services schemes, providing access to credit and housing finance, rent control, land titling, infrastructure improvements and utility subsidies.
- Programs aimed at improving the income of the poor such as job training, micro-enterprise development, and the provision of childcare.
- Safety net programs targeted to the most vulnerable such as cash transfers, food stamps, feeding programs, fee waivers, subsidies, and public works programs.

Some of these services render with different names i.e. Andhra Pradesh urban-based services for the poor (APUBSP) funded by DFID, Jawaharlal Nehru National Urban Renewal Mission (JNNURM) which provides a new paradigm for inclusive city development and building inclusive urban communities based on a holistic approach. Integrated Housing and Slum Development Programme (IHSDP).

- Security of tenure at affordable prices,
- Improved housing,
- Water supply,
- Sanitation,

- Education,
- Health,
- Social security,

Swarna Jayanti Sahari Rojgar Yojana (SJRSY), which is currently in operation with effect from 1-12-1997, is a substitution of the earlier programmes like Urban Basic Services for the Poor (UBSP), Under the scheme SJSRY, the following programmes are being implemented.

- Community structure (Information Education and Communication (IEC) component.
- Urban Self-employment Programme (USEP) (subsidy).
- Development of Women and Children in Urban Areas (DWCUA).
- Thrift and Credit Society.
- Urban Wage Employment Programme (UWEP).
- U.S.E.P (Skill Up-gradation Training).
- Administration and Office expenses (A & O.E.).
- Prime Minister Integrated Urban Poverty Eradication Yojana (NRY).
- Environmental Improvement of Urban Slums (EIUs).

At present for establishing the people owned and community based management institutions/organizations like SHGs and its apex level bodies with suitable legal frame work providing micro credit and facilitating bank linkages for promoting sustainable livelihoods of the poor in municipal areas through a programme called Mission for Elimination of Poverty in Model Municipal Areas (MEPMA) with the funding support of World Bank and DFID.

In addition to the above some of the common programmes has adopted for both rural and urban poor related to nutrition through Public Distribution System (PDS), health and insurance (Rashtriya Swasthya Bima Yojana [RSBY]), a health insurance scheme, for workers in the unorganised sector has been launched in 2008. The scheme provides smart card-based cashless health insurance cover up to Rs. 30,000 annually to the people living Below Poverty Line (BPL) and also cover hospitalization charges. As on February 2011 RSBY issued smart cards to 22,806,768 BPL families in India. Similarly Janani Suraksha Yojana or JSY under the overall umbrella of National Rural Health Mission or NRHM integrates the cash assistance with antenatal care during the pregnancy period.Though the government is not reaching its target in improving the basic amenities and quality of life of poor people in urban areas and slums.

METHODOLOGY

Tirupati is a well-known sacred place of pilgrimage, which is full of temples and holy spots. It has become a great seat of learning and education The Tirupati town is well business and commercial-oriented town. According to 2001 census, the Tirupati Town (Municipality) has the population of 3, 28,202 with 54,457 households in 36 wards. This municipality contains 42 slums (38 are notified and the remaining 4 are denotified). Number of families living in these slums are 14,272 which is having 94,057 population as per 2001 census. The research design for the present study is an exploratory one, which aims to explore and understand the socio economic, living conditions, type of problems that are facing by the slum dwellers and suggestions for improving the quality of life of slum dwellers living in Tirupati town. Type of sample is purposive and selected 20 units for the study from five selected slums (Ashok Nagar, New Indira Nagar, Yerukula Colony, Sivajyothi Nagar, and STV Nagar) the interview schedule was administered as a tool and interviewing, observation and Focused Group Discussions have been adopted as methods for data collection from the study area.

MAJOR FINDINGS AND DISCUSSION

The study results reveals majority 84 per cent of the families are from lower socio economic strata that they belongs to BC, SC and ST very few of them are from OC. In addition to that their income levels are also not yet all sufficient for their family minimum needs, the income levels of the selected slum dwellers are Rs. 2,000 to Rs. 2,500 per month these earnings are not adequate with the present price raise. And these people are not getting their part from the Public Distribution System. Unfortunately, the enabling environment does not necessarily support the needs of the poor. Access to basic public services (water, health, education, sanitation, legal protection, etc.) in India is mediated through weak governance systems in which accountability mechanisms are not enforced, corruption is widespread, and patronage in the distribution of services is endemic (DFID, 1999). Poor people's capacity, irrespective of individual identities, to influence political systems is extremely restricted. They invariably have limited or no right to make demands on the political system, and often operate within frameworks which do not guarantee them their civic and political rights. Vulnerability is not synonymous with poverty, but refers to defenselessness, insecurity and exposure to risk, shocks and stress. Vulnerability is reduced by assets, such as: human investment in health and education; productive assets including houses and domestic equipment; access to community infrastructure; stores of money, jewellery and gold; and claims on other households, patrons, the government and international community for resources at times of need (Wratten 1995).

This study recognized that 66 per cent of the respondents were migrated from rural communities for the purpose of their livelihood opportunities, for better employment options and some of them were reported that for their children's education. Migrants come to the urban areas for a better future for themselves and their children. While they realize the importance of shelter and infrastructure, these are not necessarily their first priority. Earning an income is a priority and as transport costs can be high, proximity to employment opportunities is often more important than the quality of the housing. Many migrants also expect to return eventually to their village and will therefore not be interested to buy, a house, even in a squatter settlement. They are more inclined to rent accommodation, anywhere near employment opportunities. Many city-born families also are faced with a shortage of housing, and are forced to live slums and squatter settlements.

Although in many third world cities natural population growth is the major contributor to urbanization, rural-urban migration is still an important factor (de Haan 1997).

A key determinant of migration is the income differential between rural and urban regions (Gilbert and Gugler 1992). Migration is also affected by crop prices, landowning structures and changes in agricultural technologies and crop mixes in surrounding areas and distant regions. It is also influenced by other factors related to individual or household structures and survival strategies, and wider political, economic and social forces (UNCHS 1996).

Coming to the nature/type of employment 74 per cent of the families are working in private and unorganized sectors. Only 24 per cent of them are in government jobs that to in low cadres. Many urban poor are working in the informal sector. Where they don't have any job security and they may not cover under any risk coverage packages and safety for their lives and for their family members which creates lot of ambiguity in the mind set of people which ultimately resulting in the poor production capacity of a person. Employment in government, factories and offices is much sought after, but usually in short supply. To find such employment, the unemployed need to have the required education and skills, as well as the right contacts. Most of the slum people are illiterates and very few of them are having good skills and education which definitely combines and ties with the income levels as well as the grade or position of the person in the present competitive world. Some respondents shared that some times they do not know the nature of day's work.

If we look at into the basic amenities and living conditions 70 per cent of the respondents are suffering with poor living conditions, lack of sufficient basic civic amenities and particularly very poor sanitary facilities. People residing in slums face many problems like improper sanitation, unhygienic environmental conditions, social, economic, health, educational and cultural problems and many more. The basic problems inherent in slums are health hazards. Lack of basic amenities like safe drinking water, proper housing, drainage and excreta disposal services, make slum population vulnerable to infections. These further compromise the nutrition requirements of those living in slums. These slum people said that poor sanitary conditions and poor quality of water lead to illnesses like diarrhoea and other water borne diseases, affecting the life expectancy of slum-dwellers.

The present study reveals that 59 per cent of the respondents expressed that they are suffering with different communicable diseases due to unhygienic environment and pollution through water, air and other solid wastes. These water and sanitation diseases are responsible for 60 per cent of environmental health. Among water borne diseases, diarrhoea disproportionately affects children under the age of five. The high concentration of slum populations, inadequate water and sanitation facilities, poor drainage and solid waste management, and indoor pollution contribute to acute respiratory diseases, diarrhoeal disease and a wide array of other infectious diseases (e.g., tuberculosis, hepatitis, dengue fever, pneumonia, cholera and malaria) (Montgomery and Hewett, 2004). Poor quality housing conditions also contribute to poor health outcomes and increase vulnerability (Cattaneo, et al., 2007). Poor health among children adversely affects the attendance rate at schools. In dense, overcrowded urban conditions it is often difficult for people to find space to build latrines. Many have to defecate in the open or share whatever limited facilities are available which tend to offer no privacy, safety or hygiene. Because of human waste and refuse collecting in stagnant pools spread disease and contaminate water sources. The problem is made worse during the rainy season when rubbish and excrement are washed into cramped living areas. In these conditions it is virtually impossible to remain healthy and clean. Diseases spread rapidly among the crowded conditions and the little money that slum dwellers earn often has to be spent on medicines to help the sick recover. The determinants of health in urban areas are complex, but social and cultural factors, including composition of the family and cultural restrictions are important (Fustukian 1996). Poor health can reduce capacity to earn an income, and health treatment can use up scarce savings or lead to debt. Ill-health is the most important trigger pushing households into poverty and destitution, particularly when the person sick is the adult wage earner (Harriss et al. 1993, Beall 1995b) is male.

The slum environment is the perfect breeding ground for a wide range of social problems. High unemployment often causes men to stay around the home growing increasingly frustrated with their pathetic situation and the worsening poverty. Cramped conditions mean that there is nowhere to go when tensions rise, a factor that regularly leads to domestic violence. Sometimes the situation goes to the other extreme, where people abandon their homes, lured by the prospect of oblivion through alcohol or drug abuse. Once people develop such problems the prospects of finding work diminish. They fall deeper into poverty and the cycle continues.

The study shows that 33 per cent of the respondents reported that the youth and children were addicted to substances like drugs and alcohol; respondents also shared that nearly 10 per cent of the children from these slums were dropped to school turned as child labours and engaged in antisocial activities like robbery, gambling and prostitution. Many children in the slums started working at a very early age with no prospect of getting any education. They make money by rag picking (trawling through rubbish dumps to retrieve anything that can be sold), selling newspapers in traffic jams, peddling drugs or begging. They are at risk of exploitation as well as all the health problems that accompany their lifestyles. In India, an estimated one million workers move out of agriculture every year, yet the organized service sector generated only 76,000 new jobs annually over the past decade (Glinskaya and Narayan, 2007). Child labour is also of concern, "children, mainly girls, are trafficked for commercial sexual exploitation in urban centers such as Mumbai, Calcutta and New Delhi" (US Department of Labour, 2006).

Then the slum-dwellers 15 per cent of them were replied that due to low incomes some of the women, and youth were involved in commercial sex and running homes for that also with the support of some influenced persons in the secret places; because Tirupati is a famous pilgrimage and centre for business and heart for educational institutions. There is lot of demand for such type of activities which attracts the low income population for easy earnings to survive and for satisfying minimum essentials of their family.

Then the slum dwellers nearly 90 per cent of them expressed that the performance of municipal authorities and execution of sanitary workers are very poor. These concern municipal staff may not respond even any asks for not attending their work regularly as well as the officials also not answer the problems of people. Hence these slum people stopped to question the scavengers and officers. Which resulting in high spreading of diseases and most of the income of these poor are spending to health problems. It is very worse during rainy season.

CHALLENGES FOR CONTROLLING THE URBAN POVERTY

Inequality in access to services, housing, land, education, health care and employment opportunities can have socio-economic, environmental and political repercussions.

Inequality also appears to increase with city size, density of population, though this has not been tested widely. The highly visible disparities in wealth, services and opportunities, can create frustration, tension and a sense of exclusion for the poor. The dimensions of exclusion as defined in the literature are grouped into three categories:

(i) Economic exclusion to equitable access in economic/financial, social, human and natural resource assets.

(ii) Exclusion from access to basic services.

(iii) Social exclusion restricting people from participating on fair terms in local and national social life (World Bank, 2006). For the urban poor, exclusion is extremely evident in day to day life ranging from educational inequality across schools to spatial barriers in access to jobs.

Many of the problems of urban poverty are rooted in a complexity of resource and capacity constraints, inadequate Government policies at both the central and local level, and a lack of planning for urban growth and management. Given the high growth projections for most cities in developing countries, the challenges of urban poverty and more broadly of city management will only worsen in many places if not addressed more aggressively. The given areas are the key areas of challenge for urban poverty. There is urgency to rectify and act immediately on these aspects to reduce the extent of urban poverty.

- Poor coordination among officials and NGOs or civil societies, lack of ownership among people on government programmes.
- Lack of role clarity and professional competencies in staff.
- In sufficient budget allocation and time constraint in availability of funds at the time of need.
- Corruption/illegal land occupying by the politicians.
- Low levels of people's participation or involvement in planning of urban poverty programmes – because feeling of non locality/out siders.
- Limited opportunities for policy advocacy.

The next of part of the paper discussed with the various alternative methods and approaches for controlling the poverty in urban areas with suitable strategies.

APPROACHES FOR REDUCING URBAN POVERTY

In order to achieve the MDG we should introduce/adopt certain innovations and interventions for tackling of urban poverty.

One of the powerful gears is Social protection. The World Development Report (World Bank, 2000) places emphasis on three types of action to reduce poverty — opportunity, empowerment and security. The latter aims to improve poor people's security through "Social Risk Management" measures, which are defined as activities by secondary stakeholders (governments, the private sector and civil society) to assist individuals, households and communities in managing income risks in order to reduce vulnerability, improve consumption smoothing and enhance equity, while contributing to economic development in a participatory manner (Ravallion, Martin, 2003).

- The social protection measures will focus on preventing or reducing risk, mitigating risk through portfolio diversification and insurance, and introducing mechanisms to cope with risk, including social safety nets.
- In order to provide water supply services of required standards in slums, it is recommended to provide individual pipe connections to each slum household, promote rain water harvesting, replace damage pipes and improve delivery pressures at public stand posts and remove illegal connections.
- Similarly, to improve sanitation standards, it is essential to construct community toilets where individual toilets are not possible, to extend sewerage networks to slum areas and connect toilet outlets with that, and community management of toilets in common places.
- A demand led approach for improvement of access to public transport should be adopted. Appropriate technology should be used for developing road network depending on the geographical conditions and climate etc. People's participation needs to be promoted in operation and maintenance of public transport.
- Solar, bio-gas and non-conventional energy needs to be promoted for street lights as well as in household energy use wherever possible and feasible. Complete coverage of slum households through electric connections should be ensured.
- In order to ensure proper drainage systems, flood prone habitats should be shifted to higher elevation, canal banks should be raised and protected and retaining walls constructed wherever required.
- Good urban governance is necessary to ensure that no one is excluded from participation in decision-making and from the benefits of urban policies and programmes. Improving people's participation in design and implementation of the basic services in slums through Self-Help promoted groups and their apex level institutions like clusters and federations which are having a great control over the community.

In addition to the government interventions the NGOs can play a vital role in improving the existing conditions of slums. NGOs should work for the underprivileged segments in the slums. NGOs should work in close coordination with government and make sure that the following facilities are available to the slum-dwellers

- Counseling services to minimize crime and other problems.

- Basic amenities like schooling, proper sanitation, potable water, health facilities and common electricity with minimal charges.
- Free weekly medical and healthcare facilities etc.

SUGGESTIONS

The respondents also suggested some points to improve their situation only through improving their incomes and along with availing the better and adequate infrastructure and basic amenities (shelter, water, sanitation, electricity at their localities by the municipal authorities then only they will come out of their existing problematic situations. Based on the author's experience and exposure of field she is also suggesting some of the ways for improving the living standards of the poor in urban slums as follows:

(i) Poverty reduction and human development are incremental processes and have to be accepted as such. Achieving adequate housing can only be realized progressively.

The urban poor are the major resource in poverty reduction and urban development. They should drive the process of incremental development of housing and settlements. Government should enable and support the process. Apartment type of colonies must be developed with high ventilation in the place of slums.

(ii) Roads and streets must be spaciously widened.

(iii) Health and hygiene awareness must be created in the slum-dwellings.

(iv) Underground drainage system, toilets must be constructed and managed in a proper way.

(v) Vaccinations must be administrated to the slum dwellers for epidemic and endemic diseases.

(iv) The role of the government is to mobilize resources of the public and private sector and of civil society for the benefit of the town or city as a whole, by acting as effective and efficient managers of the resources. Providing income generation opportunities through promotion of people's institutions or community based and managed organizations for achieving self sustainability with tie ups with formal financial institutions like banks and micro finance Institutions.

The despair of the underprivileged has to be replaced with hope, their fear with security, and their ignorance with knowledge. Give them an opportunity to secure good health, immunity from curable diseases, employment opportunities, sufficient and nutritious food, clean water and a clean environment, capability to protect their children against exploitation and discrimination. Their children should have the right to get adequate education for becoming responsible citizens of India. Slum-dwellers should be empowered to enable them to improve the quality of their own lives.

CONCLUSIONS

India has entered the Eleventh Plan period with an impressive record of economic growth.However, the incidence of decline of urban poverty has not accelerated with GDP growth. Infact, urban poverty will become a major challenge for policymakers in our country as the urban population in the country is growing, so is urban poverty. Therefore, a need has arisen to develop new poverty reduction tools and approaches to attack the multi-dimensional issues of urban poverty. For this, policymakers at the national and local levels should have a good understanding of the nature of urban poverty as well as accurate data on various issues relating to it, in order to develop programme/policies to manage urban poverty in a systematic manner. India Urban Poverty Report using human development framework provides a good insight on various issues of urban poverty such as basic services to urban poor, migration, urban economy and livelihoods, micro finance for urban poor, education and health, unorganized sector and livelihoods.

REFERENCES

Beall, J. 1995b, 'In Sickness and in Health: Engendering Health Policy for Development', *Third World Planning Review*, Vol. 17 No. 2.

Cattaneo, M. S., P. Galiani, S. Gertler, Martinez, and R. Titiunik, 2007, "Housing, Health, and Happiness." *Policy Research Working Paper No. 4214*, World Bank, Washington, D.C.

Census of India 2001, http://www.censusindia.net/.

De Haan, 1997, 'Rural-Urban Migration and Poverty: The Case of India', *IDS Bulletin*, Vol. 28 No. 2, Brighton: Institute of Development Studies.

DFID., (1999); *India Country Strategy Paper*, Department for International Development India: Delhi.

Fustukian, S., 1996, 'Strategies to Strengthen Urban Health and Social Development', in N. Hall, R. Hart and D. Mitlin, *The Urban Opportunity: The Work of NGOs in Cities of the South*, London: ITDG.

Glinskaya, E. and D. Narayan, 2007; "Ending Poverty in South Asia: Ideas that Work", World Bank, Washington, D.C.

Gilbert, A. and J. Gugler, 1992, *Cities, Poverty and Development: Urbanization in the Third World*, Oxford: Oxford University Press.

Harriss, J., C. Rosser, and S. Kumar, (1993); *Slum Dwellers and the Cuttack labour Market*, Report for DFID India.

Montgomery, Mark R. and C. Paul Hewett, 2004, "Urban Poverty and Health in Developing Countries: Household and Neighborhood Effects," *Policy Research Division Working Paper No. 184*, Population Council, New York City, New York.

Ravallion, Martin, 2003, "The Debate on Globalization, Poverty and Inequality: Why Measurement Matters", *International Affairs*, 79 (4), 739–753.

Ravallion, Martin, Shaohua Chen and Prem Sangraula, 2007, "New Evidence on the Urbanization of Global Poverty," *Policy Research Paper No. 4199*, World Bank, Washington, D.C.

Ravallion, Martin and Shaohua Chen, 2007, "China's (Uneven) Progress Against Poverty," *Journal of Development Economics*, 82 (1): 1-42.

Sen, Amartya (2000); *Development as Freedom*, New York, 2000.

UNCHS (HABITAT), 1996, *An Urbanizing World: Global Report on Human Settlements 1996*, Oxford: Oxford University Press.

U.S. Department of Labor, Bureau of International Labor Affairs, 2006, "The Department's of Labor's 2005 Findings on the Worst Forms of Child Labor," Washington, D.C.

World Bank, January 2006, India Water Supply and Sanitation: Bridging the Gap Between Infrastructure and Service. Background Paper, Urban Water Supply and Sanitation, pp. 18-19.

World Bank 2000, *World Development Report*, World Bank: Washington.

Wratten, E. 1995, 'Conceptualising Urban Poverty', in IIED, 1995, 'Urban Poverty: Characteristics, Causes and Consequences', *Environment and Urbanization*, Vol. 7 No. 1.

Slumisation in India

Problems and Challenges – Strategies for Social Work Intervention

Dr. R. Srinivas

INTRODUCTION

Slumisation is corollary of urbanization. It is examined as a process of increasing total population as well as increasing slum population in a city as percentage of total population in the city. "Slums are in fact, universal phenomena and are the product of urban explosion, which has accompanied industrialisation and has caused physical and social stress to the urban environment. Particularly in the developing countries that have failed to cope with ever-tide and uncontrolled growth of urban morphology" (Singh, 1984).

People settled in slums do not usually have accessibility to basic material needs food, housing, education, health and occupation and environmental conditions particularly with reference to drainage, garbage disposal and sewerage.

CONCEPT OF AN URBAN AREA AND SLUM

An urban area and the related process of its growth is largely contingent upon certain parameters, viz., number and density of people in a region, of persons engaged in secondary and tertiary activities as well as administration. There is wide variation in the exact number of persons that differentiate urban from rural. In India defines an area as urban under the following criteria (Census, 2001):

(i) An area having population of five thousand or more,

(ii) An area with 75 per cent of its population engaged in non-agricultural activities,

(iii) An area with density of population of 400 persons per square kilometre.

Moreover, a region with more than 50 per cent of economically productive population engaged in non-agricultural occupation is termed as urban. Even a settlement with less than 5,000 persons can become urban if it has a municipality and a cantonment board or notified area. Urbanization is thus, the process of change and shift from rural society to urban settlements that involves quantitative transformations of demographic and economic aspects.

The increasing urbanization enhances growing demand for basic services to meet the growing consumerism of urban population. There is lack of space for building purposes and thus, cities face inadequacy of housing facilities for immigrants who later find dwelling spaces on footpaths, fly-over/s. railway lines, etc., and encroach upon public lands. These areas become the habitat choices. These degenerated areas with shanty houses, miserable health, sanitation, nutrition and illiteracy throw a pathetic picture around the city, These are called slums.

TREND OF SLUMISATION IN INDIA

In India, there are 607 towns reporting slums, which have a population of 1783.9 lakhs. The number of towns reporting slums in India were highest in Andhra Pradesh (76), followed by U.P. (65), Tamilnadu (63), Maharashtra (62) and West Bengal (51). The population of towns reporting slums (in lakh) was highest in Maharashtra (336.2), followed by U.P. (187.9). Goa (1.7) reported to be a state with lowest population of to India.

The State with percentage of slum population above national average (22.76%) was reported in Meghalaya (41.33%), followed by Andhra Pradesh (32.69%), Maharashtra (31.66%), Chhattisgarh (29.27%). West Bengal (26.82%), Madhya Pradesh (24.31%). Uttar Pradesh has 22.12 per cent of slum population, which is a proportion below the national average.

That the total slum population in million-plus cities in India was 718.5 lakh. Among the four major metropolitan cities, the highest slum population is in Greater Mumbai (119.1), followed by Delhi Muncipal Corporation (98.1) Kolkata (45.8) and Chennai (42.1). Among the other million-plus cities in Peninsular India, Bangaluru is leading with total slum population of 42.9 lakh, followed by Ahmedabad (35.1), Hyderabad (34.5), Pune (25.4), Surat (24.3), Nagpur (20.5), Vadodara (13.0), Thane (12.6), Kalyan Dombivli (11.9) and Nasik (10.7).

In the northern central part of the country, the big cities with a million-plus slum population are Kanpur (25.3), Jaipur (23.2), Indore (15.9), Bhopal (14.3), Ludhiana (13.9), Patna (13.7), Agra (12.5), Varanasi (11.0), Meerut (10.7), Faridabad (10.5), Henra (10.0) and Pimprichinchwad (10.0) (Table 4.1).

The percentage of slum population is 23.86 in India. The cities with the percentage of slum population above the cities with the percentage of slum population above the national average is in Greater Mumbai (48.8) followed by Faridabad (46.5), Meerut (43.8), Nagpur (35.4), Thane (33.3), Kolkata (32.5) and Chennai (25.6). Below the national average by percentage of slum population, the million plus cities are Ludhiana (22.5), Pune (20.9), Delhi

Table 4.1:Slum Population in Million-Plus Cities of India (Muncipal Corporation) – 2001

Name of the City	Total population (lakh)	Slum population (total in lakh)	Percentage as Total
Greater Mumbai	119.1	58.2	48.88
Delhi (urban)	98.1	18.5	18.89
Kolkata	45.8	14.9	32.55
Bangaluru	42.9	3.4	8.04
Chennai	42.1	10.7	25.60
Ahmedabad	35.1	4.3	12.51
Hyderabad	34.5	6.0	17.43
Pune	25.4	5.3	20.92
Kanpur	25.3	3.6	14.56
Surat	24.3	4.0	16.68
Jaipur	23.2	3.5	15.07
Nagpur	20.5	7.2	35.42
Indore	15.9	2.5	16.25
Bhopal	14.3	1.2	8.81
Ludhiana	13.9	3.1	22.56
Patna	13.7	0.03	0.25
Vadodara	13.0	1.0	8.21
Thane	12.6	4.2	33.31
Agra	12.5	1.2	9.67
Kalian-Dombivli	11.9	0.3	2.92
Varanasi	11.0	1.3	12.55
Nasik	10.7	1.4	13.20
Meerut	10.7	4.7	43.87
Faridabad	10.5	4.9	46.55
Henra	10.0	1.1	11.72
Pimprichinchwad	10.0	1.2	12.85
Total	**718.5**	**171.7**	**23.90**

* *Source:* Census India 2001, Office of the Registrar General of India.

Municipal Area (18.8), Hyderabad (17.4), Surat (16.6), Indore (16.2), Jaipur (15.0), Kanpur (14.5), Nasik (13.2), Pinprichinchwad (12.8), Ahmedabad(12.5), Varanasi (12.5), Henra (11.7), Agra (9.6), Bhopal (8.8), Vadodara (8.2), Bangaluru (8.0), Kalyan (2.9) and Patna (0.2).

MEASURES FOR SLUM IMPROVEMENT

The scheme of Environmental Improvement of Urban Slums (EIUS) came into operation in 1972 and thereafter, received much attention under minimum needs programme. Any slum area selected for improvement under the scheme should have at least two-thirds of the slum families in the poor and low-income groups with an income of less than Rs. 250 per month. There should be no likelihood of any slum clearance or redevelopment programme being taken up in that area for a period of at least 15 years in case of *pucca*-built slums and 10 years for hutment type slums, so that adequate benefit is secured from the money spent on improvement.

The Central and State governments, Municipalities and private industries should take responsibility of providing funds for various schemes under slum improvement programme:

- Housing is a major problem in towns and cities particularly for weaker sections and low income groups. Since, government alone cannot meet the shortage of houses, private building activities should be encouraged by providing plots, long-term loans with low interest rates, subsidies etc.
- The World Bank, UNICEF and other agencies must be approach for financing housing schemes for weaker sections.
- Urban land ceiling plans should be strictly enforced to regulate the prices of urban lands.
- Low-Cost houses with cheap materials should be designed and encouraged.
- A separate slum improvement finance corporation should be set-up to advance long-term loans with low interest rates.
- The Central Government should take of the responsibility of providing houses for slum dwellers in cities.
- Strict enforcement of master plans is necessary to avoid further growth of slums.
- Rural-urban migration should be regulated by creating alternative avenues of employment in rural areas.
- Efforts may be made to rehabilitate the slum-dwellers in their existing locations without up-rooting their economic and social life.

- The rents payable by the slum dwellers for the allotted houses should with in their reach. The Government and local authorities may provide necessary and minimum services like roads, water supply, bathroom, drainage, schools, hospitals etc.
- Efforts may be made to educate the slum-dwellers for inculcating civic sense and to understand the dangers of slum life.
- The slum-dwellers ultimately should realize the value of cleanliness and healthy surroundings and eschew what is called "slum mentality" in the words of Sociologists.
- The ultimate solution to the removal of slums lies in eradication of urban poverty.

STRATEGIES FOR SOCIAL WORK INTERVENTION

Social work is particularly concerned with the removal of human sufferings by providing help and support to the individual, the groups and community. Social work endeavours to being about environmental manipulation or desirable change in the community and society. Social workers view the slums not as a problem but as people's solution to the shelter problem, but slums are not ideal solutions to human settlement. The social workers should help the slum community to describe, identify and articulate its aspirations and mobilize the community to strive to achieve them. Social workers should intervene in slums for planned development. A particular slum can be adopted by the schools of social work for its total development. Slum area adoption by the institute of social work helps to identify the social workers with the slum dwellers and work with them for better social and economic life. The main of the slum area adoption is to improve quality of life of the residents:

- Social workers may organize sanitation drive from time to time by involving the residents of locality and concerned officials.
- Social workers should undertake the responsibility of creating awareness among the slum-dwellers about their rights and responsibilities.
- Social workers should involve themselves in arousing consciousness among the people towards health, sanitation, nutrition etc.
- Vocational guidance and counseling services can also be organized in slum area, particularly for the youth.

In order to solve the problems of slums in Indian society three ways are suggested by social thinkers:

1. By physical improvement of the slums.
2. By establishing welfare service centers in slum areas to solve the problems of the slum.
3. By making provision of economic opportunities to the slum-dwellers.

REFERENCES

Ahuja, Ram Social Problems in India 2004, Rawat Publication, New Delhi.

Aggarwal, S.K., (Ed) 2007, *Urbanization Urban Development and Metropolitan Cities in India Concept Publishing Company*, New Delhi.

Census of India Series 1: Tables on General Population, Registrar General 2001 and Census Commissioner, India, Government of India.

Pant, S. K., 2006, *Human Development Concept and Issues in the Context of Globalization*, Rawat Publication, New Delhi.

Dwelling Conditions in Tirupati Urban Slums

T. Mallikarjuna,
Dr. Janaki Ramaiah,
Prof. V. Reddeppa Naidu

INTRODUCTION

Industrialization results in increasing urbanization. The accumulation of wealth and availability of more economic and job opportunities in the urban centres have resulted in the concentration of the population in the congested metropolitan areas and thus the formation and growth of big slum areas. These slum centers, when combined with industrial sectors, become house less from the standing point of living degradation and pollution etc.

Urbanization brings in its wake, multitude of problems affecting the quality of life of the urbanities. It was felt that the inadequacies and gaps in the provision of services which affect the quality of life of the urban people are access to water, sanitation, roads, street lights etc. As per the Census 2001, about 25.11 per cent of urban people are living in slums and it is 6.79 per cent in when compared to State total population. The percentage of slum population as against the total population of the State is 6.80. The average literacy rate in the slum areas of the State is 70.70 per cent whereas it is 61.11 per cent for the State as a whole. The literacy rate figures give an indication of the rural literacy migration to the urban areas in search of employment.

Slum dwellers share something with people caught in a war zone, where the infrastructure of society has been interrupted or destroyed. They have to scrounge and improvise, just to have the basics primary need shelter, food, heat, water, sanitation, drainage. To survive, they have to be inventive. But the people in the war zone can look forward to the end of war, the restoration of society and its services. The slum-dwellers have no such prospect. For them the war, its brutalities and atmosphere of cruelty and indifference to human life, never ends.

Slum-dwellers are the most substantial but overlooked section of the Indian society. At a size able 26 per cent of India's population; they represent the poorest of the urban poor. Different States have different meanings of the word Slum. But a few characteristics are hard to escape. Minuscule living areas, a bourgeoning population living below the poverty line, nil drinking water, and latrines shared among hundreds, a non-existent sewage system; the record is endless. The existence of slums in every major city of India is due to the imbalance in the urban economy. The government, fully aware of a size able portion of its poverty-stricken population that lives under despicable sanitation and housing conditions conveniently turns a blind eye to its cause.

India is urbanising very fast and along with this, the slum population is also increasing. India's urban population is increasing at a faster rate than its total population. With over 575 million people, India will have 41 per cent of its population living in cities and towns by 2030 from the present level of 286 million and 28 per cent. However, most of them do not have access to basic facilities like drinking water and sanitation. Among the urban poor, the slum dwellers are the poorest. The very definition of slums points at the acute drinking water and sanitation crisis for the slum dwellers. A slum in India is defined as 'a cluster inside urban areas without having water and sanitation access'.

The National Sample Survey Organisation (NSSO) survey conducted in 2002 found that in 84 per cent of the notified slums the main water source is through tap water supply. But these numbers mask differences across the States of India. In Andhra Pradesh none of the slums get water via the tap.

Tirupati is famous for the Venkateswara Swamy temple dedicated to Lord Venkateswara, located about 10 kilometres Northwest of Tirupati in the Tirumala hills at an elevation of 853 metres. One of the most important pilgrimage centres in India, the temple draws millions of pilgrims and is the busiest pilgrimage centre in the world. Tirupati town itself has several temples and is famous for its red wooden toys, copper and brass idols. Also, the town is a major economical and educational hub in the southern region of the state.

Tirupati is a sacred place of pilgrimage and is situated in the latitudes of 13º40'N and Longitudes of 79º27E and at a height of 500 feet above the mean sea level in Chittoor district of Andhra Pradesh. Tirupati rests in the midst of an amplitheatre encircled by a range of eastern ghats. It covers a geographical area of 24.28. Sq. km. and 2,50,852 lakhs population (2001 census). It is famous for Lord Sri Venkateswara's temple, which attracts 10-16 million pilgrims every year. Tirupati growth as a pilgrimage, educational, and industrial centre has led to a substantial increase in commercial activity during the past decades. This has also resulted in rapid proliferation of slums, mainly due to large-scale migration from the neighbouring district of Andhra Pradesh. At present 42 slum areas with 94.057 population and 19.289 households living slums of Tirupati city. It is also connected to the three State capitals of the southern states by road and it is about 580 km from Hyderabad; 137 km from Chennai and 248 km from Bangaluru. The district headquarters Chittoor is about 69 km southwest of Tirupati.

The Tirupati commissioner and other senior officials were instructed to supply water through tankers in the towns. Among the other things that the officials brought to the Minister's notice were the huge number of illegal water connections and an equally large number of BPL families in slums, which could not afford a connection. The Minister suggested that the tap connection charges of Rs. 1,200 be collected in 12 equal instalments for slum dwellers. Making it clear that paucity of funds would never be a problem in improving civic amenities, he recalled that the Government had sanctioned Rs. two crores for all civic bodies, thus breathing life into the ailing ones, and even released half of the said amount initially to help them improve infrastructure and meet the needs of the denizens.

Tirupati city is not a district headquarters but a *mandal* headquarters. It is the seat of the administratior of Tirumala-Tirupati Devasthnams' management as several of its offices are located here. It derives its importance and growth mainly due to its location as a piligrim centre. It has also grown up as an important centre of education with the location of Sri Venkateswara University, Sri Padmavathi Mahila University, N.G. Ranga Agriculture University, Veterinary, Medical and several engineering and educational colleges and also famous hospitals such as SVIMS, BIIRD etc.

At present Municipal Corporation spread over an area of 24.28 sq.km with 20 Revenue Wards and 50 Election wards with 42 Poor slums. In this 42 slums 38 slums are notified from the Tirupati urban development authority, the reaming the 4 slums are not notified Tirupati urban development authority even today.

GEOGRAPHICAL AREA

Tirupati is located in the southern part of Andhra Pradesh. It has an average elevation of 162 metres (531 feet)· The Tirumala hill is 3,200 ft (980 m) above sea level, and is about 10.33 square miles (26.8 km^2) in area.

Climate

Tirupati has an extreme type of climate. Monsoon remains moderate and summer experiences temperatures ranging from 42 to 45º Celsius (107.6º F and 113º F). In winter the minimum temperatures will be between 10 and 18º Celsius (50º F to 64.4º F). Usually summer lasts from March to June, with the advent of rainy season in July, followed by winter which lasts till the end of February.

Population

Tirupati has a population of about 2,50,821 (with urban agglomeration, 3,03,521). Males constitute 53 per cent of the population and females 47 per cent. It has an average literacy rate of 81 per cent, higher than the national average of 59.5 per cent: male literacy is 82 per cent, and female literacy is 72 per cent. sixteen per cent of the population is under 6 years of age. According to 2001 Census, 41 per cent of the population of Tirupati live in slums whereas the BPL population is only 28 per cent.

Language and Culture

Telugu is the official and principal language of the town whereas Tamil is widely spoken. Most of the temples in Tirupati have been built using Dravidian architecture. Hinduism is the major religion here. *Dhoti* (*Pancha/Veshti*) and *Saree* are traditional attire of people here. Dresses like *churidar* and pants-shirt have become common in recent decades. Practices of tonsure and using *tilaka* are very popular among devotees of Lord Venkateswara. Songs and prayers of Lord Venkateswara are generally heard all over the town. Near the bus stand, stands the statue of Bharatharatna M.S. Subbulakshmi.

List of Slums and Population in Tirupati

S. No.	Name of the slum	Population per hec	Area in hec	Population Density
1	2	3	4	5
1.	Sapthagiri Nagar	3520	4.80	733
2.	Suraiah Katta	1121	0.20	5605
3.	Sivajyothi Nagar	4586	2.40	1910
4.	Yerramitta	3691	2.00	1845
5.	Korlagunta, Maruthi Nagar	8444	4.40	1919
6.	Sanjay Gandhi Colony	6422	1.20	5351
7.	Chandrasekhar ReddyColony	527	2.40	219
8.	Kothapalli	551	0.80	688
9.	Yerukula Colony	97	0.80	121
10.	Ashok Nagar	5377	1.20	4480
11.	Scavengers City	314	2.00	157
12.	Murikineela Gunta	2382	6.00	397
13.	Yosodha Nagar	4094	1.20	3411

(Contd...)

1	2	3	4	5
14.	Tataiah Gunta	3879	1.20	3232
15.	Mallaiahgunta Katta	1023	1.21	845
16.	Chintalachenu	704	1.20	586
17.	Uppanki Harijanwada	869	2.40	362
18.	Laxmipuram	1178	1.16	1015
19.	Gandhipuram	430	0.30	1433
20.	Dasarimatam	2158	1.51	1429
21.	New Indira Nagar	3173	0.48	6610
22.	Pedda Harijanawada	5742	1.00	5742
23.	S.T.V. Nagar	4164	4.04	1030
24.	Bhagat Singh Colony	552	0.50	1104
25.	Pachigunta	171	0.24	712
26.	Chenna Reddy Colony	5620	2.96	1898
27.	Ambedkar Colony	215	1.45	148
28.	Haridwar Colony	60	0.20	300
29.	Singalagunta	1922	2.97	647
30.	Sanjeevaiah Colony Beside Maty. Hospital	337	0.58	581
31.	Giripuram	1172	1.50	781
32.	Sanjeevaiah Colony opp.to Medical College	1222	0.60	2036
33.	Nehru Nagar	7367	7.28	1011
34.	Bommagunta	943	1.40	673
35.	Ramakrishna puram	165	0.89	185
36.	Poola Thota	1568	0.12	13066
37.	Kummarathopu	3164	0.28	11300
38.	Indira Nagar	3173	3.69	859
39.	Parvathipuram	1504	0.56	2685
40.	Lenin Nagar	246	0.35	702
41.	Ambedkar Society Colony	66	1.00	66
42.	Chinnagunta	144	0.94	153

TIRUPATI IN A GLANCE

Area of the City	24 km^2
As per 2001 censes the population of town	2,27,6772,
Floating Population	237.00lakhs / Annum
Male population of the town	1,17,806
Female population of the town	1,09,871
Total No. of households in the town	54,457
Slum population	94,057
Total No. of slum households in the town	19,289

Objectives of the Present Study

1. To Study the dwelling conditions of Tirupati slums.
2. To identify the number of slums in Tirupati city.
3. To examine the debt and savings of the slums-dwellers.
4. To know the city area and its population size.
5. To collect population information of the selected slums in Tirupati.
6. To make cautions and give suggestions to future developments.

METHODS AND MATERIALS

The present investigation is based on both secondary and primary data. The secondary data pertaining to slums, land-use and population have been collected from the Tirupati Municipal Authority office and Tirupati Urban Development Authority office. The census collected through the census handbooks of Chittoor district (1971, 1981 1991 and 2001).

The primary data relating to the structure, pattern and growth of slums and socio-economic aspects of slum-dwellers have been collected with the help of the structural schedules, participatory and non-participatory observation.

In the present study simple Random sample, stratified Random sample and statistical techniques are applied to describe the significance of slums in Tirupati. The sample size is 150 households in selected four slums such as Tataiahgunta, Chenna Reddy Colony, Korlagunta, Maruthi Nagar, and Giri Puram.

Analysis of Data

Table 5.1 shows that housing structure of the slum dwellers 24.7 per cent of the respondents having *pucca* houses, 46.0 per cent of the respondents having semi-*pucca* houses. Remaining of them having katcha houses.

Table 5.1: Housing Structure of the Slum-Dwellers

House Type	No of Respondents	Percentage
Pucca	37	24.7
Semi Pucca	69	46.0
Katcha	44	29.3
Total	**150**	**100**

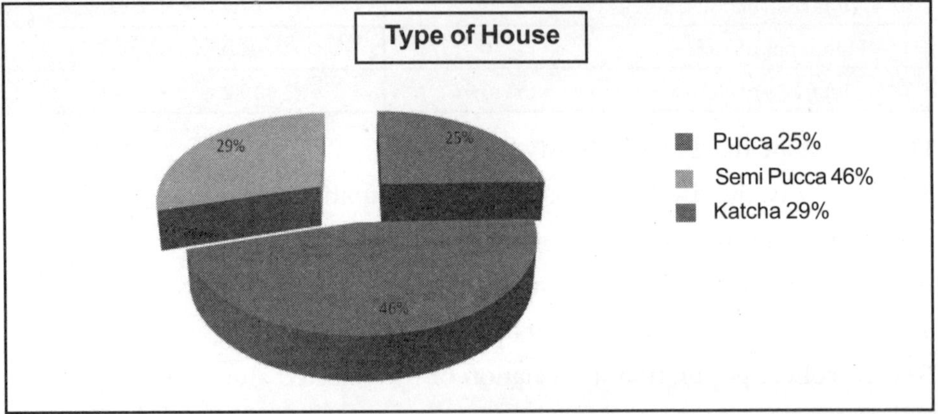

Table 5.2 shows that house status of the respondents. 28.7 per cent of the respondents have own houses, 54.7 per cent of the respondents living in rental houses and 16.6 per cent of the respondents in living share houses.

Table 5.2: Housing Statuses of the Respondents

Status of House	No.of Respondents	Percentage
Owen house	43	28.7
Rent house	82	54.7
Share house	25	16.6
Total	**150**	**100**

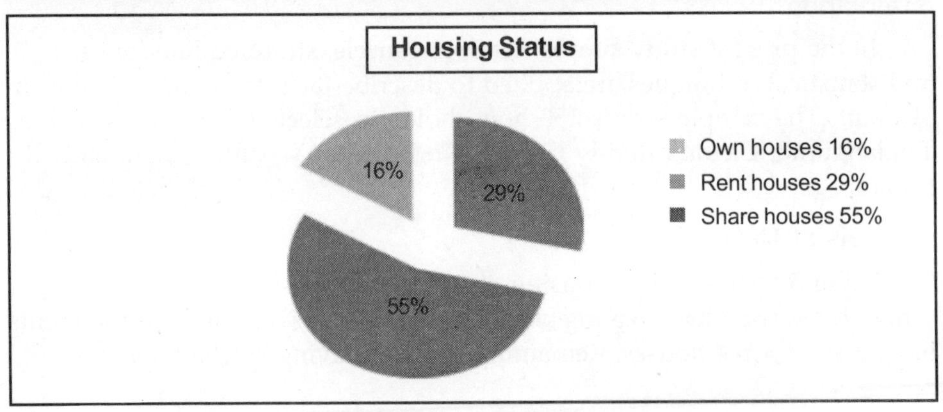

Table 5.3 shows that minimum housing facilities 71.4 per cent of households having attached kitchen facility, 28.6 per cent are not having attached kitchen facility. Thirty eight per cent of the households having attached lavatory, 62.0 per cent of the households using common lavatory Forty four per cent of the households having proper ventilation facility, 56.0 per cent of the households have no proper ventilation facility and 59.3 per cent of the households have drainage facility, 40.7 per cent of them have no drainage facility. Because of this things slums are become dumping bins.

Table: 5.3 Housing Facilities of the Respondents

Item	Yes	Percent	No	Percent	Total
Attached Kitchen	107	71.4	43	28.6	150
Lavatory facility common/attached	57	38.0	93	62.0	150
Ventilation	66	44.0	84	56.0	150
Drainage	89	59.3	61	40.7	150

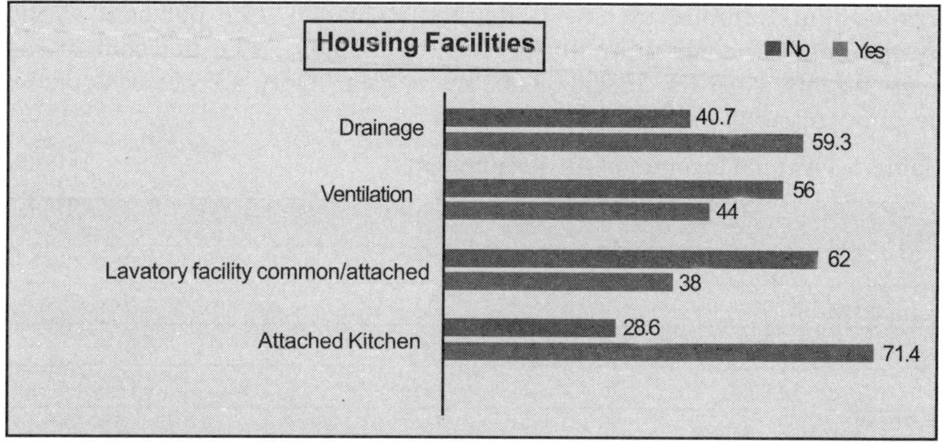

Table 5.4 show that the economic source of the respondents 21.4 per cent of the respondents earn through the jobs, 49.3 per cent of the of the respondents got money from daily wages,14.0 per cent of the respondents through the rickshaw pulling and 15.3 per cent of the respondents income source domestic work.

Table: 5.4 Economic Sources of the Respondents

Occupation	Respondents	Percentage
Jobs	32	21.4
Daily wages	74	49.3
Rickshaw Pulling	21	14.0
Domestic workers	23	15.3

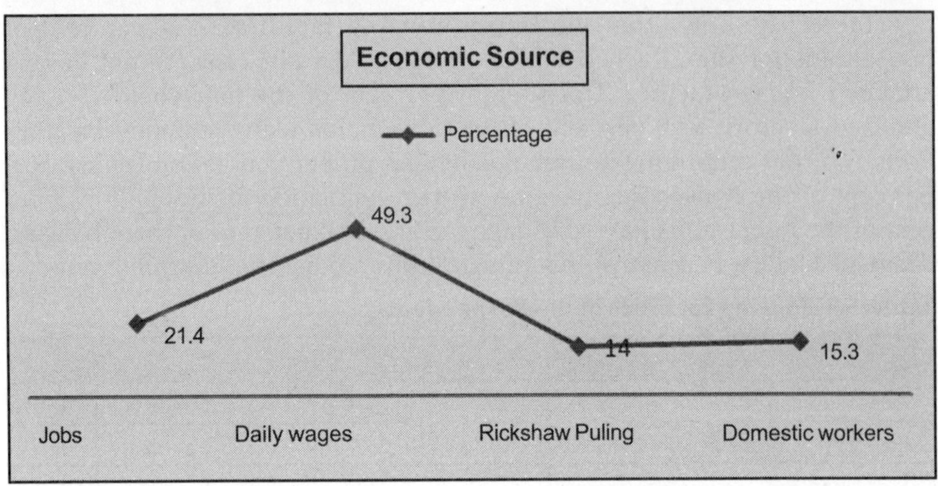

Table 5.5 reviews the annual income of respondents ie 41.3 per cent of the respondents income is Rs. 10,000-15,000 annually, 20.6 per cent of the respondents, annual income is Rs. 15,000-20,000, 18.6 per cent of the respondents, income annually is Rs. 20,000-25,000, 14.6 per cent of the respondents, earn Rs. 25,000-30,000 every year. Only 4.7 per cent of the respondents earn more than 30,000 yearly.

Table: 5.5 Annual Incomes of the Respondents

Annual Income	No. of Respondents	Percentage
10,000-15,000	62	41.3
15,000-20,000	31	20.6
20,000-25,000	28	18.6
25,000-30,000	22	14.6
More than 30,0000	07	4.7

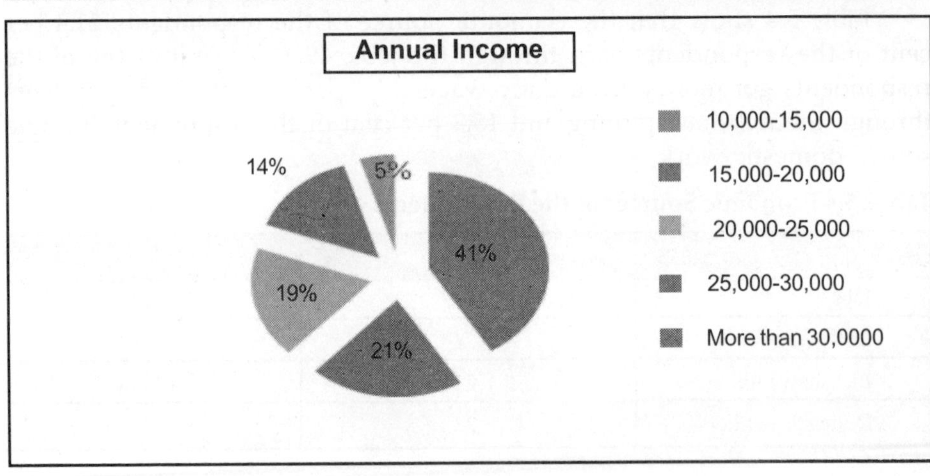

Table 5.6: Four Slums Population According to 2001 Census

S.No	Ward No.	Name of the slum	Population per hec	Area in hec	Population Density
1.	4	Korlagunta, Maruthi Nagar	8444	4.40	1919
2.	13	Tataiah Gunta	3879	1.20	3232
3.	27	Chenna Reddy Colony	5620	2.96	1898
4.	29	Giri Puram	1172	1.50	781

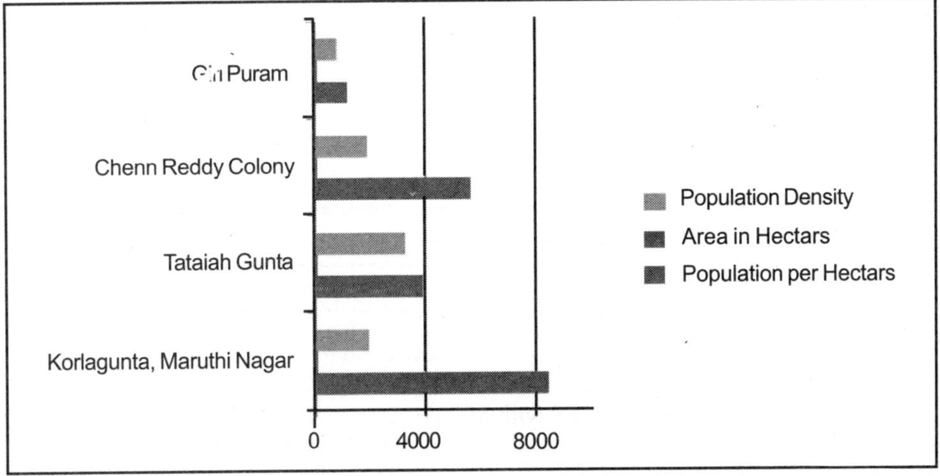

SUMMARY AND CONCLUSION

In these slums socio-economic conditions and quality of life are also very poor. The poor pilgrims coming to the city generally stay in the slum areas, where certain people dwelling in slums give lodging and board to the pilgrims, Ex. Nehru Nagar, Parasala Veedi etc. Korlagunta slum is the biggest one in terms of population (8444). Poolathota, Kummarathopu, New Indira Nagar, Pedda Harijanawada, Suraiah Katta and Ashok Nagar are identified the denser slums. These slums are causing an ill-health environment to the town in terms of over crowding, unclean environment, drainage water stagnation, presence of mosquitoes, disease proneness and favourable conditions to the spread of diseases etc. If the situation continues, unknown diseases come with the strangers and go with the strangers if they stay in the unhygienic conditions of the slums. It is more a danger for the city and for the pilgrims. If these slums are not developed in a planned way, it becomes a disease spreading centre instead of pilgrim centre causing people to be afraid to come to Tirupati, and it loses its sanctity and importance.

A slum is like a pawn to political parties. An entire slum could sway its vote-bank towards one party and bring them to power in the centre. Elections after election, political parties woo slums with their promises of making life better for them. They pledge material items and reservations; are assured in aplenty. But once in the power chair, the people are left high and mighty dry.

SUGGESTIONS

1. Apartment type of colonies must be developed with high ventilation in the place of slums.
2. Roads and streets must be spaciously widened.
3. Hygienic awareness must be created among the slum-dwellers.
4. Underground drainage system, toilets must be constructed.
5. Already two large INDIRAMMA housing colonies are developed in Tirupati sub-urbs and urban housing development planners have to plan such huge housing colonies in the sub-urban areas.
6. Old age homes, child care centers, Vocational training centers for youth must be provided in all slums.

REFERENCES

Biswaroop (2010) *Das Slum Dwellers in Indian Cities: The Case of Surat in Western India*, Queen Elizabeth House, University of Oxford.

Eswaramma, P,. (2000) M. Phil Thesis on "Urban Growth in Tirupati city with Special Reference to Slums", S. V. University, Tirupati.

Krishnaiah, K., (2003), "Tirupati City with Many Slums; an Ill-Health Environment to the Pilgrim Centre", *Third International Conference on Environment and Health*, Chennai, India.

Kumar, S., K. Shigeo and H. Harada (2003), Living Environment and Health of Urban Poor, A Study in Mumbai, *Economic and Political Weekly*.

Janardhana Raju, N., and Krishna Reddy (2006), Urban Development and the Looming Water Crisis—A Case Study from Tirupati, South India, *The Geological Society of London*, 2006.

National Sample Survey Organization (2004) *Housing Condition in India*.

National Sample Survey Organization (2003) *Condition of Urban Slums–2002*.

Pradhakrishna, B., 2004, Man-Made Drought and the Looming Water Crisis, *Journal of the Geological Society of India*, 63, 477-481.

Planning Commission, India (2002) *India Assessment 2002: Water Supply and Sanitation*.

Retnaraj, D., 2001, "Fast Growing Cities, Spurt in Land Prices and Urban Slums: The Kerala Experience", IASSI Quarterly 20(2):123-133.

Registrar General of India, 2001, *Analytical Report on Housing Amenities, Series I*, Census of India, Delhi.

Registrar General and Census Commissioner, 2001, *Census of India: Slum Population*, in Series 1, New Delhi.

Siddiqui, N. Roomana, (2001), Perception of Economic and Environmental Stressors by Urban Slum Dwellers, *Psychology and Developing Societies*, pp. 93-103.

The Hindu, NEWS Thursday, January 09, 2005.

Urban Development State of Environment, Andhra Pradesh EPTRI, Hyderabad.

United Nations, (2005), *United Nations Development Programme Report*, 2005.

Living Conditions in Urban Slums of India

Need for Improvement

Dr. Saraswati Raju Iyer

INTRODUCTION

Almost all the houses in slums in India are in bad, and sometimes dilapidated, conditions. The houses are usually inadequately ventilated. The designs are such as to afford bare shelter, leading to acute congestion. In squatter settlements, houses are constructed using materials like mud, unburnt bricks, tin-sheets, asbestos sheets, bamboo, gunny bags, plastic sheets etc. and are usually single-room units with inadequate space standards.

Private toilets do not exist in a majority of slum areas and even common toilets are available only in a few. Where there are no toilets, people defecate in the open which, besides being an environmental nuisance, poses hardships for, especially women. Community latrines, even where available generally remain filthy and in sanitary and virtually a menace to the areas in which they exist.

Most of the houses in slum areas do not have individual water supply. In some slum areas, public taps do exist but the number of persons using each such tap is generally very high. Many slums, especially in the outskirts of the cities, have open wells as their only source of water for drinking, bathing and cleaning. These wells are generally in sanitary. No attention is paid to the maintenance of wells, or even of public taps. A considerable number of slum dwellers have to fetch water from outside the slum areas.

The drainage system in almost all the slums is very poor. With the exception of *pucca* buildings in old city areas, slum settlements generally do not have any drainage. Further more, a majority of unauthorized colonies and squatter settlements are located on low-lying lands. As a result, sullage water cannot flow away. The situation becomes particularly worse during the rainy season when storm water finds its way into these low lying settlements and get mixed-up with the sullage water, making extremely unhygienic environment.

Roads and lanes are narrow and often unpaved. Puddles and slush are common-place after every rain shower. The facility of roads and street lights is generally inadequate. This adversely affects the safety and security of residents and is generally believed to be largely responsible for high rates of night-time crimes.

There is a complex relationship between environment and health. A number of studies have shown that the unhygienic slum environments make slum-dwellers more susceptible to certain types of diseases like respiratory diseases, gastro-intestinal disorders, skin diseases, malarial fever, tuberculosis, etc. Unfortunately, the economic circumstances of the slum-dwellers are such as they do not allow them to improve their living conditions. A majority of the sum-dwellers are employed in the unorganized or informal sector. A large proportion of them work on a daily wage basis and, therefore, have little or no job security. A significant proportion is employed in construction work. Due to low income, their standard of living is also low and they are left with little surplus income for housing after meeting their families' basic needs of food and clothing.

DEFINITION OF SLUM

A slum, as defined by the United Nations agency UN-HABITAT, is a run-down area of a city characterized by substandard housing and lacking in tenure security. According to the United Nations, the percentage of urban dwellers living in slums decreased from 47 per cent to 37 per cent in the developing world between 1990 and 2005. However, due to rising population, and the rise especially in urban populations, the number of slum-dwellers is rising. One billion people worldwide live in slums and the figure will likely grow to two billion by 2030.

The term has traditionally referred to housing areas that were once relatively affluent but which deteriorated as the original dwellers moved on to newer and better parts of the city, but has come to include the vast informal settlements found in cities in the developing world.

Many shack dwellers vigorously oppose the description of their communities as 'slums' arguing that this results in them being pathologised and then, often, subject to threats of evictions. Many academics have vigorously criticized UN-Habitat and the World Bank arguing that their 'Cities without Slums' Campaign has led directly to a massive increase in forced evictions.

Although their characteristics vary between geographic regions, they are usually inhabited by the very poor or socially disadvantaged. Slum buildings vary from simple shacks to permanent and well-maintained structures. Most slums lack clean water, electricity, sanitation and other basic services.

GROWTH OF SLUMS AND COUNTER MEASURES

Past years have seen a dramatic growth in the number of slums as urban populations have increased in the Third World.

In April 2005, the director of UN-HABITAT stated that the global community was falling short of the Millennium Development Goals which targeted significant improvements for slum-dwellers and an additional 50 million people have been added to the slums of the world in the past two years. According to a 2006 UNHABITAT report, 327 million people live in slums in Commonwealth countries almost one in six Commonwealth citizens. In a quarter of Commonwealth countries (11 African, 2 Asian and 1 Pacific), more than two out of three urban dwellers live in slums and many of these countries are urbanizing rapidly.

The number of people living in slums in India has more than doubled in the past two decades and now exceeds the entire population of Britain, the Indian Government has announced. The number of people living in slums is projected to rise to 93 million in 2011 or 7.75 per cent of the total population almost double the population of Britain Many governments around the world have attempted to solve the problems of slums by clearing away old decrepit housing and replacing it with modern housing with much better sanitation. The displacement of slums is aided by the fact that many are squatter settlements whose property rights are not recognized by the state. This process is especially common in the Third World. Slum clearance often takes the form of eminent domain and urban renewal projects, and often the former residents are not welcome in the renewed housing. For example, in the Philippine slums of Smokey Mountain, located in Tondo, Manila, projects have been enforced by the Government and non-government organizations to allow urban resettlement sites for the slum-dwellers. According to a UN-Habitat report, over 20 million people in the Philippines live in slums, and in the city of Manila alone, 50 per cent of the over 11 million inhabitants live in slum areas.

Moreover new projects are often on the semi-rural peripheries of cities far from opportunities for generating livelihoods as well as schools, clinics etc. At times this has resulted in large movements of inner city slum-dwellers militantly opposing relocation to formal housing on the outskirts of cities. See, for example, Abahlali based Mjondolo in Durban, South Africa.

Critics argue that slum clearances tend to ignore the social problems that cause slums and simply redistribute poverty to less valuable real estate. Where communities have been moved out of slum areas to newer housing, social cohesion may be lost. If the original community is moved back into newer housing after it has been built in the same location, residents of the new housing face the same problems of poverty and powerlessness. There is a growing movement to demand a global ban of 'slum clearance programmes' and other forms of mass evictions.

SLUMS IN INDIA

Condition of slums in India is very bad and need improvement. Slums are defined as "Habitations located on disputed as well as unused government, municipal and private land and characterized by a serious lack of basic amenities and sanitation with dense and overcrowded housing conditions. In other words a slum is taken to mean 'hutting areas with squalid surroundings where huts are erected in a haphazard manner without proper access, minimum basic amenities are lacking, protected water supply and drainage arrangements do not exist. There are number of reasons for slums to emerge in India and the chief among them being change in agricultural scenario, no prospects in rural areas, bigger opportunities in cities, preference on labour market than agriculture. The results of slums are poverty, poor living conditions, no education, very poor hygiene and poor health care. Facts reveals that slum population all over India is 40,297,341 (40 million), four per cent of total Indian population lives in slums, almost quarter of Indian metro cities live in slums, sadly five million of this population are young children (0-6 age group). Occupation in slum suggest the following figures in per centage which are proportion of all earners across India. 4.36 per cent are in State government employment, Union government employment is 7.19 per cent, Non-earners is 3.74 Per cent, Self-employed professional and worker is 5.71 per cent, 0.42 per cent are wage earners and other than own account workers those in business are 4.46 per cent, non-government salaried employment is 0.15 per cent, self-employed is 0.96 per cent and slum population in 4 metros in India shows an alarming growth of slums in India 55 per cent Mumbai, 44 per cent Meerut, 40 per cent of Pune: India's top list on slum population. Pune is considered as the growing city of slums with a total Area of 244 sq.km, population being 15 Lakh approximately and the population in slums is 6 lakh encroachment of slums is 6 per cent (15 sq.km) and the total growth in slum population in the city since 1991 is 176 per cent.

INDIA—HEALTH AND LIVING CONDITIONS IN EIGHT CITIES

A study by Kamla Gupta, *et al.* (2009) on Health and Living Conditions in Eight Indian Cities. National Family Health Survey (NFHS-3), India, 2005-06. Mumbai: International Institute for Population Sciences; Calverton, Maryland, USA: ICF Macro analyzes health and living conditions in eight large Indian cities (Chennai, Delhi, Hyderabad, Indore, Kolkata, Meerut,

Mumbai, and Nagpur). The report is based on data from India's 2005-06 National Family Health Survey (NFHS-3). A special feature of NFHS-3 is that the sample was designed to allow separate estimates of population, health, and nutrition indicators to be generated for each of these eight cities, as well as for the residents of slum and non-slum areas in these cities. In addition, a wealth index was constructed for households in urban India as a whole, using NFHS-3 data on household assets and housing characteristics.

For the purposes of this report, the urban poor population is defined as those persons belonging to the lowest quartile on this wealth index. The study examines the living environment, socio-economic characteristics of households and the population, children's living arrangements, children's work, the health and nutrition of children and adults, fertility and family planning, utilization of maternal health services, knowledge of HIV/AIDS, attitudes of adults toward schools providing family life education for children, and other important aspects of urban life for the eight cities by slum/non-slum residence and for the urban poor.

The analysis shows that more than half of the population in Mumbai lives in slums, whereas the slum population varies widely in the other seven cities. Major differences in the estimation of the size of the slum population are found depending on how slum areas are defined (according to the 2001 Census designation or observation of the area by the NFHS-3 team supervisor at the time of the fieldwork). The poor population in these cities varies within a narrower range, from seven per cent in Mumbai to 20 per cent in Nagpur. The analysis finds that a substantial proportion of the poor population does not live in slums and that a substantial proportion of slum-dwellers are not poor (that is, they do not fall into the bottom quartile on the NFHS-3 wealth index). In some cities, the poor are mostly concentrated in slum areas, whereas the reverse is true in other cities.

Although slum-dwellers are generally worse off than non-slum-dwellers, this pattern is not consistently true for all indicators in every city, and the differentials are quite small in some cases. However, there are large disparities in health and living conditions between the poor and the non-poor in these cities. Although there is an obvious need to improve living conditions and the health of slum-dwellers, it is equally apparent that programs that focus solely on slum areas will not be able to address the urgent needs of the large poor population not living in slums.

LIVING CONDITIONS OF URBAN SLUMS IN INDIA

Sanitation in India is said to be going under improvement. Their main water facility is hand pumps but now some are getting it by tap. Most of them do not have access to neither; so what they do is that they travel to places where there are faucets like the ones the hose are attached too, and they put buckets underneath. Then they wait for like 2-3 weeks for water to come out. Sometimes they have to wait more depending on how many families are waiting for it and have already reserved the faucets.

Water aid is extremely important to Indian slums because the lack of water is the cause for children not receiving education and lost work days. Lost work days is something that no slum-dweller wishes because they do not earn enough, so one day missed is like a huge amount of money wasted and unearned.

A child not getting education is something sad that unfortunately is happening in these places. Children do not miss school because they do not have the money to go, but because of water. Water plays a huge role in the lives of every kid. The reason why they do not attend school is because they need to go with their parents to fetch water in order to survive. According to the study" a bathtub may hold up to 151 L of water and a person living in the slums may only get 30L of that water for all of their needs".

NEED FOR IMPROVEMENT

It is needless to say that there is a need to improve the living conditions of slums. The slum dewellers face lots of problems with regard to housing, water, santitation, education health and hygiene and it is important to improve their living conditions by taking up several projects. The various needs of the slum dwellers are to be met and slum improvement projects have to be taken up more vigourously.

INITIATIVES

1. Different governments have different ways to handle the problem of growing slums.
2. Various NGOs are also taking initiatives to help government in dealing with this issue.
3. Agencies like Jawaharlal Nehru National Urban Renewal Mission (JNNURM) and Slum Rehabilitation Authority (SRA) plan the Rehabilitation of the slums in metros.

SOLUTIONS

Short-term

1. Rehabilitation of major slums in better hygienic places.
2. Re construction of the middle level slums in the same area with proper drainage system and water supply.
3. Provision of basic amenities, medical and health care, education to eradicate poverty completely.

Long-term

1. The objective should be to reduce the migration from rural areas.
2. Providing the basic amenities and better opportunities in rural areas
3. Encouraging agricultural and small-scale industries.

CONCLUSION

In conclusion we may say that slum dwellers are faced with insecurity of tenure, lack of basic services, especially water and sanitation, unsafe building structure, over-crowding, limited access to credit and formal job markets. Normally slums exist on polluted land. They suffer from water-borne diseases. It is also believed that slums are places of high level of crimes. This is not universally true. The poverty is the main reason for slums. At the same time slums also provide low cost accommodation to poor migrants and necessary support to city. In the light of the above discussion it is evident that the Indian urban slum dwellers are living in a poor condition. Hence it is needless to say that there is a need for improvement of the living conditions of urban slums of India need for intervention has to be felt by government as well as non governmental organizations so as to make urban slums a better place of living.

REFERENCES

Blum, Elisabeth / Peter Neitzke: *Favela Metropolis, Berichte And Projekte aus Rio De Janeiro und São Paulo*, Birkhäuser Basel, Boston, Berlin 2004.

Birkinshaw, Matt *A Big Devil in the Jondolos: 2008 A Report on Shack Fires.*

Cassidy, D. "How the Irish Invented Slang", p. 267, Counter Punch Press, 2007.

Davis, Mike (Scholar): Planet of Slums London, New York 2006.

Dyos, H.J.; Cannadine, David and Reeder, David (1982), 131 *Exploring the Urban Past: Essays in Urban History*, Cambridge University Press.

Fabrizio, Floris 2007, Puppets or People? A Sociological Analysis of Korogocho Slum, Pauline Publication Africa, Nairobi Floris Fabrizio ECCESSI DI CITTÀ: Baraccopoli, Campi Profughi, Città Psichedeliche, Paoline, Milano.

Millenium Development Goals—News, 5 April 2005.

Measure Evaluation / NIPORT (2006) Slums of urban Bangladesh: Mapping and Census, 2005, Centre for Urban Studies / Measure Evaluation / Nationaldiei /.

Neuwirth, Robert's Article *Squatters and the Cities of Tomorrow.*

Neuwirth, Robert's Shadow Cities, New York, 2006, Routledge.

Politics in the Slum, *New York Indymedia*, 2008.

Page Jeremy, (2007-05-18). "Indian Slum Population Doubles in Two Decades", *The Times* (London).

Slums of the World UN-HABITAT Report.

Slum-Dwellers to Double by 2030 UN-HABITAT Report, April 2007.

UN-HABITAT, dados de 2005–http: / / www.unhabitat.org / stats / Default.aspx.

UN-HABITAT 2007 Press Release on its Report, "The Challenge of Slums: Global Report on Human Settlements 2003".

Ward, Wilfrid Philip (2008), The Life and Times of Cardinal Wiseman, Volume 1 Biblio Bazaar. p. 568.

Wohl, S. Anthony (2002), The Eternal Slum: Housing and Social Policy in Victorian London, Transaction Publishers, p. 5.

Socio-economic Conditions of Slum Dwellers

A. Jyotsna,
B. Venkata Subba Reddy

INTERDICTION

Independence and After

According to our estimation, the urban population of India in 1947 was 53 million, or 15.7 per cent of the population. Between 1951–61, the urban population increased to 68 per cent of increasing of towns. The urban population as a proportion of the total population increased from about 18 per cent in 1961 to about 20 per cent in 1971. In terms of increase in percentage points, the rate of urbanization during 1961–71 cannot be regarded as high. However in terms of absolute numbers, the urban population increased by about 30 million from 78.9 million in 1961 to 109.1 million in 1971. In other words, during these 10 years, the urban population of India increased by 38.2 per cent or in other words at the rate of 3.3 per cent per annum. Thus from the point of view of the urban growth rate, urbanisation has indeed been rapid during 1961–71 decade. The urban population of India as recorded in the 1981 census-excluding Assam and Jammu and Kashmir) was 156 million. This constituted 23.73 per cent of the total population of the relevant areas of India covered by the census. According to provisional figures for the 1991 census, the total population of India is 844 million (as 0f 1st March 1991). The total urban population in 1991 spread over 4,689 towns and cities is 217 million. The urban population in 1991 is 26 per cent of the total population.

In the 1970s and 1980s, the Indian government had a policy of 'no slums cities' this warranted forceful resettlement and rehabilitation of slum dwellers. However, this didn't help in making cities slums-free. Then the goverr.ment started implementing slum up-grade programmers' under which infrastructure upgrade programmes under which infrastructure development was encouraged. Since 1972 the Government of India initiated a programme called "Environmental Improvement of Urban Slums" under which priority to drinking water and sanitation was given again in 1996 government initiated the National Slum Development Programme with substantial fund allocation. It was estimated that 46 million slum-dwellers benefited from it. In 2005 government started the Jawaharlal Nehru Urban Renewal Mission (JNNURM) an initiative to encourage reforms and fast track planned development of certain cities. It has a financial commitment of $1,50, 00 crores during 2006–2012.

The slum question is not margins to urban development it is at its very heart. Urban growth takes place primarily in developing countries in which populations leave from rural to urban regions at a very fast pace. According to UN–Habitat, some 923,986,000 people, or 32 per cent of the world's total urban population, live in slums: some 43 per cent of the urban population of all the developing regions combined live in slums: some 78 per cent of the urban population in the least developed countries live in slums. Some six per cent of the urban population in developed regions lives in slums. The total number of slum-dwellers in the world increased by about 36 per cent during the 1990s, and in the next 30 years the global number of slum-dwellers will increase to about two billion.

The slum population is constantly increasing it has doubled in the past two decades. The current population living in slums in the country is more than the population of Britain. India's slum-dwelling population raise from 27.9 million in 1981 to over 40 million in 2001. As per the 2001 census of India, 640 towns spread over 26 States and union territories have reported existence of slums. This means one out of every four persons reside in slums in our cities and towns. The NSSO (The National Sample Survey Organization) survey in 2002 has identified 51,688 slums in urban areas of which 50.6 per cent of urban slums have been declared as "Notified Slums". This growing slums population and the lack of basic facilities will broadly impact on socio-economic and health sector.

The most common problem facing the urban population in a majority of the developing countries is the limited access to almost all the basic services such as health, shelter and particularly water supply and sanitation facilities. The Central and State Governments have been introducing number of urban welfare programmers for improving the socio-economic conditions of urban slum-dwellers in India, even though, in India. In most of the cities one-fourth to one-half of the population live in poverty and are deprived of the basic needs. The basic poverty continuum demonstrates itself in low incomes, inadequate nutrition levels and basic services, limited no education and low skills. The urban poor, according to many studies in India, are those a household income of $650-700 a month, who live in low income settlements which mostly lack of adequate sewerage facilities, water supply and healthcare.

The National Sample Survey Organization has estimated that the population in urban-slum areas has been increased and paced by leaps and bounds in the recent past. Based on the 65th phase sample survey, NSSO has proclaimed and released a report on "Basic features of slum areas, 2008-09, which revealed that as per the 2008-09 estimates the populace in urban-slum areas has been increased to the soaring heights. It also stated that there are 48,994 slum areas that includes notified and unnotified slum areas. In Andhra Pradesh only there are 3,964 notified slum areas besides 1,285 unnotified slum areas. It is incredible and amazing to know that there are 5,249 slum areas in total. In the light of the NSSO's report in 2011, government has constituted a committee to make a survey on slum areas and other perennial problems.

The committee stated that the population in slum areas was 72,54,399 in 2001, but the same committee has been estimating that the population in slum areas may increase to 81,88,022 by the end of the year 2011. In this connection, the committee has changed the definition of slum areas whoever from the present definition and the same has been submitted to the Central Government. In this context and process, the Central Government has written letters to all the States seeking their cooperation in identifying the slum areas.

The State and Central Governments have been introducing number of welfare programmes especially for urban poor to improve the socio-economic status of slum dwellers in urban areas. Today the Indian Government implementing Urban Basic Services for the Poor (UBSP), Prime Minister Integrated Urban Poverty Eradication Yojana, Environmental improvement of Urban Slums (EIUS), Urban Self Employment Programme (USEP), Thrift and Credit Society, Development of Women and Child in Urban areas (DWCUA), Urban Wage Employment Programme (UWEP) and Urban Community Development (UCD) Programmes, even though we are not able to get good results in urban slum dwellers life.

METHODOLOGY

In the light above factors, a study was carried out with few objectives as follows:

- To assess the socio-economic, demographic conditions of the respondent.
- To assess the health status of the respondents.
- To find out the slum problems faced by the respondents.
- To know the expectation and solutions of the respondents on slum issues.

Sampling

The study was carried out at urban slums in Nellore city. Nellore is also known as Simhapuri, Nellore town stands unique among other places of Andhra Pradesh as it is supposed to be the place of Sri Potti Sriramulu,

Telugu patriots and activist, who fasted to death for formation of Andhra State. Nellore is famous for rice and aquaculture the place such as rocket launching centre Sriharikota, Kristnapatnam Port, Penna river. According to 2001 Census the total population of Nellore town was 404775. The Nellore district having 47 large and medium industries, among them 17 industries existing in Nellore town, due to growing of industries many people migrate to Nellore town from rural areas and they are staying in slum areas. There are 68 slums in Nellore Municipal Corporation. Out these the researcher selected three different slum areas i.e. Venkateswara Puram (in east phase), Ranganay-akulapeta (in west phase), Wood Sangam (in north phase). From each slum area 50 samples were collected randomly.

Tool used for the study

Well-structured interview schedule was used to collect the data regarding socio-economic conditions of slum-dwellers in Nellore city and pertaining to objectives of the study. Schedule consists of two parts and the total number of questions are 40. The researcher first informed to the respondents about the purpose of the study and collects the data from them. Interview method, observation, was used to gather the information. Further collected data necessary information from local key persons wherever requires.

Analysis of the Data

The collected data were tabulated and percentages were calculated.

Results and Discussions

Demographic and socio-economic status of the respondents and problems faced by the respondents, and their expenditure status, expectation of the respondents on slum issues which are presented in Table 7.1

It is clear from the results (Table 7.1) that a majority i.e., 47 per cent were in the age group of 35 years and above and 52 per cent were male, and a little above i.e., 53 per cent were illiterate. Further the study stated that 44 per cent were belongs to scheduled caste. Forty eight per cent were having *kachha* houses, and a little above three fifth i.e. 64 per cent were having 3 or 4 family members, and a little above four-fifths i.e. 83 per cent were having the ration card. At the same time a little below three-fifths i.e., 69 per cent were having the health card but due to political influence, 31 per cent of them were not having the health card hear. Nearly three-fifths i.e., 59 per cent of them are not utilized the health card due to lack of awareness about that like how to utilize the card and how to approach the hospitals and what type of treatments will be given by the card.

Table 7.2, explains about the economic conditions of the respondents. The study reveals that nearly three fifths i.e., 58 per cent were belongs to

Table 7.1: Socio-Demographic Characteristics of the Respondents

		Number	Percentage
1.	**Age**		
	20 – 25	26	17
	25 – 30	24	16
	30 – 35	30	20
	35 and above	70	47
	Total	**150**	**100**
2.	**Education**		
	Illiteracy	80	53
	Primary Education	46	31
	Secondary	14	09
	Degree and above	10	07
	Total	**150**	**100**
3.	**Caste**		
	Forward	26	17
	Backward	48	32
	Scheduled Caste	66	44
	Scheduled Tribes	10	07
	Total	**150**	**100**
4.	**Gender**		
	Male	78	52
	Female	72	48
	Total	150	100
5.	**Type of House**		
	Pucca	15	10
	Kaccha	72	48
	Semi Pucca	63	42
	Total	**150**	**100**
6.	**No. of family members**		
	1 or 2	15	10
	3 or 4	96	64
	4 or 5	34	23
	5 and above	05	03
	Total	**150**	**100**

Contd...

7. **Ration Card**		
Availing	125	83
Not Availing	25	17
Total	**150**	**100**
8. **Rajiv Health card**		
Availing	104	69
Not Availing	46	31
Total	**150**	**100**
9. **No. of respondents used Health Card**		
Used	62	41
Not Used	88	59
Total	**150**	**100**

daily wage workers in companies, hotels, rice mills etc. and a little above three-fifths, i.e. 61 per cent were having the monthly income of less than Rs. 5,000 per month. Nearly above half, i.e. 55 per cent of the families having membership in self-help groups. Nearly three-fourths, i.e. 73 per cent were not having any saving, remaining 27 per cent of the respondents have a savings in SHG's, Bank/post office, Insurance, money lending. Further the study stated that nearly three-fifths, i.e. 59 per cent of the respondent having debts and 35 per cent of the respondents depending on their relatives for their needs incase if they have insufficient of economic crisis.

Table 7.2: Information Pertaining to Economic Status of the Respondents

	Number	Percentage
1	2	3
1. **Occupation**		
Wage Labour	87	58
Driving Field	29	19
Self Employment	27	18
Private Job	07	05
Total	**150**	**100**
2. **Family Monthly Income (Rs.)**		
< 5,000	92	61
5,000 – 10,000	30	20
10,000 – 15,000	21	14
15,000 and above	07	05
Total	**150**	**100**

Contd...

1		2	3
3.	**Membership in S.H.G**		
	Yes	82	55
	No	68	45
	Total	150	100
4.	**Savings**		
	Yes	41	27
	No	109	73
	Total	**150**	**100**
5.	**Mode of Savings**		
	S.H.G	29	19
	Bank/Post Office	07	05
	Insurance/Money lending	05	03
	None of the above	109	73
	Total	**150**	**100**
6.	**Debits**		
	Yes	89	59
	No	61	41
	Total	**150**	**100**
7.	**Sufficient of Economic sources**		
	Yes	19	13
	No	131	87
	Total	**150**	**100**
8.	**Sources of support during economic crisis**		
	Children	40	27
	Relatives	52	35
	Money Lenders	50	33
	Banks/ Chits	08	05
	Total	**150**	**100**

Table 7.3, explain about what type of facilities they are not having in their slums. The study reveals that a little blow three-fifths, i.e. 57 per cent were not having Municipal tap water connection and a little above three-fifths, i.e. 61 per cent were not having the individual toilets the same per cent were not having drainage facility.

Table 7.3: Information Pertaining to the Facilities in their Slum

Facilities	Number		Percentage		Total
	Yes	No	Yes	No	
Tap Water	65	85	43	57	150
Individual Toilets	58	92	39	61	150
Drainage	58	92	39	61	150
Waste Disposal					

It is clear from the results (Table 7.4) that four-fifths, i.e. 88 per cent of the respondents were expressed that they are facing lack of sanitation facilities like proper drainage facility, dustbins etc. and a little above four-fifths, i.e. 81 per cent were suffering with lack of drinking water facility problem and a little above half, i.e. 52 per cent of the respondents were expressed that they are facing mosquitoes and other poisonous insects problem. Further the study stated that a little below three-fifths, i.e. 57 per cent were expressed that they have not sufficient street light. Though the State Government has been supplying the rice for two rupees to the white card holders, the true fruits are not reached to needy. The same anomaly has been revealed in this study i.e. 61 per cent of the respondents facing the inadequate supply of rice due to the deaths of questioning capacity and a vast majority, i.e. 92 per cent of the respondents have stated that the local leaders do not extend their co-operation to mitigate the local slum issues. Further the study revealed that 100 per cent of the respondents also expressed their opinion on official supervision or support that officials do not have supervision regarding slum issues and four-fifths, i.e. 88 per cent of the respondents have said that they are not provided with health services and four-fifths, i.e. 84 per cent said that they do not have sufficient drinking water due to in proper administration and negligence of the Municipal authorities.

Table 7.4: Information Pertaining to Problems faced by the Respondents

Problems	Number		Percentage		Total
	Yes	No	Yes	No	
1. Lack of sanitation	132	18	88	12	150
2. Lack of Drinking Water	121	29	81	19	150
3. Mosquitoes and other poisonous insects	78	72	52	48	150
4. Street Light	86	64	57	43	150
5. Inadequate supply of rice	92	58	61	39	150
6. Lack of support of local leaders on slum issues	138	12	92	08	150
7. Lack of health supply	150	—	100	150	
8. Drinking Water	132	18	88	12	150

Figure 7.1: Monthly Expenditure of the Respondents

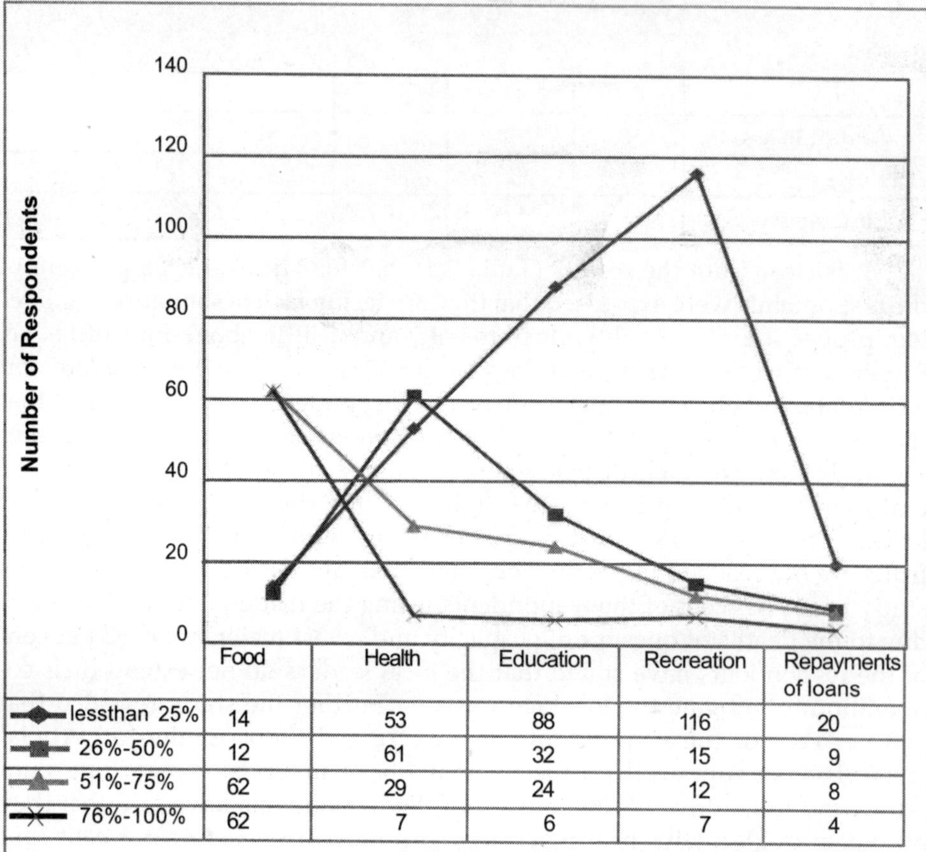

	Food	Health	Education	Recreation	Repayments of loans
lessthan 25%	14	53	88	116	20
26%-50%	12	61	32	15	9
51%-75%	62	29	24	12	8
76%-100%	62	7	6	7	4

Figure 7.1: explains about the monthly expenditure of the respondents that is out of the total respondents. A majority 62 of the respondents are spending (76 per cent to 100 per cent) in their monthly income for the purpose of their food needs, less than 25 per cent is 14 respondents, 26 per cent to 50 per cent is 12 respondents and 51 per cent to 75 per cent is 62 respondents.

Health

Out of the total respondents majority 61 of the respondents are spending (26 per cent to 50 per cent) in their monthly income for purchase of medicine, treatment, 53 respondents are spending less than 25 per cent in their monthly income, 29 respondents are spending 51 per cent to 75 per cent and 7 respondents are spending 76 per cent to 100 per cent.

Education

Out of the total respondents 88 of the respondents are spending less than 25 per cent in their monthly income fort their children education, 32 respondents are spending up to 26 per cent to 50 per cent, 24 of the respondents are spending 51 per cent to 75 per cent and 06 respondents are spending 76 per cent to 100 per cent.

Recreation

Out of the total respondents a majority 116 of the respondents spending less than 25 per cent in their monthly income for their recreation purpose, 15 respondents is 26 per cent to 50 per cent, 12 respondents is 51 per cent to 75 per cent and 07 respondents is 76 per cent to 100 per cent.

Repayment of Loans

Out of the total respondents 20 of the respondents are spending less than 25 per cent in their income for repayment of loans, 9 respondents are spending 26 Per cent to 50 Per cent, 8 respondents are spending 51 per cent to 75 per cent and 4 respondents are spending 76 per cent to 100 per cent from their monthly income for repayment of loans

CONCLUSION

The ever increasing number of slum dwellers is forced to leave life in below poverty line. The main reason of their poverty is illiteracy and lack of opportunities to improve their conditions. They look for the government support in the form of loans, relief, employment, basic amenities, housing etc., In this context government has to provide the above services to needy slum-dwellers. At the same time they are not having good education, health, sanitation facilities also. The study revealed that a majority of the respondents was belonging to Scheduled Caste with low income, working as daily wage workers having Illiteracy with out any gaining occupation. Further the study observed that the majority of slum-dwellers were having health card, but majority of them are not utilized health card due to lack of awareness and majority of them having debits and they are depending on their relatives for their needs in case if they have insufficient of economic crisis. Regarding the problems faced by the respondents majority of the respondents facing lack of sanitation, drainage facility, street lights, inadequate supply of rice, lack of support of local leaders, health, lack of health services, drinking water. Regarding monthly expenditure of the respondents majority of them are spending their major percentage of income on food, health, debits.

Though the government have been implementing number of welfare programmes for urban slum people, to improve their socio-economic status, is not up to mark as the number of slum-dwellers are increasing day by day. If the government properly implemented the urban development and slum improvement programmes with a strong commitment towards slum-dwellers problems, we can mitigate their problems. In this context, both government and nongovernmental organizations and public participation is essential where the social worker can work along with above mentioned agencies to overcome problems of slum dwellers both at familial, community level through self help and community organization agencies.

Recommendations

- Reduce the percentage of migration from rural urban through providing employment opportunities.
- Strengthen the local municipalities on slum issues
- Government has to take the initiation to improve the literacy rate in slum areas through designing special programmes.
- Central Government has to allocate more budget to the state governments for improving basic needs in slums.
- Through providing the more women income generative programmes, we can empower the women living in slums.
- N.G.Os should work for the underprivileged in slums.

REFERENCES

Ahuja, Ram,"Social Problems in India" , Rawat Publication, India p.p. 282–283.

Ghosh, Archana ,"Urbanization in Developing Countries-Status of Basic Services in Indian Cities", p. 147.

Mohanthy, Bidyut,"Urbanization in Developing Countries–Urbanization in India" (1951 – 2002), , Concept Publishing Company, New Delhi p.p. 107–108.

N.S.S.O Report on Slums in Andhra Pradesh (Sakshi Telugu Daily News Paper 04–05– 2011, p. 5.

Thudipara, Jacob Z., "Urban Community Development II Edition", Rawat Publication, New Delhi p.p. 52–53.

Sharma, R.N., K. Sita , "Cities, Slums and Government, *Economic and Political Weekly"*, October 14, 2008.

UGC-SAP(phase-2), Urbanization: Emerging Issues.

www.rameshkumar.co.in (science to social welfare).

www.wateraid.org

http: / / en,wikipedia.org

Slums

The Reality Today

V. Usha Reddy, N. Anitha and
Dr. T. Ramashri

INTRODUCTION

The origin the word 'slum' is thought to come from the Irish phrase '*Slomé* (pron. slum ae) meaning "it is a bleak or destitute place." — A 1812 English dictionary defined slum to mean "a room".

Slums are "Habitations located on disputed as well as unused government, municipal and private land and characterized by a serious lack of basic amenities and sanitation with dense and over crowded housing conditions".

In other words

A slum is taken to mean 'hutting areas with squalid surroundings where:

- huts are erected in a haphazard manner without proper access.
- minimum basic amenities are lacking.
- protected water supply and drainage arrangements do not exist.

LIVING CONDITIONS IN SLUMS

In many slums, especially in poor countries, many live in very narrow alleys that do not allow vehicles (like ambulances and fire trucks) to pass. The lack of services such as routine garbage collection allows rubbish to accumulate in huge quantities. The lack of infrastructure is caused by the informal nature of settlement and no planning for the poor by government officials. Additionally, informal settlements often face the brunt of natural and man-made disasters, such as landslides, as well as earthquakes and tropical storm. Fires are often a serious problems.

CHARACTERISTICS

The characteristics and politics associated with slums vary from place to place. Slums are usually characterized by urban decay, high rates of poverty, illiteracy, and unemployment. They are commonly seen as "breeding grounds" for social problems such as crime, drug addiction, alcoholism, high rates of mental illness, and suicide. In many poor countries they exhibit high rates of disease due to unsanitary conditions, malnutrition, and lack of basic health care. However, some like Dharavi, Mumbai, are a hive of business activity such as leather work, cottage industries, etc. Rural depopulation with thousands arriving daily into the cities makes slum clearance an uphill struggle.

Reasons of Slums

- Change in agricultural scenario.
- No prospects in rural areas.
- Bigger opportunities in cities.
- Preference on labour market than agriculture.

Results of Slums

- Poverty.
- Poor living conditions.
- No education.
- Very poor hygiene conditions.
- Poor health-care.

Facts Reveal That

- One billion people worldwide live in slums and the figure will likely grow to 2 billion by 2030.
- Slum population all over India is 40,297,341 (40 million).
- Four per cent of total Indian population lives in slums.
- Almost quarter of Indian metro cities live in slums.
- Sadly five million of this population are young children (0-6 age group).

Occupation in Slums

- The heavy shifts of population are the result of the lack of adequate employment opportunities in the villages and the attraction of relatively high wages and amenities in the towns.

  Figures in percentage are proportion of all earners across India are as follows:

State government employment	4.36
Union government employment	7.19
Non-earners	3.74
Self-employed professional and worker	5.71
Wage labour and other than own account workers	0.42
Business	4.46
Non-government salaried employment	0.15
Self-employed in primary sector activities	0.96

Alarming Growth of Slums in India

- Slum population in 4 metros in India 55 per cent Mumbai, 44 per cent Meerut, 40 per cent of Pune.
- India's top list on slum population.
- Pune: the growing city of slums
- Total Area: 244 sq.km
- Population: 15 lakh approx
- Population in slums: 6 lakh
- Encroachment of slums: 6 per cent (15 sq.km)
- Total growth in slum population in the city since 1991 is 176 per cent.

Initiatives

- Different governments have different ways to handle the problem of growing slums.

- Many governments around the world have attempted to solve the problems of slums by clearing away old decrepit housing and replacing it with modern housing with much better sanitation.
- The displacement of slums is aided by the fact that many are squatter settlements whose property rights are not recognized by the State.
- This process is especially common in the Third World. Slum clearance often takes the form of eminent domain and urban renewal projects, and often the former residents are not welcome in the renewed housing.
- Various NGOs are also taking initiatives to help govt in dealing with this issue.
- Agencies like Jawaharlal Nehru National Urban Renewal Mission (JNNURM) and Slum Rehabilitation Authority (SRA) plan the Rehabilitation of the slums in metros.
- The government should also concentrate on dissemination (or) awareness of human survival, development, protection and participation of children in slums. To realize the goals of the programmes related to improve the quality of life in slums needed heightened political commitment.

SOLUTIONS

Short-term

- Rehabilitation of major slums in better hygienic places.
- Re construction of the middle level slums in the same area with proper drainage system and water supply.
- Provision of basic amenities, medical and health care, education to eradicate poverty completely.

Long-term

- The objective should be to reduce the migration from rural areas.
- Providing the basic amenities and better opportunities in rural areas.
- Encouraging agricultural and small scale industries.

SOCIAL RESPONSIBILITY AND ROLE OF MEDIA

- During the last two decades there is drastic change in the media.
- Media is fast developing and it is proved that it has lot of impact on the public.
- Media is the fourth estate so it should be socially responsible for the citizens of the country to inform about the activities of NGOs.
- Non-Governmental Organizations (NGOs) play an important role in the development of society.

- The Media should focus on the development programmes, and they have to motivate philanthropists to come forward and support financially.
- The media is focusing on sensational journalism to increase their circulation.

PRESENT SCENARIO IN OUR COUNTRY

Unfortunately multi-national companies entered and too much concentration on getting interest in short-term on renewals and neglecting original poor people and their sight is on source of repayment either by force more than running interest rates comparison with scheduled banks. We can see this type of evil attitude in our country.

The implementation in the proper way micro finance is not worse system.

CONCLUSIONS

So the slums are reality of today and cities are collective future of human beings. We should take collective responsibility for their future development. We want to inspire people globally to aid and help cure the unsanitary conditions in Indian slums by educating them about the conditions and the life of a slum-dweller.

REFERENCES

www.unhabitat.org/slum report.

www.google.com

9

Growth of Urbanization and Slums

P. Murali Dhar and
V. Nirmala

INTRODUCTION

Urbanization

It is the physical growth of urban areas as a result of global change. Or an urban area can grow because of immigrants or people in search of a better job or a better life. Urbanization is also defined by the United Nations as movement of people from rural to urban areas with population growth equating to urban migration. The United Nations projected that half of the world's population would live in urban areas at the end of 2008. Urbanization is often identified with urban growth; urban growth usually leads to urbanization. Though both the concepts are interrelated processes, they are different. Therefore a distinction between the two concepts is essential. Urbanization refers to proportion of the total population concentrated in urban settlements. It has been viewed as transitional phase in the switch over from tradition to modernity is witnessed.

Slums

The areas which are seen to be over crowded dilapidated, faulty laid out and lacking in essential services generally termed as slums. These areas are in official terms, "illegal" or "informal." Slums are differently known in different countries and cities. "*Hoods*" of New York, "*bidon vielles*" of Abidjan, "*jhopad patties*" and "*jj colonies*" in Indian cities are some of the names by which slums are known. The worst part is that such area is found even in the developed world.

Location and Extent of Study Area

Geometrically, Tirupati is situated on the latitude of 13°39′0"N and longitude 79°25′12"E (survey of India map of 57 O/6) in the river Swarnamukhi basin forming the part of eastern coastal plain at an elevation of 240 mts above mean sea level and an extent of 16.21 km^2. Tirupati is located immediately to the south of the foothills of Tirumala hills also known as Palakonda Seshachalam ranges which form part of the Eastern Ghats. Administratively, Tirupati is located in Chittoor district of Southern Andhra Pradesh.

The Study Area

This study area, Tirupati urban settlement, is one of the biggest cities of Andhra Pradesh occupying 14th place in the size of urban population. It is the biggest of all 13 towns in Chittoor district. A unique feature of Tirupati is that it has been treated as a town right from the very first census taken in 1871-72. Starting with the total population of 15,485 in 1901, the town reached more than two lakh population, indicating 15 times increase in the last hundred years. The spectacular increase of Tirupati urban dwellers had not been merely due to natural growth but due to heavy influx of rural population. This increase of population has been contributed to the growth of slums.

Urban Sprawl

In the past three decades, the neighbourhood of Tirupati has been developed as an industrial base, through which the city is fast merging with Renigunta on the East, Chandragiri on the West and Tiruchanoor on the South. On the North, Tirupati has reached maximum frontiers to foothills of Tirumala hills. In view of this fast urban sprawl Tirupati is brought under development authority in keeping with others in Andhra Pradesh.

Major Issues in Urbanization

Obviously, the impact of the growth of urban population on urban infrastructure and services has mostly been adverse. Due to over migration the major problem of urban settlements are unemployment, congestion, housing shortages, origin and growth of slums, straining of urban services, pollution, possible increasing crime rates, etc. Some cities grew so rapidly without plan or supervision that even most elementary services could not keep up with population growth. The unprecedented expansion of cities and town will have far-reaching consequences. They are unable to handle such large chunk of people and some urban facilities are even at the verge of collapse. The urban settlements with higher rates of growth of population especially the slum population would be expected to have more resources as well as planning measures to alleviate the increasing problems/demands on urban services for better urban way of life. This may call a critical evaluation of urban growth and slum development of unprecedented expansion of cities like Tirupati, a pilgrim as well as an educational urban settlement in the State of Andhra Pradesh.

Origin and Growth of Slums

Rise in the living standards and availability of more economic job opportunities in the urban centers leads to the origin and growth of slums. These areas will become unsuitable for human beings because of marked lowering of environmental quality, crowded streets and roads, slums increasing trend of murder, theft, dacoit and other crimes etc. with this perspective Tirupati city has been chosen for the study of growing urbanization and slums.

Slums are the physical and socio-cultural expression of inequalities in the distribution of the economic benefits as well as the structure, function, performance and special pattering of the urban economy. The sprouting of slums in Tirupati city due to many factors such as, the shortage of developed land for housing, the high prices of land and building material beyond the reach of urban poor, a large influx of rural migrants to the city in search of jobs and better wages. Another significant feature of slums is that most of it's inhabitants have low thresholds of income and invariably belong to socially backward strata of society.

Objectives of the Study

1. The main objective of the present study is to bring out a systematic account on two aspects namely Urban growth of Tirupati city, and Slum development.
2. In this process, the vital aspect of the present study is to focus upon origin and evolution of slums, structural and functional characteristics of slums and socio-economic dimensions of slum dwellers of Tirupati city.

It is hoped that this diagnostic study will help evolve both prophylactic and curative measures and ultimately to upgrade the slums and improve the quality of life of slum dwellers of Tirupati city.

DATABASE AND METHODOLOGY

The present study is based upon both primary and secondary data. The secondary data pertaining to ward wise population, land use, slums, etc., have been collected from Tirupati Municipal authority office and Tirupati Urban Development Authority office. Secondary data was also collected from the census handbooks of Chittoor district.

The primary data relating to the structural and socio economic characteristics of slums and slum-dwellers was generated with the help of personal interviews. Here, slum-dwellers are the basic and real operational unit for micro analysis of slums.

GROWTH OF POPULATION OF TIRUPATI

Tirupati is one of the largest towns of the Rayalaseema and it is the largest of all 13 towns in Chittoor district. As per 2001 census figures, the population of Tirupati reached to 2,26,551 occupying the 14th place among the cities of Andhra Pradesh. A unique feature of Tirupati is that it has been treated as a town right from the very first census taken in 1871-72 with a total population of 15,483.

The population of Tirupati town has been increasing from 1901 onwards. However, the increase has not been significant and there has been fluctuations in the decadal variations. The increase of population up to 1941 was very small and the decadal variation was also significant. During 1941-1951, there was a significant increase of decadal variation accounting 25.14 per cent. From Table 9.1 it is clearly noticed that the growth of population of Tirupati was small in the pre-independence period. In the post-independence period, the growth was very striking particularly in the past four decades (1971-2011). During this period the sudden spurt in population can be ascribed to the effects of increasing developmental and welfare activities undertaken both by the Government of Andhra Pradesh and the Tirumala Tiruapti Devasthanams (TTD) not only in the centre of the town but also in the peripheries. In the outskirts, where a number of colonies are being built for housing the middle income group people and most of whom are employees. The value of lands in the peripheries is one third of the value of the land located at core. Both Renigunta and Chandragiri are located at almost equal distance on either side of Tirupati. The value of land in the peripheries has been spectacularly increased an account of extensive industrial and infrastructural activities taken.

Renigunta is a big Railway junction located at the confluence of South Central and Southern Railways. It serves as gateway to Tirupati. Between Tirupati and Renigunta, the value of land is high as compared to other sites, namely, towards Chandragiri, SVU located on the road leading to Chandragiri. Industrial expansion is permitted on Renigunta side and it is developing into an industrial satellite town.

Two factors have helped Tirupati grow to it's present size and magnitude. They are:

(i) The establishment of Sri Venkateswara University in 1954 and Sri Padmavathi Mahila University in 1985.

(ii) An increase of pilgrim population on account of boon in transport and communication sector in post-independent era specially after the formation separate Andhra Pradesh state in 1956. Revolving around these two very important aspects, the town has developed in to a religion-academic centre within a span of two to three decades.

Along with pilgrim influx the facilities like hotels, banking institutions and various other important tertiary services have come to be located at Tirupati, mainly to serve the pilgrims. Apart from private services, public services both from the Municipality and TTD have increased in many folds. The services rendered by TTD both at Tirumala and Tirupati were financed by the contribution received from the pilgrims. Enormous increase in the public and private services and facilities also brought large number of unique grants to move these services.

Table 9.1: Growth of Population and Classification of Tirupati City: 1901-2011

Year	Persons	Absolute Decadal variation	Per centage of decadal variation	Male	Female	Class of Tirupati city
1901	15,485			7541	7944	V
1911	16701	+1216	+7.85	8239	8462	V
1921	17434	+733	+4.39	8631	8803	V
1931	19138	+1704	+9.77	9493	9645	IV
1941	20143	+1005	+5.25	9981	10162	III
1951	25207	+5064	+25.14	12793	12414	III
1961	35845	+10638	+42.0	19230	16615	II
1971	65845	+29998	+83.69	34841	31002	II
1981	115292	+49401	+75.02	60360	54884	I
1991	174393	+59101	+51.26	90741	83652	I
2001	226551	+52158	+29.90	116640	109911	I

Tirupati is classified as a class-I town for the first time in 1981. Table shows the growth of population sex-wise from 1901-2001. As the importance of the place is increasing, the scope for the increase of both males and females is uniformly competitive. From the table it is found that the highest decadal variation both in male and female population was during 1971.

It is significant to state that the per centage of decadal variation was higher in male population in the earlier decades 1921-31. But in 1941 and 1961 to 1991 the percentage of decadal variation was higher in the case of female population than the male population. It may be attributed to the early migration of more male population for seeking job opportunities in the town keeping their families in the rural areas. And also recently the equal opportunities created to the females in diversified economic sectors for their sustenance. During 1961-71 the decadal variation of female population was considerably high which accounted for 86.5 per cent compared to 81.08 per cent in the case of male population. It is indeed a significant variation in the growth rate of male and female population.

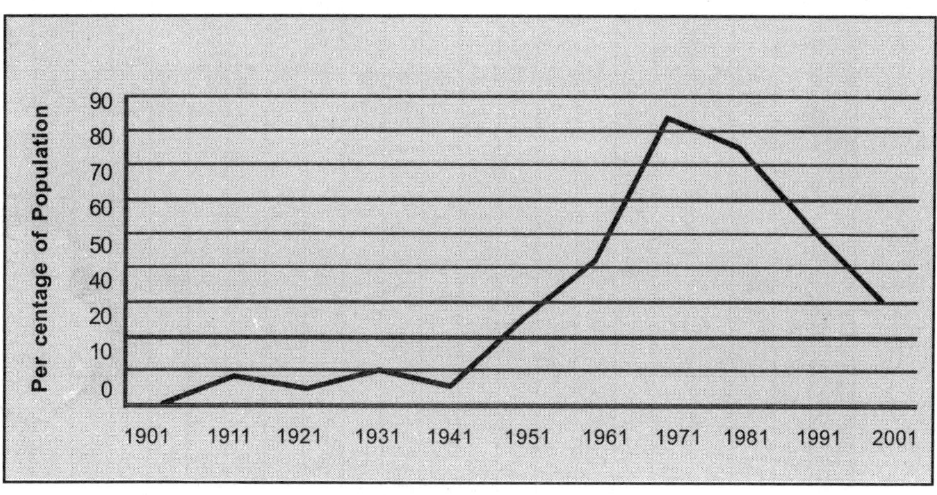

Decadal Growth of Population in Tirupati (1901-2001)

GROWTH OF SLUMS IN TIRUPATI

Tirupati is one of the most important cultural centers of South India and has become one of the sacred places for pilgrims in India. In fact Tirumala is the richest temple in the country.

In terms of urbanization, Tirupati town is one of the fast growing towns in India during the last four decades. The town has witnessed a substantial increase in urban population which is partially natural growth but heavily with the increase of slums and slum-dwellers.

At present there are 42 slums within the Municipal limits of Tirupati town. Out of 42 slums identified in the town, 22 slums are located in the old town and 20 slums in the new town.

It is clear from Table 9.2 that there are no slums in the wards 2, 3, 5, 7, 8, 9, 10, 11, 12, 14, 15 and 16. The slums in the old town such as Nehru Nagar, Bommagunta, Giripuram, Kummarathopu, and Singalagunta are the oldest slums. The slums in the old town have come up adjacent to the market and business areas taking advantage of the Government and Municipal lands available for encroachment.

Most of the above slum areas have cropped up on Government and Municipal lands especially on road margins and Government porambokes. Bulk of the dwellers belong to the poorer sections of the society and uneducated. It may be explained from the table that 18.75 per cent of the town dwellings and 18.3 per cent of the total population of the town are located in the slums. Although the slums are scattered all over the town, there is a distinct concentration in the socially backward areas which are associated either with the industrial areas (Renigunta) or historic core of the town.

Table 9.2: Spread of Slums in Tirupati City

SI. No.	Name of the Slum	Ward No.	Area of Slum	Age of Slums (in years)	No. of Houses	No. of Households	Population
1	2	3	4	5	6	7	8
1.	Indira Nagar	1	9.23	32	191	818	3628
2.	Kummara Thopu	1	0.70	30	97	290	1307
3.	Giripuram	4	3.74	32	111	218	1064
4.	Ramakrishnapuram	4	2.23	30	30	43	192
5.	Nehru Nagar	4	18.20	35	558	1578	6967
6.	Bommagunta	4	3.50	35	65	221	1024
7.	Haridwar Colony	6	0.50	17	26	29	115
8.	Pachigunta	6	0.60	15	45	45	183
9.	Marrichenna Reddy Colony	6	7.40	18	325	527	2290
10.	Singalagunta	6	7.43	25	403	729	2756
11.	Ambedkar Colony	6	6.13	25	67	256	1162
12.	Sanjeevaiah Nagar	6	3.50	28	198	198	693
13.	Sanjeevaiah Colony	6	1.46	20	-	99	289
14.	Mallaiah Gunta Katta	13	3.00	50	124	289	1263
15.	Tataiah Gunta	13	3.00	40	360	500	2399
16.	Pocla Thota	17	0.30	35	79	223	939
17.	Yasoda Nagar	18	3.00	30	32	257	1196
18.	Sajjthagiri Nagar	18	12.00	30	460	460	2223
19.	Surayya Katta	18	0.50	30	48	83	318

Contd..

20.	Murikineella Gunta	18	15.05	35	419	517	2144
21.	Scavenger's Ccloay	18	5.11	25	6	208	830
22.	Hhagat Singh Colony	19	1.24	20	69	112	609
23.	Pedda Hari] anawada	19	2.50	32	85	261	1161
24.	Uppanki Harijanawada	19	6.00	35	75	204	932
25.	Gandhi Puram	19	0.74	35	60	153	659
26.	Lakshmi Puram	19	3.90	30	70	390	1779
27.	Dasari Matham	19	3.74	30	70	294	1321
28.	New Indira Nagar	19	1.19	30	113	565	2610
29.	Chintala Chenu	19	3.00	40	79	200	923
30.	Parvathi Puram	19	3.00	25	-	200	1036
31.	S.T.V.Nagar	19	9.00	32	280	669	3051
32.	Sivajyothi Nagar	20	6.00	8	70	449	1893
33.	Yerramitta	20	5.00	18	64	422	1774
34.	Yerukula Colony	20	1.90	15	45	40	204
35.	Chandra Sekhar Reddy Colony	20	6.00	18	165	244	1030
36.	Ashok Nagar Extension	20	3.00	35	129	391	1487
37.	Maruthi Nagar	20	11.00	40	569	851	3482
38.	Kothapalli	20	2.00	30	430	96	395
39.	Sanjay Gandhi Colony	20	3.00	25	70	274	1036
40.	Ambedkar Society Colony	6	1.50	20	42	165	454
41.	Lenin Nagar	19	1.00	20	28	145	320
42.	Chinna Gunta	5	1.00	20	65	220	625

CONCLUSION

In the recent times i.e., in the last three decades the urban growth as well as the urban spread was more striking and spectacular. The process of urbanization has gained a significant momentum and it may further continue to do so, because Tirupati town has become a nodal centre for many socio-economic activities. After considering Tirupati Town as a centre of pilgrimage, academic Excellency, tourism, industrial hub, the Government of Andhra Pradesh has been taking several measures to solve the problems of rapid urbanization. In this Endeavour the Government of Andhra Pradesh constituted the Tirupati urban development authority in 1982. The objectives of the authority are well designed and raised hope of getting better environment and picturesque for Tirupati as a modal town. But the implementation of the objectives, especially relating to housing, water supply, sanitation, slum clearance, has not been taking place at the expected rate due to many reasons of its own. Hence, both TTD and Municipal administration have combined to take up the infrastructural developmental programmers for providing the necessary civic amenities of the town. Here, the utmost concern of the public is that these three administrative bodies do not have systematic linkage, understanding and co-ordination in the operation of developmental programmers for solving urban problems in a phased manner. Hence, it is pre-requisite to emphasize for systematic linkage of these three governing bodies for the well being of the people of Tirupati town.

It is interesting to state that the Tirupati town has been dominating with the activities of tertiary economy. It speaks that the secondary economic activity once flourished i.e., two decades back has lost its base at present with the sickness of many industrial units. Hitherto there was no encouragement both from the public and private sectors for the revival of the secondary. Economic activities for providing better employment opportunities for large influx of rural-urban migrants, diversification of economy are the essential base for sustainable processes of urbanization which help not only the site but also the situation environs.

It is truism that the sprouting of slums occurs due to many factors which have been jeopardizing urban environment. In the case of Tirupati town many of the slums have recent origin and found with so many problems, especially the housing, water supply, drainage, sanitation town, child labour, alcoholism, illiteracy, health, caste conflicts, family planning, crime rate and unemployment. The physical environment in slum areas of Tirupati town is not satisfactory for the people living there. The slum environment which is bad not only affecting of its own site but also polluting the urban environs. Since Tirupati is identified as a religious and renowned pilgrimage centre, thousands of people coming from all over the country visit the town daily. It speaks volumes on cleanliness of the town from all aspects especially from slum based environmental problems. Housing is the major problem of the slum-dwellers for which the governing bodies of town have to take serious concerned for the construction of new colonies at the outskirts of the town with all basic services. In the case of Tirupati town it is of paramount importance to go for satellite townships either at Renigunta side or at Chandragiri side in order to avoid congestion. The pollution of different kinds of illegal occupation of someone's land or the public land allotted for developmental activities by slum dwellers is a serious problem in the town. This has become a business for slum people. This must be arrested by the concerned by alternatively providing pucca house sites. There is a need to improve the quality of life of slum dwellers through welfare measures. Out of all it is imperative to bring a change in the behavior of the slum dwellers which gives a long way for wealthy and healthy environment. It is very clear to say that the slum dwellers should not be treated as untouchable and Second-rate citizens of the town. The World Bank says that the city authorities in the developing world given their limited resources should adopt policies that promote low-cost basic services for the many rather than for high priced services for the few. These can and do include private sector and community provision of many basic services. Therefore, the robust slum development and improvement policy with stringent rules and regulations and more importantly enough powers must be in place if something has to be done towards emancipating the slum poor in Tirupati town.

Suggestions for Up-gradation of the Tirupati Slums

- The Government of Andhra Pradesh must establish a slum clearance board exclusively for this pilgrimage town and allot more funds to clear and rebuild the existing slums.
- At present the governing bodies of the town should not allow the further growth of new slums in and around the town.
- Top most priority should be given for urban housing especially for the slum-dwellers by adopting low cost technology.
- New slums with readymade hutments which suddenly spring up either in the heart of the town or in the planned developmental areas should be immediately dismantled.
- House land ownership should be given to those who occupied the government lands long ago and at the same time land grabbers must be discouraged by punishment.
- Regular water supply, construction of pucca roads with drainage I facility, public lavoratories and solid waste disposal units or essential basic services have to be provided in each slum for improving the general slum environment.
- Compulsory primary education is to be made for slum children in order to avoid child labour for which the government has to take utmost care in attracting boys and girls of the slums by providing all necessary help

for clothes, books, food and also establishing children parks for recreation.

- Everything cannot be done by the government. Hence adoption of slums by non-governmental organizations, charitable institutions, universities, autonomous bodies, clubs should be encouraged and strengthened for bringing change in socio-economic cultural set up of the slum-dwellers.
- Family planning measures are to be strictly brought among the slum people to avoid large family structure and economic burden.
- Hygienic problem is a serious one in the slums. To make the healthy slum living, some awareness is to be brought about in the minds of slum people, about seasonal diseases which occur through pig rearing, mosquito breeding in the water logging spots, etc. Free health camps are to be frequently conducted in the slums by the voluntary organizations.
- Many of the slum-dwellers are affected by alcoholism. This results in family quarrels, rowdyism, street fights, crime rates and ultimately affecting law and order. Most of their wages are spent towards this alcoholism pushing back all other necessary basic needs such as nourished food, clothes, medicines and children care.
- Due to the money lending at higher interest rate is becoming a common phenomena ultimately leading to suicide and unrest in the families, the slum-dwellers need constant counseling.
- It would be better if the local government commit seriously to the goals suggested by world leaders met in 2000 at U.N. and forged a charter millennium goals, which includes to improve the lives of 100 million slum dwellers worldwide which is 10 per cent of total slum population.

REFERENCES

Gupta, I. and A. Mitra, (2002), Rural Migrants Segmentation and Labour: Micro-Level Evidence from Delhi Slums, *Economic and Political Weekly*, January 12.

Jones,. Gavin W. and P. M. Visaria (1998), *Urbanization in Large Developing Countries: China, Indonesia, Brazil, and India* (International Studies in Demography).

Kapadia-Kundu, N. and T. Kanitkar, (2002), Primary Healthcare in Urban Slums, *Economic and Political Weekly*, December 21.

Kumar, S., K. Shigeo and H. Harada, (2003), Living Environment and Health of Urban Poor, A Study in Mumbai, *Economic and Political Weekly*, August 23.

Montgomery, Mark, R. Stren, B. Cohen, and H. Reed (eds.)., 2003, *Cities Transformed: Demographic Change and Its Implications in the Developing World*, Washington, D.C.: National Academy Press.

National Sample Survey Organisation, (2004), Housing Condition in India.

National Sample Survey Organisation, (2003), Condition of Urban Slums–2002.

Planning Commission, India (2002), *India Assessment 2002: Water Supply and Sanitation*.

Urbanization and Role of Health in Slum Areas

Dr. Marri Padmaja

Louis Wirth is of the opinion that an urban may be defined as a relative large and socially heterogeneous human settlement. There are large cities in ancient times in countries like India and China. Urbanization or Urban drift is the physical growth of urban areas as a result of global change. Urbanization is also defined by the United Nations as movement of people from rural to urban areas with population growth equating to urban migration. The United Nations projected that half of the world's population would live in urban areas at the end people to live in urban slum areas is also important. World Health Organization (WHO) described health as a "State of complete physical, mental and social well being and not merely are absence of disease or infirmity". This definition is subsuming individual and community aspects of health and including the promotive, preventive, curative and rehabilitation dimensions. Slum areas of substandard housing which are without proper civic amenities. The poor housing and civic conditions create many physical and health hazards to the inhabitants of slums. The data is collected in the slum areas of Tirupati piligrim city. Random sampling method was selected. The present paper attempt to interpret the right to health care, in terms of Community Development Programmes and health problems and the methods for preventing and controlling them: promotion of food supply and proper nutrition: and adequate supply of safe water and basic sanitation: maternal and child health care, including family planning, immunization against major infectious disease: prevention and control of locally endemic diseases: appropriate treatment of common diseases and provision of essential drugs. According to 2011 census India consists 41 per cent of children population.

Children are main backbone citizens to the country. So childcare is an important aspect for future human generation. Community developmental programmes place a major role for mother and child care. Maternity hospital, RUYA Hospital and DWACRA mainly extend their health services to the poor and needy in slum area of Tirupati people.

Health visitors visit door to door and provide medicines in the slum areas. They enquire about the children who are below five years regarding Pulse Polio Vaccines. The data collection of the sample was 100 children who are below 15 years and collected in the slum areas of Sundaraiah Katta and Pachigunta areas of Tirupati. The environment is polluted with garbage and drainage in these slum areas. They lack proper ventilation in the houses and housing structure is in rigid manner. The children below 15 years are suffering from Kwahiyarkar and Marasmus fever, Motions, Malaria, Typhoid and skin diseases.

Table 10.1. Children Population Below 15 Years

S.No.	Gender	Total
1.	Male	96
2.	Female	89
Total		**185**

The area comprises 185 children who are below 15 years out of that 96 are Male and 89 are Female children.

EDUCATION BACKGROUND OF THE CHILDREN

When we take the history of the education before 10 years only 15 per cent of the children have education. But now 35 per cent of the children have education. Free and compulsory education below 14 years is applicable here because TTD schools are very nearer to this slum area and joined their children. Many of the persons in slums began their life as hawkers, auto drivers and daily wage workers and their female partners also work as servant maids and vendors. Women self-help groups some what enhanced their economic status and few joined their children at private english medium schools.

Table 10.2. Below 15 Years Education Background

S.No.	Type of Education	Male	Female	Total
1.	Infants	10	10	20
2.	Anganvadi Schools	13	12	25
3.	1st to 10th Class	39	34	73
4.	Drop Outs	10	15	25
5.	Private English Medium Schools	20	10	30
6.	Illiterates	04	08	12
	Total	**96**	**89**	**185**

Table 10.2 consists of 185 children out of that Infants Male are 10 and Female are 10, Anganvadi school going Male are 13 and Female are 12, 1st to 10th Class school children Male are 39 and Female are 34. Private English Medium school education children Male are 20 and female are 10 and 25 members are dropouts and 12 members are illiterates.

Table 10.3 comprises 96 male and 89 female. Out of 40 children, 20 male and 20 Female are suffering from Kwashiorkor and Marasmus. Out of 25 children, 15 male and 10 female suffering from Scabies, 30 members equally male and female suffers frequently from Fever. Out of 25 children 11 male and 14 female suffering from Diarrhoea. The reasons behind the this are mainly lack of sanitation and Hygiene in the family and round the environment. Lack of balanced diet leads to Marasmus. This is a common deficiency disease in India. The first sign of malnutrition among the children is failure to gain weight and much worse is loss of weight. Diarrhoea and other diseases also make the condition still worse. Some of the early signs of malnutrition include: the muscles look wasted and the child looks thin; the belly looks prominent; the child is listless and does not respond when the mother plays with him; the child looks short for his age; and the hair looks light or reddish instead of dark. To put short, failure to gain weight every mouth is an early sign of malnutrition. The child becomes normal with simple treatment at this stage. Due to lack of systematic research investigations very little information on dietary habits and nutritional status of slums are available. Malnutrition is common among slums and affects the general physique of the Slums and lowers the ability to resist infections and leads to chronic illness. In the post-weaning period it leads to permanent brain impairment. Among most of the slum population the staple diet is rice. Diets are deficient in calcium, Vitamin-a, Vitamin-c, Riboflavin and animal protein. In some South Indian people the diet is deficient in calories and protein.

Table 10.3: Healthy Composition of the Children Below 15 Years

S.No.	Type of Disease	Male	Female	Total
1.	Kwahiyorkor & Marasmus	20	20	40
2.	Skin Diseases	15	10	25
3.	Fever Frequently	15	15	30
4.	Diarrhoea	11	14	25
5.	Healthy Children (Absence of disease)	35	30	65
	Total	**96**	**89**	**185**

Deficiency diseases such as Anemia, Kwashiorkar, Marasmus and vitamin deficiency signs like Bitot's spot and angular steatites were prevalent among tribal population: Nutritional anemia, which lowers resistance to fatigue, and increases susceptibility to other diseases is common among slums.

Maternal mortality was reported to be high among in India. The chief causes for maternal mortality were unhygienic conditions and primitive practices for parturition. Urban Health Centre one is to be upgraded to a community health centre with 30 beds and 4 specialties of Gynecology, Pediatrics, Surgery and Medicine. Tirupati being pilgrim centre there is always floating population and Urban health centers should pay much attention regarding health and hygiene.

PROBLEMS OF THE DISEASE PREVENTION AND CONTROL

If early malnutrition is not treated, it may develop into Marasmus or Kwashiorkor or a combination of these two conditions. Marasmus normally occurs in children be-low one year and is due to eating an insufficient quantity of food.

Symptoms of Marasmus include: greatly retarded growth; the skin becomes loose as in case of old people because there is little fat underneath the skin; flabby muscles on thighs and buttocks and the child is always hungry crying a lot.

Kwashiorkor symptoms include: retarded growth; swelling on the feet and legs; the child appears 'moonfaced'; the hair often turns red or gray and is easily pulled out; and the child has no appetite and is difficult to feed. Kwashiorkor normally occurs in children above one year. It is due to an imbalanced diet containing foods which are low in protein.

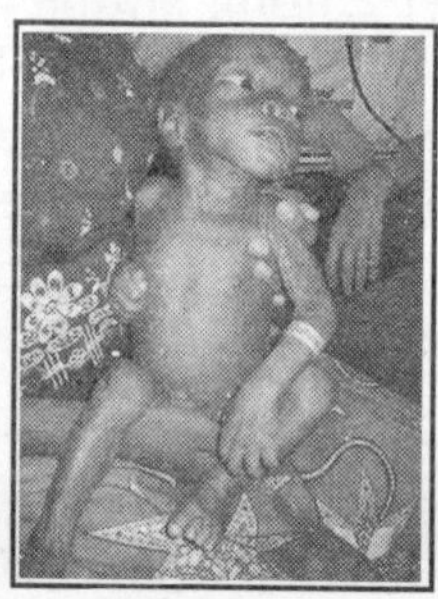

A Child suffering from Kwashiorkor

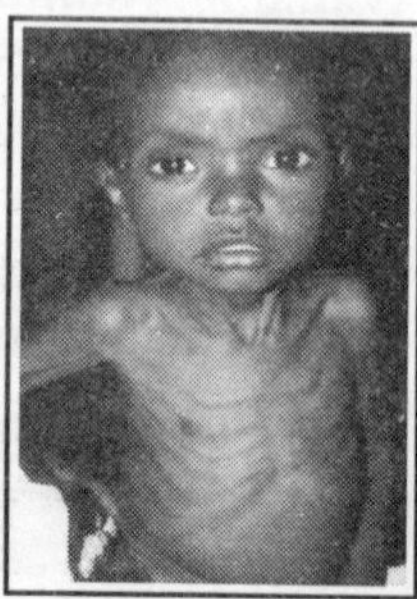

PREVENTION AND CONTROL

- Balanced diet given to the Children.
- Anganvadi food supplement should provide to this children.
- Peanuts, milk, egg, vegetables and meat added in the diet which provides more proteins.

Anemia: Iron deficiency in the blood causes anemia. It is very common in India particularly among mothers and children. There are many causes of anemia which include malnutrition; lack of iron and folic acid in the diet; and blood loss due to injuries, hookworm or malaria.

Vitamin 'A' Deficiency: 'A' Vitamin is necessary for the normal function of the eyes. Deficiency of Vitamin 'A' leads to loss of vision and eventually to blindness. We can prevent it by taking leafy vegetables carrot, Lever and Papaya Which are Rich in Vitamin 'A'. The micro nutrients which place growth and development need more to adolescent girls. The maternal and child care centres provides milk powders, and variety of pulses powder rich in vitamins and also supply threptin biscuits. Hare Rama Hare Krishna Temple provides mid-day Meal Programmes to this school children and it is very rich in nutrient.

Fevers are of different kinds caused by malaria, typhoid and viral infections. A person has fever when the body temperature is more than 37°C or when the body is too hot. Proper diagnosis and medication necessary for treatment by A qualified physician. In this slum area one year back majority of the people suffered from chicken Guniya. Malaria is an endemic disease. It is caused by infection of the blood by a parasite. High fever and chills are the symptoms. The mosquito bites a person with Malaria and sucks up the parasite. It later bites a healthy person and injects the malaria parasite into the blood. Slides are prepared with the blood smear of suspected cases to confirm the positive cases. Chloroquin is the medication administered.

Warm Infections: These include, pinworms, round worms, hook worms and whip worms and they give trouble in stomach.

Headache and Body Ache: These are often associated with fever. If the movements of neck are normal, aspirin or paracetamol tablets are supplied by the health visitors and Anganvadi workers in the slum areas. If it is not control they advise to go to hospital.

Cough: Cough, by itself is not an illness. It is a sign of some other sickness affecting the throat, lungs or airways tubes in the chest. If the cough is present for two weeks or more or if the sputum is blood stained doctor's diagnosis and treatment are necessary. If not sulphadimidine tablets are advised.

Scabies: It is an infection of the skin. It causes severe itching and tiny blisters or cracks in the skin, especially between the fingers, on the wrists, around the waist and on the genitals. Scabies is caused by tiny mites which make tunnels under the skin. It spreads rapidly from one person to another. Therefore, if one person in the family has scabies, everyone in his family should be treated.

Prevention: Scabies can be prevented by personal cleanliness. It is important to bathe and change clothes regularly and to prevent children from playing in dirty and muddy surroundings.

Lice Infestation: Infestation of the hair with lice is very common in tropical countries including India. It is more likely to occur if the hair is not properly washed or combed. It spreads from one person to another especially when the same comb is used by many and causes itching of the scalp a day. It should be washed at least once a weak and more often in the hot weather. It is better to avoid the comb used by others. Particularly in this slum area this type of lice infestation is common.

Diarrhoea is one of the major causes of health among the children. It is diagnosed when a person passes frequent watery stools. Diarrhoea could be fatal in children below two years of life. It is more common in undernourished children than the healthier ones. As the severity of malnutrition increases, the incidence of diarrhea increases and it becomes more severe.

Etiology: Diarrhoea is caused by germs (bacteria or viruses) or by parasites. These germs live in dirt in dust, dirty water and stools. Dirty hands carry germs as the germs get under the finger nails. When the food is touched and eaten by dirty hands one contracts diarrhoea. Germs also stick to flies when they sit on stools. If flies sit on uncovered food, they carry these germs to the food. Dirty water also contains these germs. Dirty feeding bottles and bottle feeds prepared with unclean water can also cause diarrhea. Thus, diarrhea occurs in dirty, unhygienic conditions.

Prevention: Sugar Salt solution one glass of boiled water is cooled and then added one spoon of sugar and salt. This solution is given to the Diarrhea patient once in two hours. The surroundings must be clean. Proper sanitation, sewage and waste disposed and personal hygiene are necessary to prevent worm infestation. Defecation must be made in proper sanitary latrines and not in open fields. Vegetables should be washed thoroughly before cooking. The water used for drinking should be clean and disinfected by chlorination and boiling. Hands should be washed with clean water and soap after play and defecation and before eating. Finger nails should be cut regularly and kept clean. Walking barefoot in places used for defecation should be avoided.

SUGESTIONS AND SOLUTIONS

The Ministry of Health and Family Welfare provided Centrally Sponsored schemes for control of Malaria, Fileria, Tuberculosis, Leprosy and Blindness. A specific provision is made to carryout research into diseases to which slum areas are prone. Towards the end of Second Five Year Plan Government of India launched a National Goitre Control Programme (NGCP) to control Goitre among urban population. Indian Council of Medical Research (ICMR), (Ministry of Health and Family Welfare, Government of India) set up regional centres at Andhra Pradesh to study the health problems. Integrated Child Development Services provided supplementary nutrition, immunization, health check up and referral services to children in age group of 0-6 years and also to pregnant and nursing mothers In the slum areas with a population of 700 persons an Anganwadi can be set up. A number of MCH Schemes have been initiated by Government of India to provide maternal" and child health care and to reduce mortality and morbidity among the population.

The Schemes should be continued in Extension with some more Development

1. Health education.
2. Prophylaxis against nutritional anemia.
3. Prophylaxis against blindness due to Vitamin-A deficiency.
4. Medical Termination of Pregnancy (MTP).
5. Universal Immunization.
6. Oral Rehydration Therapy (ORT).
7. Acute Respiratory Infection control.
8. Minimum Needs Programme (MNP).
9. 2020 Health Vision.
10. Safe water programmes.
11. Especially in slum areas DDT powerful chemicals should be sprayed.
12. Free Medical checkups.
13. Rajiv Arogya Sri should be continued.
14. Pranadana Schemes should be continued.
15. AIDS Awareness Programmes especially in slums.
16. Women Welfare Programmes like DWACRA, SHG's.
17. Tirupati being Vatican city Urban Community Development should maintain sanitation.
18. Pollution control board should take much attention regarding environment.
19. Health awareness programmes should conducted in the slum areas regarding balanced diet rich in proteins.
20. Child health-care services especially in slum areas have to reach poor and needy.

The above schemes enrich the health status in the Urban communities and Woman welfare programmes enhance the economic status of the family to drove poverty. The family should concentrate mainly on health of the children. Children are the main backbone of the country and the bright future of country is in their intelligent hands.

So health is wealth.

REFERENCES

Chaurasia, B.D. Human Anatomy

Khan, Prof. M.R. & Dr.M.K.Rhlasur Rahman, Essence of Pediatrics

Jain, A.K. Physiology

Pramukh, Raj Medical Anthropology

Rao, Subba Health and Society

Social Welfare Journal 2010

Standard of Living of Persons with Disabilities Residing in Urban Slum

Khim Kumari Kausila

INTRODUCTION

"Slums are the emerging human settlements of the 21st century", states the "State of the World's Cities 2006/7" report released by the U.N.-Habitat at Vancouver. In fact, the report states that at the present rate of growth of rate of slum dwellers in the world, there will be 1.4 billion slum-dwellers by 2020, According to the Census of India, 2001, we have about 40,297,341 people living in slums in about 607 towns across India which have a population of more than 50,000.

(i) The Census of India, 2001 Classifies a Slum as: A compact area of at least 300 populations or about 60-70 households of poorly built congested tenements, in unhygienic environment usually with inadequate infra-structure and lacking in proper sanitary and drinking water facilities.

Hyderabad alone has about six lac people living in 811 slums with more than half of them below poverty line.

(ii) More than one-third of the city's population resides in slum, squatters and other poor settlements.

(iii) Standard of living is measured in terms of availability of food, proper sanitary and drinking water facilities, proper housing and sufficient clothing, access to health services, necessary social service and ensured social security.

Everyone has the right to a standard of living adequate for the health and well-being of himself and of his family, including food, clothing, and housing and medical care and necessary social service, and the right to security in the event of unemployment, sickness, disability, widowhood, old age or other lack of livelihood in circumstances beyond his control. (Article 25, UDHR).

Persons with disabilities means a person suffering from not less than 40 per cent of any disability as certified by a medical authority. It includes low vision, blindness, hearing impairment, locomotor disability, leprosy cured, mental retardation and mental illness. (PWD Act., 1995).

According to UNCRPD, Article 28 states that States Parties recognize the right of persons with disabilities to an adequate standard of living for themselves and their families, including adequate food, clothing and housing, and to the continuous improvement of living conditions, and shall take appropriate steps to safeguard and promote the realization of this right without discrimination on the basis of disability.

Background Description of Rasoolpura

The Rasoolpura slum, designated as a notified slum by the government is the one of the largest in Hyderabad with an area of 4.89 s.q. km having population of 96,000 and 16000 household. Separate settlements within it include Sri Lanka, Gun Bazaar, Indirammanagar, Anna Nagar, Krishnanagar and other colonies. The survey has been conducted in the slum of Rasoolpura. The area is under the jurisdiction of the Secunderabad Cantonment Board (SCB), which is under the Ministry of Defense.

The Secunderabad Cantonment (SC) Slums, Colonies Integrated Development and People's Welfare Association demanded that the civic administration of the Cantonment Board be included under the jurisdiction of the Municipal Corporation of Hyderabad. The occupants of these slums are migrants from neighboring places like Siddipet, Narsapur etc.

Standard of Living of Person with Disabilities Residing in Rasoolpura

Most of the persons with disabilities residing in the slum are below poverty line. They are facing difficulty in day to day life even to meet their basic needs. Many NGOs comes to aids and raise their standard of living. Some of the NGOs working in Rasoolpura are Bhumi, Family Planning Association of India (Hyderabad), APSA, CFCA, MV Foundation, Mahita organisation, etc. The NGO Bhumi begun its work from the year 2006, concentrating in 5 areas such as health and wellness, education, sanitation, livelihood and women empowerment and is particularly working for persons with disabilities in Rasoolpura area. According to the survey conducted by Bhumi NGO in collaboration with National Institute of Mentally Handicapped carried out on 6th, 8th and 9th of February 2010 there are total 80 persons with disabilities identified. Out of which 26 Mental Retardation, 13 Cerebral Palsy, 22 physically Challenged, 13 Hearing Impairment, 4 Visual Impairment, two Mental Illness cases has been identified.

The standard of living of the persons with disabilities is measured in terms of food supply, proper sanitary and drinking water facilities, proper housing and sufficient clothing, access to health services, necessary social service and ensured social security. These are the following observation:

Food is a Basic Necessity

Right from the ancient ages we have regarded food as one of the basic necessities for survival and every individual should get it on regular basis. Most of the resident of the slum are able to manage food for themselves and their family members regular. It is also available to the persons with disabilities who are dependent on other member of the family. But it is a matter of problem of managing food for few persons with disabilities that are not dependent on other family member. Even if they are getting food regularly but the nutritional value of the food they eat is low. Sometimes they are being provided food by their neighbor or some NGO working in their area. NGO Bhumi was concentrated on the nutritional aspect of children with disabilities and started a programme of providing high protein nutritional diet breakfast to children with disabilities.

Water and Sanitation

Water supply according to most of the respondents is not much a big problem that the resident of Rasoolpura faces. Different provisions of water exist in Rasoolpura. They are water pipelines, bore wells, tankers and private sources. The person with disabilities along with their other family members depends on the same water. The water supply is shared by 10-15 house each and though readily available is not appropriately treated to make it safe for drinking purpose. Especially the children with disabilities suffer frequently suffers from water born disease due to consumption of ill treated water. Also the availability of water for other household activities is not sufficient.

Some of the houses in the slums have shared sanitation facilities due to its low cost for construction and maintenance. There are also personal toilets for many households but even that also poorly maintained. The toilets of maximum of the residents surveyed in the slum are under unhygienic and poor conditions. The households in the slum have underground sewerage system. Every house has a septic tank that filters the sewerage and releases it in to the drains on the main road. Finally the sewerage of the entire area ends up in open drains, running through the area. They have acute problems with the drainage system wherever there is one and still the constructing pipeline is still ongoing process.

Clothing and Housing

The maximum requirements of clothes of persons with disabilities are fulfilled by the earning member of the family. Sometimes nearby NGO helps by distributing the clothes to them and also neighboring people gives away the unused clothes to them. Houses in the slums are pucca houses made of bricks and cement but the roofs of maximum houses are made of asbestos and tin material. There is particularly problem of space in the locality and each house hold is shared by a large family members.

Health and Rehabilitation Services

There is no government health center in the locality and initiatives are taken by the NGO working in the area providing free health services by arranging health professionals. NGO Bhumi is working extensively for providing rehabilitation services in the slum.

Aids and Appliances

Aids and appliance required by the person with disability is provided under government schemes. Though the appliances are available but the utility in the locality does not support the mobility of such devices like wheelchair mobility.

Social Security Programmes

Disability certificate are issued to the person with disability and the NGO assists them to get the required disability certificate and the pension also.

REVIEW OF LITERATURE

Quantitative Techniques for Health Equity Analysis—Technical Note, Measuring Living Standards: Household Consumption and Wealth Indices.

In approaching the issue of living standards measurement, it is important to be aware of the limitations and potential problems of alternative measures. This requires an understanding of not only the conceptual differences between different approaches, but also of the problems that can arise in the construction of living standards variables. With this in mind, this note has four purposes:

(i) To outline different approaches to living standards measurement.

(ii) To discuss the relationship between and merits of different living standards measures.

(iii) To discuss briefly how different measures can be constructed from survey data.

(iv) To provide guidance on where further information on living standards measurement can be obtained.

Sen, A, The Standard of Living, The Tanner Lectures O N Human Values, Delivered at Clare Hall, Cambridge University.

There are at least two basic questions in any evaluative exercise: What are the objects of value? How valuable are they? Strictly speaking, the first-what objects? is an elementary aspect of the second-how valuable? The objects of value are those that will be positively valued when the valuation exercise is fully performed. This may not, however, be the most helpful way of seeing the "what" question. To clarify the contrast, consider for the sake of illustration the general view of the standard of living as pleasure. This would indicate that pleasures of different types are the objects of value and the standard of living consists of pleasures.

Objective

- To study the standard of living of persons with disabilities in slum of Rasoolpura.

Presemt Study

Rasoolpura is a huge slum settlement in the Hyderabad with an area of 4.89 sq km having population of 96,000 and 16000 household. The study would cover six basic standards of living for persons with disabilities including

- Food.
- Water and Sanitation.
- Clothing and Housing.
- Health and Rehabilitation Services.
- Aids and Appliances.
- Social Security.

Research Design

The present study is a Descriptive research study.

Research Method

Survey method was used for collecting the data from persons with disabilities.

Sample

Persons with disabilities residing in the slum of Rasoolpura are the sample of this study. The responses are collected from the either from the head of the family or the parent of the household having person with disability.

Sample Size

The sample size is of thirty persons with disabilities from slum of Rasoolpura.

Sampling Technique

Random sampling technique-The respondents have been selected randomly from different parts of this huge area to get as diverse a picture of the slum as possible. Different lanes have been covered as most problems are common although a few are native only to one particular lane. People residing in the slum area, civil society organizations and official authorities have been interviewed to know the reality and corroborate the facts.

Tools

A tool in the form of questionnaire containing was developed for this study. It consists of personals details and six items Part I, Part II, Part III, Part IV, Part V and Part VI.

Scoring

The scoring for yes is (1) and No is (0).

Data Collection Procedure

First consent is taken from the subjects or samples to participate in research study with their willingness and the response is collected from the respondents on the validated questionnaire through personal visits.

Statistical Analysis

Data were analyzed with the help of Microsoft Excel and the data are interpreted.

RESULT AND DISCUSSION

Table 11. 1 represents the preponderence of male person with disability over female in the sample size. It shows that there are 18 male and 12 female in sample of persons with disabilities. It is graphically represented in figure 11.1.

Table 11.1: Sample Distribution According to Gender

Gender	Frequency	Percentage	Cumulative %
Male	18	60%	60%
Female	12	40%	100%

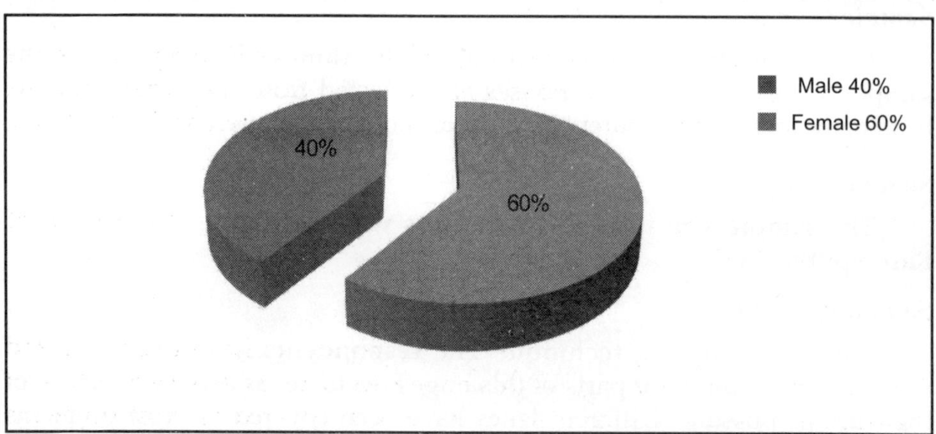

Figure 11.1: **Sample Distribution-According to Gender of Person with Disability**

Table 11.2 represents the sample distribution according to age which shows that there are 30 samples for this study and they are distributed in 4 groups. It shows that 8 samples are between age 0-4 years, 11 sample are between age 5-9 years, 6 sample are between 10-14 years and 5 samples are above 14 years. It is graphically represented in figure 11. 2.

Table 11.2: Sample Distribution According to Age

Age (years)	Frequency	Percentage	Cumulative %
0-4	8	26.66%	26.66%
5-9	11	36.66%	63.33%
10-14	6	20%	83.33%
14 & Above	5	16.66%	100%

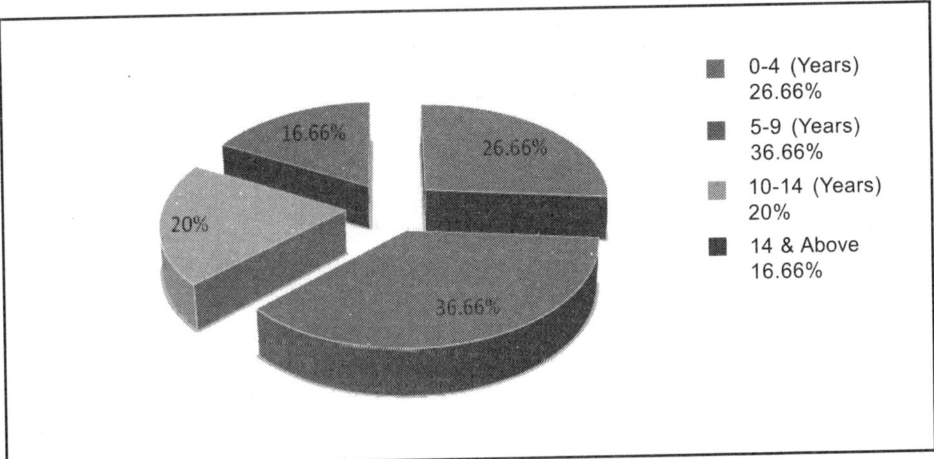

***Figure 11.2:* Sample Distribution of According to Age of Person with Disability**

Figure 11. 3 represents the percentage of item analysis of Part–I of questionnaire used in the study. Its percentage of yes and no are represented in the figure.

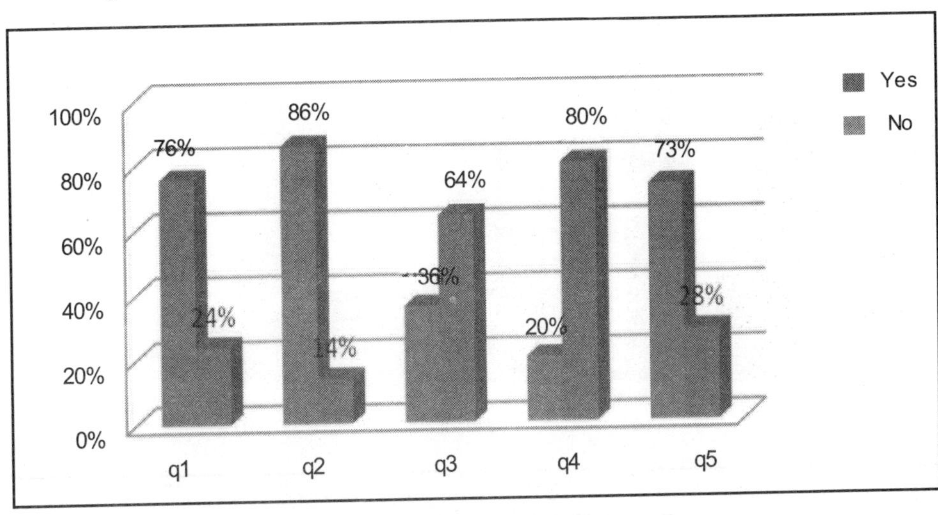

***Figure 11.3:* Item Anlysis of Part-I**

Figure 11.4 represents the average of yes and no in Part–I of questionnaire used in the study. It shows that the response percentage of yes is 58 per cent and of no is 42 per cent.

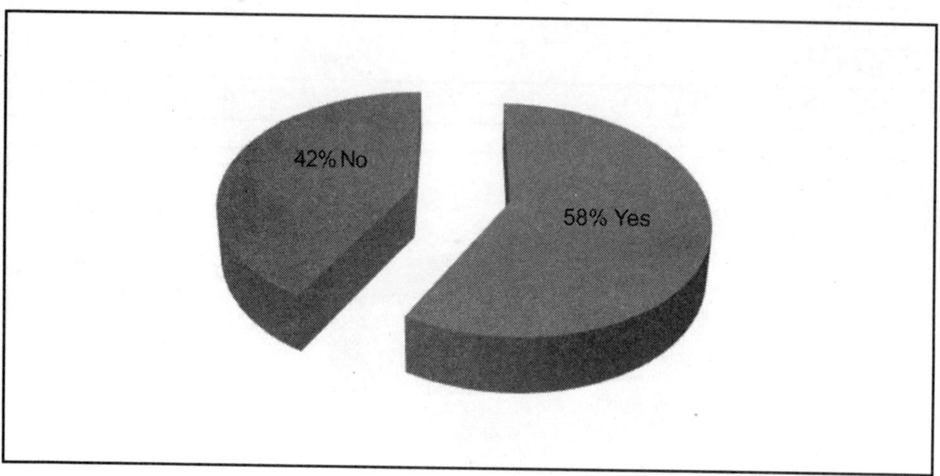

Figure 11.4: **Average of Part -1**

Figure 11.5 represents the percentage of item analysis of Part–II of questionnaire used in the study. It percentage of yes and no are represented in the figure.

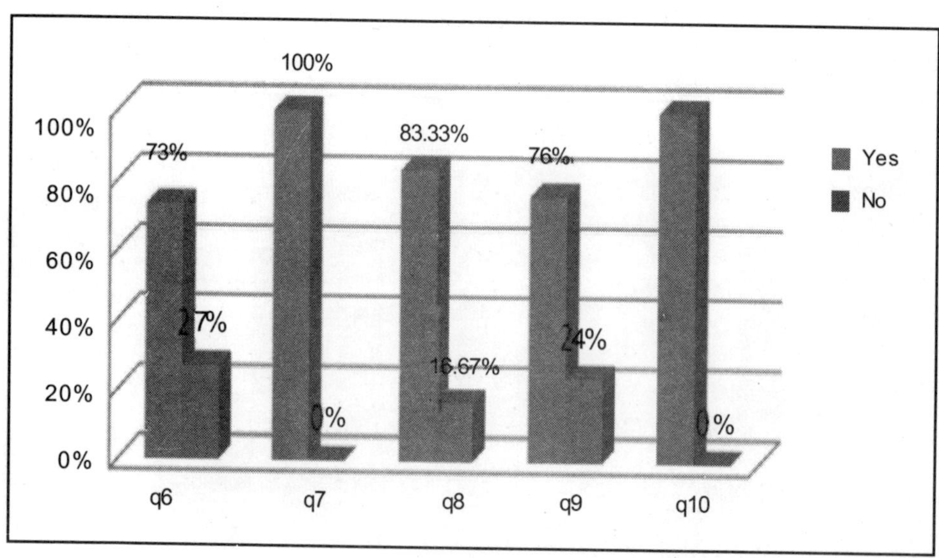

Figure 11.5: **Item Anlysis of Part-II**

Figure 11.6 represents the average of yes and no in Part–II of questionnaire used in the study. It shows that the response percentage of yes is 86 per cent and of no is 14 per cent

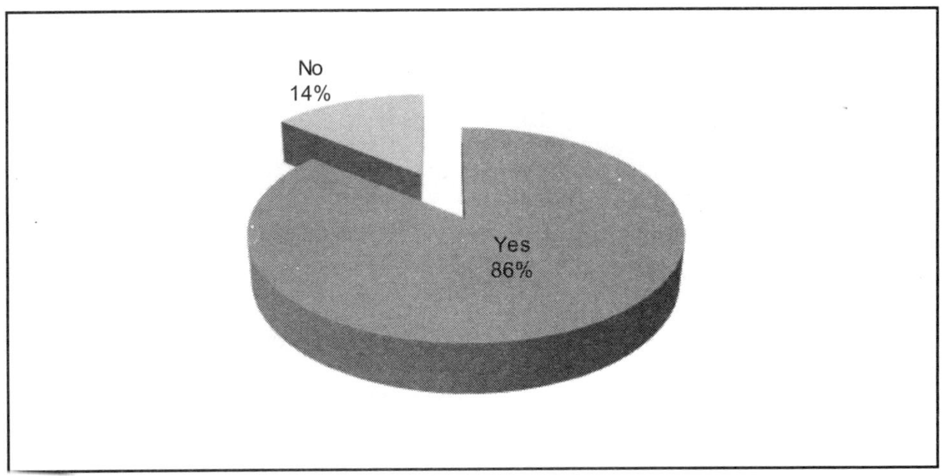

Figure 11. 6: **Average of Part -II**

Figure 11.7 represents the percentage of item analysis of Part–III of questionnaire used in the study. It percentage of yes and no are represented in the figure.

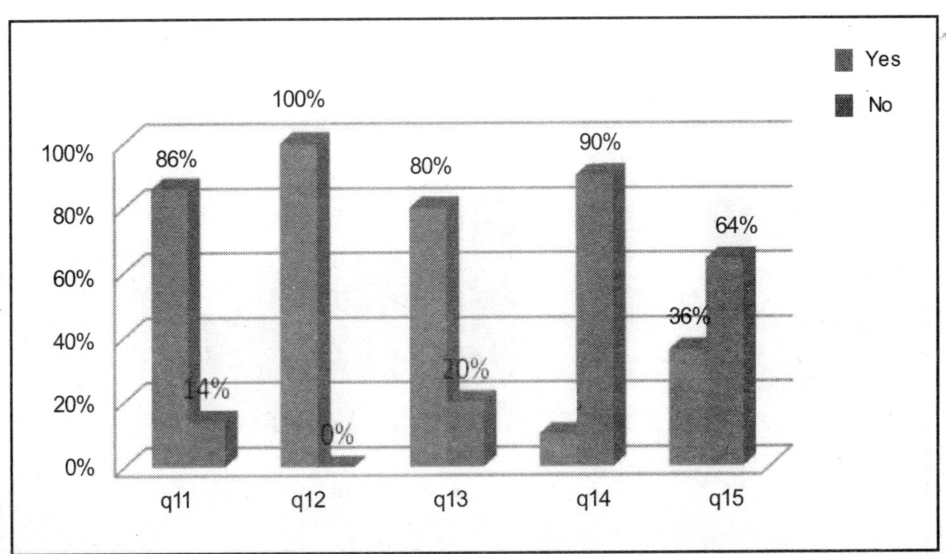

Figure 11.7: **Item Anlysis of Part-III**

Figure 11.8 represents the average of yes and no in Part–III of questionnaire used in the study. It shows that the response percentage of yes is 62 per cent and of no is 38 per cent.

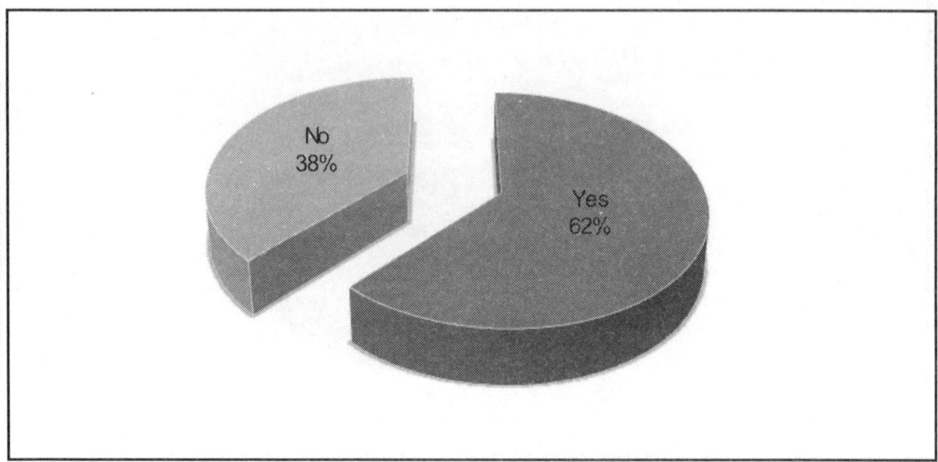

Figure 11.8: **Average of Part-III**

Figure 11.9 represents the percentage of item analysis of Part–IV of questionnaire used in the study. It percentage of yes and no are represented in the above figure.

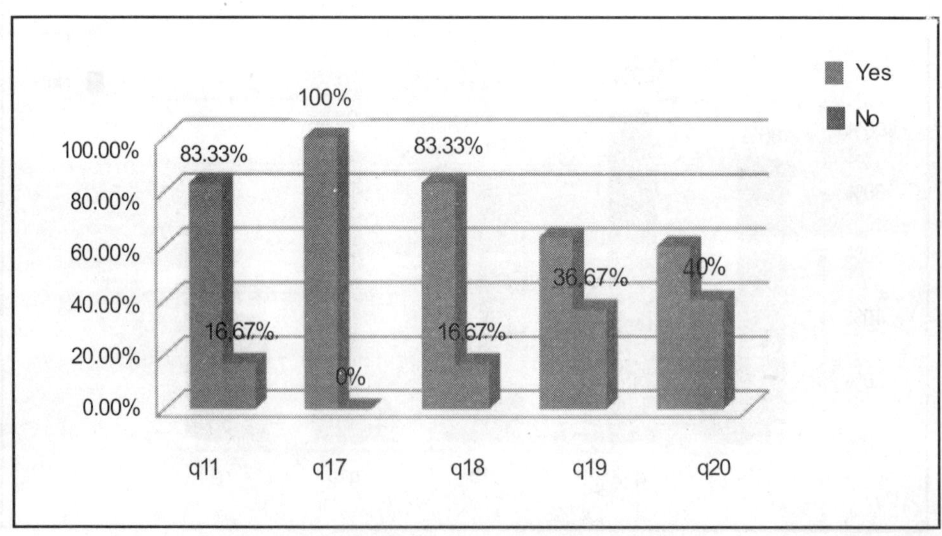

Figure 11.9: **Item Anlysis of Part-IV**

Figure 11.10 represents the average of yes and no in Part–IV of questionnaire used in the study. It shows that the response percentage of yes is 78 per cent and of no is 22 per cent.

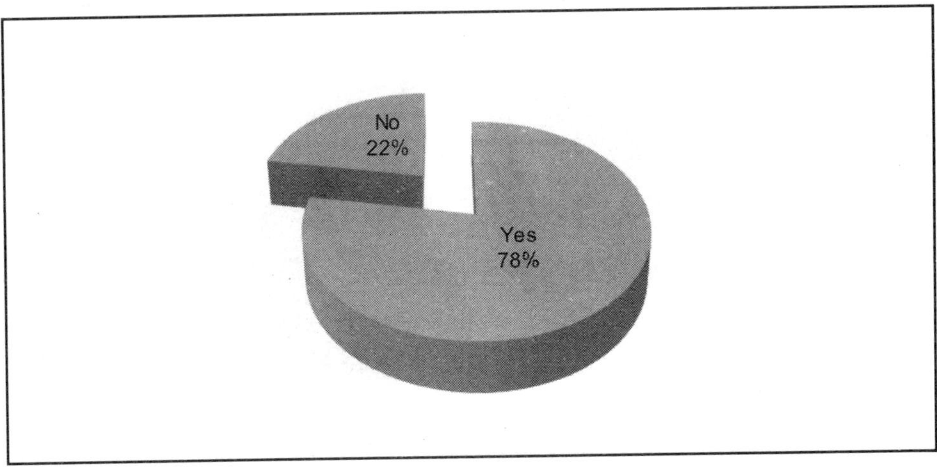

Figure 11.10: **Average of Part-IV**

Figure 11.11 represents the percentage of item analysis of Part–V of questionnaire used in the study. It percentage of yes and no are represented in the figure.

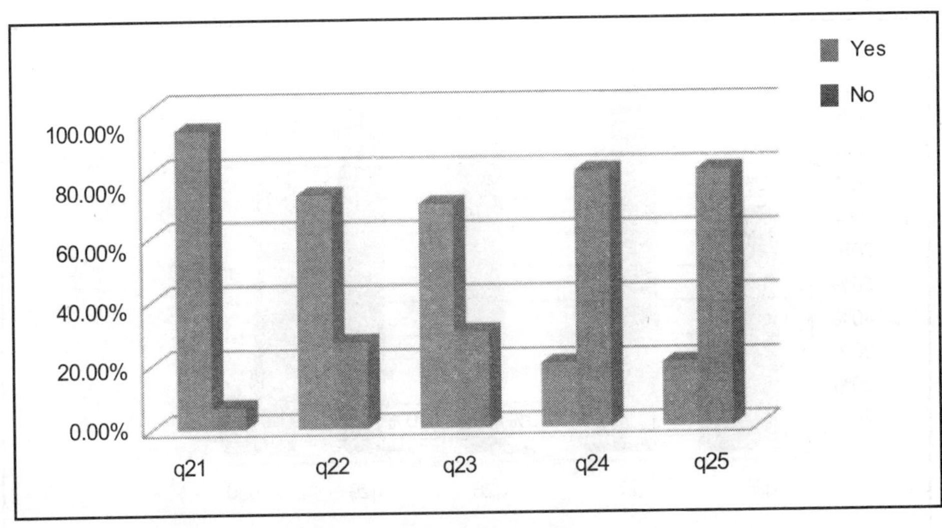

Figure 11.11: **Item Anlysis of Part-V**

Figure 11.12 represents the average of yes and no in Part–V of questionnaire used in the study. It shows that the response percentage of yes is 55 per cent and of no is 45 per cent.

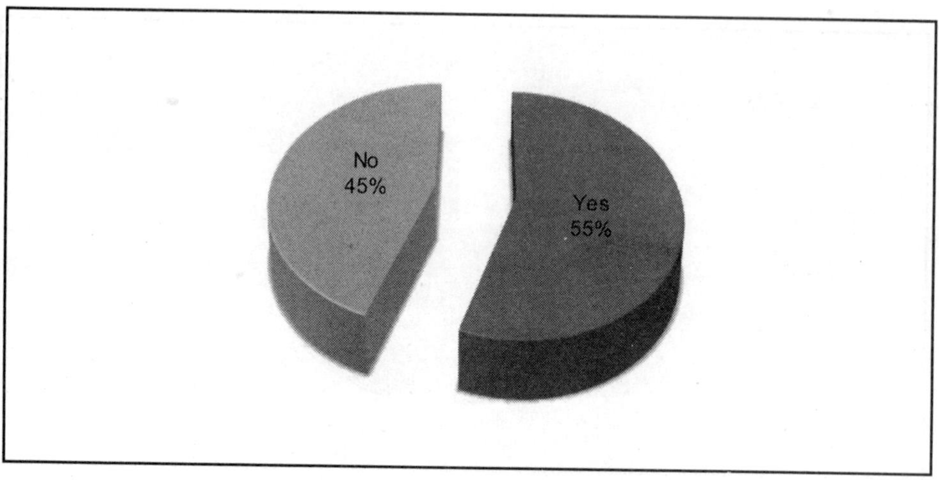

Figure 11. 12: **Average of Part-V**

Figure 11.13 represents the percentage of item analysis of Part–VI of questionnaire used in the study. It percentage of yes and no are represented in the figure.

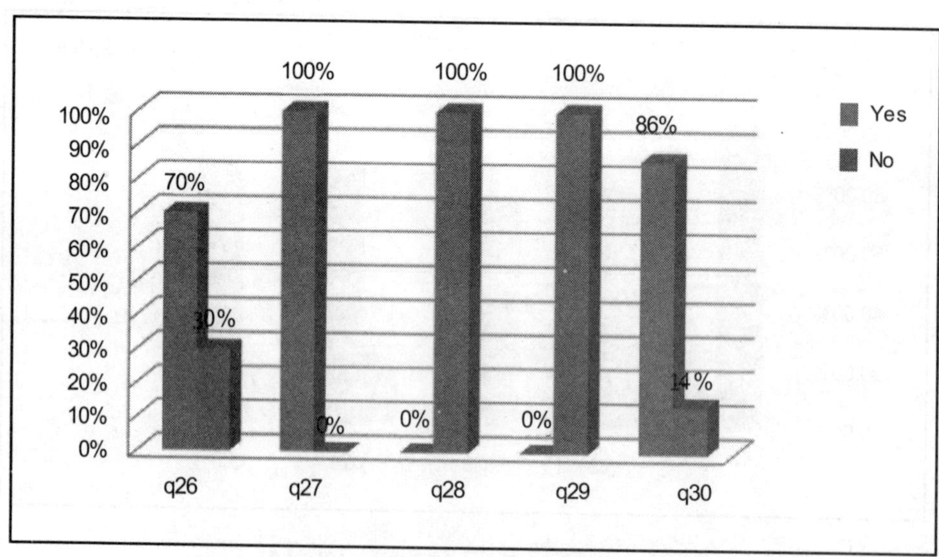

Figure 11.13: **Items Analysis of Part-IV**

Figure 11.14 represents the average of yes and no in Part–VI of questionnaire used in the study. It shows that the response percentage of yes is 51 per cent and of no is 49 per cent.

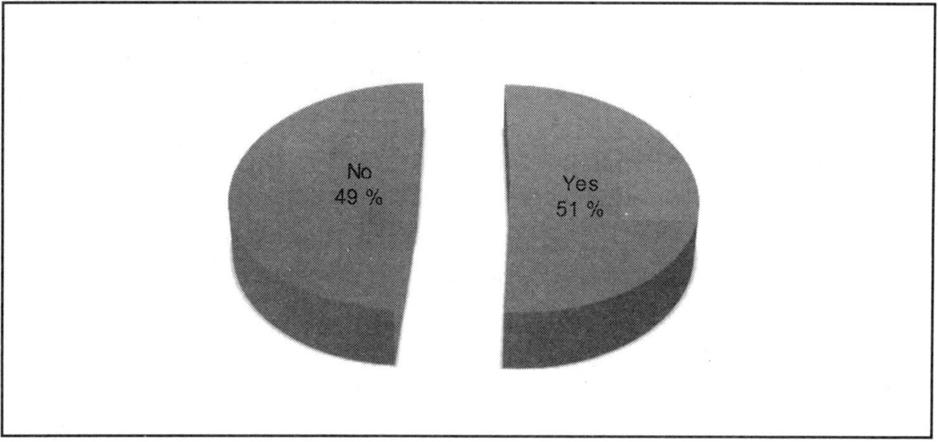

Figure 11.14: **Average of Part-IV**

Figure 11.15 represents the overall average of yes and no percentage of the questionnaire used in the study. It shows that the response percentage of yes is 64 per cent and of no is 36 per cent.

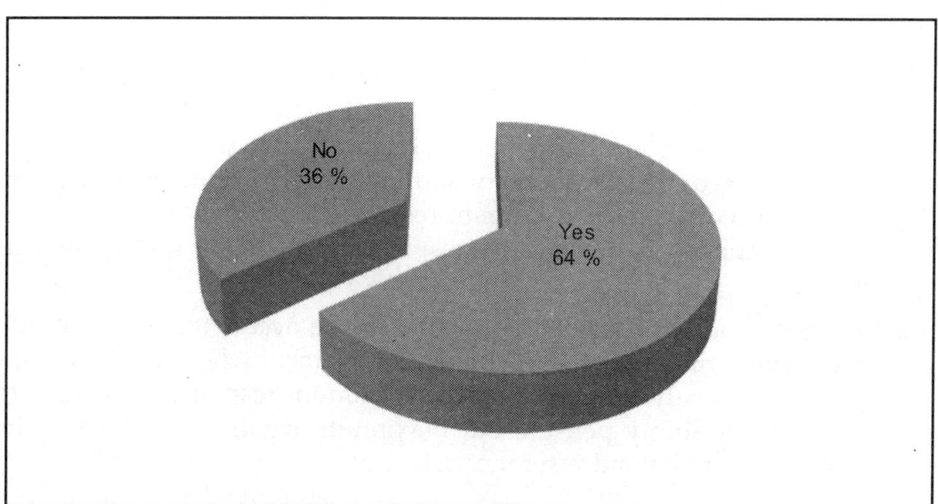

Figure 11.1: **Overall Average % of Item Analysis**

DISCUSSION

The research paper is an attempt to study the standard of living of persons with disabilities in slums of Rasoolpura in Hyderabad. Person with disabilities include Mental Retardation, Cerebral Palsy, physically challenged, Hearing Impairment, Visual Impairment and Mental Illness. The sample consists of 30 persons with disabilities. According to age the sample distribution are 0-4 years 8 PWDs, 5-9 years 11 PWDs, 10-14 years 6 PWDs and, 14 years & above 5 PWDs. According to the age 18 male and 12 female are sample. The questionnaire was developed which consists of personal details and 30 questions, which is again divided into six parts as–

Part I (Food) has items relates to the availability of food, nutrition and hygienic food. The finding of item analysis reveals that the maximum response is positive for the availability of food but negative response to the nutritional value of the food.

Part II (Water and Sanitation) has items related to the water availability, safe drinking water, sanitation facility. The findings of the item analysis reveal that the maximum response is positive for the availability of water and proper sanitation.

Part III (Clothing and Housing) has items related to the availability of clothing and proper housing in the slum. The findings of the item analysis reveal that the maximum response is positive for the availability of clothes and shelter but negative response for the adequate space.

Part IV (Health and Rehabilitation Services) has items related to the health and rehabilitation services and its access to PWDs. The findings of the item analysis reveal that the maximum response is positive for availability of health and rehabilitation services but negative response to the quality of service provided.

Part V (Aids and Appliances) has items related to the access to aids and appliances required for mobility and its uses. The findings of the item analysis reveal that the maximum response is positive to the access to aids and appliances but negative response to the proper use of it in their locality.

Part IV (Social Security) has items related to the access to social security programme running for PWD under Government scheme. The findings of the item analysis reveal that the maximum response is positive to access to disability pension but maximum negative response to the reservation under and insurance schemes.

SUMMARY AND CONCLUSION

The research paper is an attempt to study the standard of living of persons with disabilities in slums of Rasoolpura in Hyderabad. . Person with disabilities include Mental Retardation, Cerebral Palsy, physically challenged, Hearing Impairment, Visual Impairment and Mental Illness. The sample consists of 30 persons with disabilities. A closed ended questionnaire which consists of personal details and 30 questions, which is again divided into six parts is validated and administered among 30 samples through personal visits. A survey method is used for data collection.

The collected data were analyzed with the help of excel spread sheet. Item analysis of each item was done and represented with the help of graphs and tables.

The findings of the study reveal that overall 64% say "yes" in item analysis of the questionnaire used in the study and 36% say "no" which reveals that there is a need to improve the standard of living of persons with disabilities in the slum.

REFERENCES

Bliss, C, Life-Style and the Standard of Living.

Cantonment Board under Corporate Jurisdiction urged, October 29, 2005, from the Online Edtn of The Hindu, http://www.hindu.com/2005/10/29/stories/200510292 1530300.htm.

Frey., B., (2002), "Happiness and Economics How the Economy and Institutions Affect Human Well-being", Princeton University Press, USA.

Galbraith, K., (1985)," The Affluent Society, Andre Deutsch Ltd., USA.

Kumar, A.N. Freedom from Poverty, Regional Center for Urban and Environmental Studies, Osmania University. http://www.metropolis.org/Data/Files/318_Kumar. pdf.

NIMH/CR&PM/Report no-81/03-2010.

Modi, S., (2006), Poverty Premium in Rasoolpura, Hyderabad, CCS Working Paper No. 163, Summer Research Internship Program Centre for Civil Society.

Quantitative Techniques for Health Equity Analysis—Technical Note, Measuring Living Standards: Household Consumption and Wealth Indices.

Reddocrift, Michael (1992), "Sustainable Development", Japanese Edition Published by Gakuyo-syobou, pp. 40-44.

Press Information Bureaus, Press Releas, 18 August 2004, Ministry of Defense in Rajya Sabha. http://pib.nic.in/release/release.asp? Relid =3260.

Sen, A, K., (1987), The Standard of Living, The Tanner Lectures O N Human Values, Delivered at Clare Hall, Cambridge University.

V. Chapter, Hyderabad–City Development Plan, Basic Services to the Urban Poor, http://www.ourmch.com/cdp/chapter%205.pdf.

World Bank (2007), The World Bank's Living Standards Measurement Study Household Surveys, http://www.worldbank.org/lsms/manage/manual.html.

World Environment Day, Centre for Environment Education.

http://www.ceeindia.org/cee/archive/wed.htm.

Urban Poverty

V. Prakasini,
Dr. Saraswathi Raju Iyer

INTRODUCTION

Indian census authorities have adopted a strict definition of what may be called 'Urban'. Under this definition fulfillment of the following criteria are necessary for a place to be designated as urban:

1. Having in place a municipality, corporation, cantonment board or notified town area, committee etc.
2. All other places which satisfy the following criteria:
   - A minimum population of 5,000;
   - At least 75 per cent of the male working population should be engaged in non-agricultural pursuits.
   - A density of population of at least 400 persons per square kilometre.

URBAN POVERTY

The most demanding of the urban challenges, unquestionably, is the challenge posed by poverty. This challenge is of reducing exploitation, relieving misery and creating more human conditions for working, living and growth for those disadvantaged people who have already made the city their home, are in the process of doing so. The urban poor are scanty, segmented and scattered on the one end of the scale are the NSS time series data on the expenditure levels which form the basis of the estimating the number of people living below the poverty line. The other end consists of numerous micro-level studies of low-income householders and slum settlements.

The urban poor live in slums and shanty towns and not all those who live in slums and shanty towns are poor. The poor can often be found distributed throughout a city, living in servant quarters settlements and on pavements. Very often they are found in middle class and affluent areas where they perform needed services for well to do people as domestic servants, drivers, gardens, sweepers, washer men etc., on the other hand, because of the extreme shortage of housing and high rents, especially in metro-politian cities a significant proportion of slums households consists of people level but who because of their inadequate shelter lack of basic services and environmentally degraded surroundings, would be itself in many forms. The most visible of these are:

- Growth of slums.
- Growth of informal sector.
- Crushing pressure on civic amenities.
- Growing sense of hopelessness rising crime rates and group violence.

CONCEPT OF POVERTY

Poverty with reference to a country may be defined as social phenomenon in which a section of the society is unable to fullfill even its basic necessities of life. When a substantial segment of society is deprived of the minimum level of living and continues at a bare subsistence level, the society is said to be plagued with poverty. Attempts have been made in all societies to define poverty, but all they are conditioned by the vision of minimum or god life obtaining in society. In India, the generally accepted definition of poverty emphasizes minimum level of living rather than a reasonable level of living. The twin causes of poverty are under development and inequality.

CULTURE OF POVERTY

It is argued that wherever there are cities there will be slums and they are associated with poverty and a specific culture Oscar Lewis (1966) who developed the nation of the culture of poverty. Maintained that this was not just a matter of deprivation or disorganization, but a design of living with a readymade set of solutions for human problems. In the words of Lewis (1966) the lack of effective participation and integration in the major institutions of the larger society is on the crucial characteristics of the culture of poverty. We may however quote the apt statement made by Mangin even in the context of the U.S.A and Latin American Mangin (1970) writes my own interpretation of the Latin American and the United States situations is that the traits mentioned by Lewis and the phenomenon of apathy and cyclical poverty, are much more tenuous and temporary in both areas than he says.

Poverty is not necessarily associated with uncleanness (slum condition) nor is tidiness the characteristic feature of the well-to-do many middle class squatter settlements in cities like Delhi exhibit slum conditions. Squatting is not the monopoly of the poor people belonging to the middle income group often buy plots in an unauthorized area at a low cost and build pucca houses there. Since these colonies are illegal the corporation does not provide any water, electricity, drainage and sewage facilities.

The houses also get over crowded and due to the non-civic habits of the residents, slums conditions prevail. On the contrary some hutment colonies maintain greater cleanliness than colonies with pucca houses although people live in huts, the walls and floors are plastered with cow dung which is a free disinfectant they keep the surroundings and roads clean. With less over crowding the sanitary conditions do not deteriorate.

Thus, by following a civic culture, slum conditions can be avoided. Under conditions of urban living minimum of infrastructure (even given the proper attitude and concern) namely, water, drainage, sewerage and toilet and clearance of garbage and other municipal services, is necessary given these facilities, even hutments settlements can be kept clean. Hence it is a question of the poverty of civic culture that characterizes slum conditions rather than a culture of poverty.

RESOURCES OF THE POOR

It is significant to note that most urban development authorities in India not only create a very small portion of the housing supply but also cater primarily to middle and upper income groups much of legislation and rules governing so called low income housing is not only complex but such housing is beyond the income ability of the poor. It is significant that the various teams are the housing and urban development corporation (HUDCO) and the Life Insurance Corporation of India (LIC) covering so called "Low cost housing" are really irrelevant and beyond the ability of the urban poor to pay.

REVIEW OF THE PROGRAMMES FOR THE URBAN POOR

The major programmes implement by the government for the amelioration of the conditions of the urban poor.

1. Shelter-related Programmes

- *Slum Eradication Programmes*

Among the shelter related programmes, slum eradication featured as; A key approach during the first and second five years plan. In view of the resource limitations, the resistance of the local population to shifting and maintenance failures the approach abandoned in favor of slum improvement and sites and service and schemes. Housing for the economically weaker sections was taken up in the last two five year's plans.

- *National Housings and Habitat Policy (NHHP)*

1998 India is among those countries that pronounced a housing development policy way back in 1988 following the declaration of 1987 as the 'International Year of Shelter for the Homeless' by the U.N. This was followed by the national housing and habitat policy (NHHP) in 1988, which claimed to bring about housing revolution in order to minimize deprivation for housing and related services. The broad objectives of the policy or to bring about a number of changes in the housing sector;

(i) Creation of surpluses in the housing stock with shelter options to the citizens, especially the vulnerable groups, including the poor.

(ii) To remove barriers in the legal, financial and administrative processes for easy access to housing input like land, Finance and others

(iii) To ensure a progressive shift from subsidy based housing activity to cost sharing and from a target group approach to demand driven approach.

- *Valmiki-Ambedkar Awas Youjana (VAMBAY)*

The objective of VAMBAY, Introduced in 2001–2002, is to meet a long standing gap in programmes for slum-dwellers, namely, provision of shelter or upgrading of existing shelter of people living below the poverty line in urban slums. Twenty per cent of the total allocation under VAMBAY will be built for the urban poor and slums-dwellers, who will make monthly contribution of about Rs. 20 per family provision of water is also included in the scheme.

- *National Slum Development Programme*

The national slum development programme (NSDP) initiated in 1997 as a scheme of special central assistance has been providing additional central assistance to the state government for slum improvement. However, its performance has not been satisfactory mainly because of the delays at the state level in releasing funds to the implementing agencies. The monitoring of the programme at the central level requires strengthening.

2. Nutrition and Healthrelated Programmes

The programme of nutrition has been significantly expanded from the seventh year plan onwards. Special nutrition programmes, such as mid-day meal (MDM) scheme, were integrated with the integrated child development scheme (ICDS). There has been substantial improvement in access to health-care, with national programme for tackling anemia, iodine deficiency disorder and vitamin A deficiency being implemented. As a result of all these intervention, there has been a substantial reduction in serve grades of under nutrition in children and some improvements in the nutritional status of all the segments of the population.

The interventions envisaged in the tenth five year plan are;

(i) Adequate availability of food stuff.

(ii) Prevention of under nutrition of through nutrition education.

(iii) Operational zing universal screening of all pregnant women infants preschool and school children for under nutrition column.

(iv) Prevention, yearly detection under appropriate management of micro nutrient deficiencies and associated health hazards.

(v) Promotion of appropriate dietary intake and life styles.

(vi) Nutrition monitoring and surveillance.

3. Employment-oriented Programmes

- *Self-employment Programme for Urban Poor*

In 1986 the government of India started the self employment programme for urban poor (SEPUP) by year marking a sum of Rs. 200 crore as credit to be distributed to poor urban entrepreneur, whose income did not exceed Rs. 600/month. The maximum credit available is Rs. 5000. The list of economic activities per which loans are available contains 35 items including hawking handcarts laundering, welding, cycle rickshaw operations and, show making and Hair dressing.

- *Swarns Jayanthi Shahari Rojgar Youjana (SJSRY)*

The special scheme of urban self employment under the swarna jayanthi shari rajgar youjana extends assistance to the urban poor living below poverty line, it special attention to women and persons belonging to SC's and ST's to setup gainful self employment ventures. The benefits for SC's are granted keeping in the view the extent of the proportion of their strength in the local population.

The positive aspect of the SJSRY Is that it contains the to basic requirement of programme of poverty alleviation namely, community involvement and empowerment and employment generation of urban poor, formation of community groups, involvement of non government organizations ,Training for lively hoods, housing and sanitation environmental improvement, convergence of services.

4. Participatory Programmes

Urban Community Development was started as a pilot project as early as 1959. How ever, very few pilot projects survived. In 1981 the UCD, low cost sanitation and small and medium town development projects supported by UNICEF were merged into a new service called Urban basis Services (UBS). Its aim is to promote citizen participation, strengthen the service capacities of the local bodies in working with people on commonly felt needs brining about convergences of service and coordinate the resources of various agencies for the purpose of child and women care services receive special attention, with a view to improving their chances of survival and developing their learning potential.

People's participation is an important component in the management and development of cities. Through peoples participation it is possible to mobilize and put to productive use peoples untapped creativity resources and energy and to offer opportunities to people to invent new affordable and appropriate responses to their unmeet needs. How ever, barring a few exception like the UCD, the UBS and the activities of some voluntary organizations not much planned effort is visible to involve people in the urban development process.

5. Infrastructure/Environment–related Programmes

- *Accelerated Urban Water Supply Programmes (AUWSP)*

The central sponsored accelerated water supply programmes was launched in 1993-94 during the eight five year plan. it aims at providing water supply in towns with a population of less than 20,000 as per the 1991 census. A total of 2,151 towns qualify for consideration under the scheme. The project funding is shared equally by the centre and the state, the later including a 5 per cent contribution from the beneficiary town. The centre meets the entire cast in union territories. The state–wise share in the plan allocation is based on a weight age system based on population incidence of poverty, etc.

- *Low Cost Sanitation*

The centrally sponsored scheme of urban low cost sanitation for liberation of the scavengers started from 1980-81, initially through the ministry of welfare from 1989-90, it came under the jurisdiction of the ministry of urban development. The main objective of the scheme is to convert the existing dry latrines into low cost pour flush latrines and provide alternative employment to the liberated scavengers. The ministry of social justice and empowerment deals with the rehabilitation components.

- *Community Toilet Complexes Under The Valmiki Amnedkar Awas Youjana*

The housing and urban development corporation is also involved in the implementation of the pay and uses toilets programmes under the night shelter scheme, and has sanctioned 69 schemes for pay and use toilets. Under which a subsidy of Rs. 14,000 per seal toilets is provided this scheme has now been merged with the new scheme, the Valmiki Ambedkar Awas Youjana, as part of the sanitation component of the scheme, for which 20 per cent of the funds are earmarked.

Community toilets are needed for slum and pavement dwellers, rickshaw pullers and the floating population. However, the experience of maintenance and up keep of these units by municipal authorities has been dismissal, with the conditions turning so unsanitary that people prefer open–air defecation rather than use of public toilets.

CONCLUSION

A main reason is their incapacity to proportionately expand employment opportunities for this expanded labor force in the organized sector. Their infrastructures for both living and economic activity are greatly overtaxed and face huge shortages of shelter, water, sewage and drainage systems and internal transport.

Towns cities and metropolitans all over the country have grown in population size with out being able to manage the impact of this rapid population growth on their economies, both population and urban growth have only compounded the problem of social development. This has attracted considerable attention from to look for policy options to moderate urbanization and to regulate changes in its pattern.

REFERENCES

Amithab, Kundu, (1991), Micro Environment in Urban Planning Access of Poor to Water Supply and Sanitation, *Economic and Political Weekly*, Vol. XXVI (37).

Basta, S., "Nutrition and Health in Low Income Areas of the Third Word" Ecology of Food and Nutition, Vol. 6, 1977.

Chandrashekar Bhat, M.S.A Rao (1991), *A Reader in Urban Sociology*, Orient Longman.

Jacob, Z. Thudipara (2008), "Urban Community Development" Rawat Publications, Jaipur and New Delhi.

Prasad, D. Ravindra (1989), *Urban Renewal The Indian Experience*, Sterling Publishers Pvt. Ltd.

Urban Poverty in India

Dr. R.K. Anuradha, K.Tirumala,
G. Sudhakar and R. Hemalatha

INTRODUCTION

Urban poverty poses the problems of housing and shelter, water, sanitation, health, education, social security and livelihoods along with special needs of vulnerable groups like women, children and aged people. Poor people live in slums which are over crowded, often polluted and lack basic civic amenities such as clean drinking water, sanitation and health facilities.

India Urban Poverty Report using human development framework provides a good insight on various issues of urban poverty such as basic services to urban poor, migration, urban economy and livelihoods, micro finance for urban poor, education and health, unorganized sector and livelihoods.

Urban poverty with over 25 per cent of urban population is largely concentrated in small and medium towns. According Urban Poverty Report 2009, fifty per cent of India's population is expected to be urban-based by 2030.

According to the Ministry of Housing and Poverty Alleviation the urban population in year 2001 was 286.1 million (27.8% of total population of country) while the land occupied by urban India is only six per cent. The urban sector has been facing critical challenges with regard to affordable shelter, growth of slums, and disparity between demand and supply for the provision of basic services to the urban poor.

The Jawaharlal Nehru Urban Renewal Mission (JNNURM) was launched by Government in 2005 for catering to the provision of housing and basic services to urban poor in 65 specified cities and towns. JNNURM has two programmes—Basic Services to the Urban Poor (BSUP) and Integrated Housing and Slum Development Programme (IHSDP) which is aimed at the integrated provision of basic amenities and services to the urban poor and slum-dwellers like:

- Security of tenure at affordable prices.
- Improved housing.
- Water supply.
- Sanitation.
- Education.
- Health.
- Social security.

ECONOMIC DEVELOPMENT AND URBAN POVERTY

- Indian economy and tries to build a relationship between urbanisation and economic growth. Urban poverty with over 25 per cent of urban population is largely concentrated in small and medium towns.
- Urban poverty with over 25 per cent of urban population is largely concentrated in small and medium towns. Though the incidence of poverty is lower in larger cities, the poor face acute shortage of basic amenities there.
- The poverty line used by the planning commission has limitations in view of the change in consumer behaviour, compulsion of life style change, housing expenses in cities, shrinking access to health and education facilities etc. and expenses on such activities not included in the poverty line calculations.
- Urban poverty is not a spill-over of rural poverty as generally perceived and the manufacturing sector in India has not been able to provide necessary pull to rural workers.

GENDER DIMENSIONS OF URBAN POVERTY

- The magnitude and intensity of urban poverty affecting women, as well as ascertaining the discrimination and inequalities urban poor women face in terms of education and work.
- The lower levels of support structures in urban locations for most poor households, the excessive monetization in urban areas as opposed to rural areas, implications for poor households food security, access to health care, especially child care, and creditworthiness or asset ownership all get linked to the extent of women's earning capacities and productivity as well.

- Policy efforts towards provision of social security measures for the unorganised workers, with special emphasis on aspects concerning poor women worker's rights, provision of maternity benefits, toilets, security from oppressive forms of employment, violence, protection from sexual harassment and improving mechanisms for provision of justice. Improving statistics on women in general, ensuring identification of data gaps and generation of gender disaggregated data systems is a special need.

URBAN ENVIRONMENT, HEALTH AND POVERTY

The determinants of health in urban areas are complex, but social and cultural factors, including composition of the family and cultural restrictions are important. Poor health can reduce capacity to earn an income, and health treatment can use up scarce savings or lead to debt. Women play a crucial role in informal health care in low-income households and communities in their role as wives and mothers, and continue to be used as conduits to children in promotional and preventative health campaigns, for example around nutrition and immunisation.

PROPOSED SOLUTIONS TO URBAN POVERTY

- There should be greater equity in the provision of basic services as interstate and intercity disparity has acquired alarming proportions.
- Small and medium towns, particularly in backward states, should get special assistance from the Central/State government as their economic bases are not strong enough to generate adequate resources.
- Constitutional amendments for decentralization should be backed up by actual devolution of powers and responsibilities and their use by the municipal bodies.
- As much of the subsidized amenities have gone to high and middle income colonies, the restructure of these programmes and schemes is needed to ensure that subsides are made explicit through strict stipulations, targeted through vulnerable sections of population.
- There is good potential for organising slum communities as the average size of size of slum is small.
- To improve sanitation standards, it is suggested to construct community toilets where individual toilets are not possible, to extend sewerage networks to slum areas and connect toilet outlets with that, and community management of toilets in common places.
- Solar, bio-gas and non-conventional energy needs to be promoted for street lights as well as in household energy use wherever possible and feasible. Complete coverage of slum households through electric connections should be ensured.

Urban Povery Alleviation

Poverty reduction is an important goal of the urban policy. Urban growth is a result of

(i) Natural increase in population.

(ii) Net migration from rural areas to urban areas.

(iii) Reclassification of towns.

The common notion that migration largely fuels urban growth is only partially correct. Therefore, it is necessary to view urban poverty as distinct from rural poverty and not as mere transfer of rural poverty into urban areas.

Urban Poverty Leads To

- proliferation of slums and bustees,
- fast growth of the informal sector,
- increasing casualisation of labour,
- tncreasing pressure on civic services,
- increasing educational deprivation and health contingencies.

The Urban Poverty Alleviation Programmes (UPAPs) which were in operation during eighth plan are as follows:

Nehru Rozgar Yojana (NRY)

In order to alleviate the conditions of urban poor, a Centrally sponsored programme—Nehru Rozgar Yojana—was launched at the end of the Seventh Five year Plan (October 1989) with the objective of providing of employment to the urban unemployed and underemployed poor. The Central Government indicated its overall contribution while the essential task of identifying, earmarking and coordinating the relevant sectoral inputs was undertaken by the State Governments. The NRY consisted of three schemes namely:

(i) The Scheme of Urban Micro-Enterprises (SUME).

(ii) The Scheme of Urban Wage Employment (SUWE).

(iii) The Scheme of Housing and Shelter Up gradation (SHASU).

Urban Basic Services for the Poor (UBSP)

The UBSP Programme was implemented as a Centrally Sponsored Scheme during the Eighth Five, year Plan with the specific objectives of effective achievement of the social sector goals; community organisation, mobilisation and empowerment; and converence through sustainable support system. The expenditure on the programme was being shared on a 60:40 basis between the Central and the State Governments and UTs (with legislatures). Further, the per capita expenditure on any slum pocket is Rs. 75

in the first year and Rs. 50 from the second year onwards after the basic infrastructure is developed. The UBSP was targetted to cover 70 lakh urban poor beneficiaries in 500 towns during the Eighth Plan period. The programme has achieved the physical target of 70 lakh beneficiaries during the Eighth Plan period in 350 towns.

Prime Minister's Integrated Urban Poverty Eradication Programme (PM IUPEP)

Recognising the seriousness and complexity of urban poverty problems, especially in the small towns where the situtation is more grave due to lack of resources for planning their environment and development, the PMI UPEP was launched in November, 1995. The PM IUPEP was a Rs.800 crore scheme approved for the period up to the year 2000:

- House-to-house survey has been completed in 213 towns.
- Town-wise project reports have been prepared for 229 towns.
- Under the self-employment component, 20775 applications have been forwarded to banks, out of which 3080 cases have been approved.
- Under the Shelter Up gradation Component, 10386 applications have been forwarded to banks/HUDCO, out of which 4743 cases have been approved by HUDCO.
- As many as 8382 Neighbourhood Groups, 1200 Neighbourhood Development Committees and 444 Thrift and Credit Societies have been formed.

Swarna Jayanti Shahari Rogar Yojana (SJJSRY)

In pursuance of the above recommendations, during the Ninth Plan it is proposed to launch the Swarna Jayanti Shahari Rozgar Yojana (SJSRY) and phase out NRY, PMIUPEP and UBSP.

The Swarna Jayanti Shahari Rozgar Yojana seeks to provide gainful employment to the urban unemployed or underemployed poor by encouraging the setting up of self-employment ventures or provision of wage employment.

Urban Self-Employment Programme (USEP)

This programme will have three distinct components:

1. Assistance to individual urban poor beneficiaries for setting up gainful self-employment ventures.
2. Assistance to groups of urban poor women for setting up gainful self-employment ventures. This sub-scheme may be called "The Scheme for Development of Women and Children in the Urban Areas (DWCUA)".

3. Training of beneficiaries, potential beneficiaries and other persons associated with the urban employment programme for upgradation and acquisition of vocational and entrepreneurial skills.

Coverage

1. The programme will be applicable to all urban towns in India.
2. The programme will be implemented on a whole town basis with special emphasis on urban poor clusters.

Target Groups

1. The programme will target the urban poor,i.e those living below the urban poverty line, as defined from time to time.
2. Special attention will be given to women, persons belonging to Scheduled Castes/Tribes, disabled persons and other such categories as may be indicated by the Government from time to time. The percentage of women beneficiaries under this programme will not be less than 30 per cent. The SCs and STs must be benefited at least to the extent of their proportion in the local population. A special provision of three per cent will be reserved for the disabled under this programme.

Urban Wage Employment Programme (UWEP):

- This programme seeks to provide wage employment to beneficiaries living below the poverty line within the jurisdiction of urban local bodies by utilising their labour for construction of socially and economically useful public assets.
- This programme will apply to urban local bodies, the population of which is less than five lakhs as per the 1991 Census.
- The material-labour ratio for works under this programme will be maintained at 60:40. The prevailing minimum wage rate, as notified from time to time for each area, will be paid to the beneficiaries under this programme.

Recommendations

- The major recommendation is for micro-finance of housing as it can support the incremental building process and support the low income population. Micro-finance of housing has a potential for scope that is far beyond providing shelter to the urban poor and also a determinant for social engineering and inclusive growth.
- Urban poverty reduction would need a drastic revision in the present SJSRY, as well as improvement in the living conditions of the poor.

- The limited administrative capability at the city level would be better utilized if urban contractors are asked to observe laws relating to migrant labour and provide for temporary sheds under law for the labour they hire, and such conditionalities are properly enforced.
- Creating more unskilled employment without any improvement in living conditions may further aggravate the inhuman conditions in which the urban poor live.

SUGGESTIONS

- Reserve at least 30 per cent of all new housing space for the poor.
- Make it compulsory by law for all housing schemes in which more than 20 dwelling units are being constructed, whether for higher or middle income groups, to construct a certain percentage (say 30 per cent of the total number) of affordable houses of 25-30 sq km for the poor as part of the scheme.
- Make it compulsory by law for all advertisements on housing, whether from builders or government organisations, to specifically mention in what manner the poor would benefit from the housing scheme.
- A law should be passed making it incumbent for the contractors to pay for space for the labourers in the night shelter before their tenders are considered.
- Interest subsidy on bank loans for the poor should be introduced. It is ironical that the rich get income tax rebate on housing loans, but the poor get no such benefit from government.
- The poorest such as beggars and daily wage earners cannot afford even houses on a rental scheme. For them the scheme of night shelters should be revived as a centrally sponsored scheme.

CONCLUSION

The Government should not delay in granting industry status to the real estate development activity as real estate is nothing but infrastructure. The real estate activity should be included in the category of industry so as to ease financial inflow to the developers. From last many years, the Government has been making efforts to provide shelter to people belonging to Economically Weaker Sections (EWS) and Low Income Group (LIG) group of families, but the gap has steadily widened year after year as more people migrate to urban areas.

A Study on Urban Poverty Alleviation

Dr. P. Subbarama Raju,
M. Mallesh Naik and
V. Hari Babu

INTRODUCTION

The insufficient employment opportunities and inadequate income among a considerable segment of urban population in India has given rise to urban poverty. Despite the opportunities and new possibilities that the cities present due to the development process brought through urbanization, it is estimated that over 30 per cent of India's urban population live below the poverty line. Such a high degree of urban poverty highlights a serious dimension of the country's contemporary urban scenario. The miserable economic plight does not allow the urban poor to live in authorized residential areas and compel them to stay in slums. Urban poverty in India is reflected not only in the lack of productive employment but also in the inadequate living conditions and the degraded environment.

In order to alleviate urban poverty in the country, the Union Ministry of Urban Affairs and Employment (formerly known as Ministry of Urban Development) has launched a number of slum improvement and urban poverty alleviation programmes (UPAPS). Some such prominent programmes are the Environment Improvement of Urban Slums (EIUS), Integrated Development of Small and Medium Towns for (IDSMT), Urban Community Development (UCD), Small Enterprise for Urban Poor (SEPUP), Urban Basic Services for Poor (UPSP), and Nehru Rozgar Yojana (NRY). These programmes are based on the recognition of the potential contribution that urban poor are capable of making in society and the substantial development they are going to have in the future.

The NRY and the UBPS are two major programmes of the Central Government for urban poor launched in 1989 and 1990 respectively. The UBSP is based on the convergent provision of social and physical inputs in low-income neighborhood involving various specialist departments with the active participation of community groups. The principal aim of the UBSP is to improve and upgrade the quality of life of urban poor, especially women and children. NRY is a direct measure for addressing the problem of urban poverty. It consists of three main schemes:

(i) The Scheme of Urban Micro-Enterprises (SUME).

(ii) The Scheme of Urban Wage Employment (SUWE).

(iii) The Scheme of Housing and Shelter Up-gradation (SHASU).

The SUME is meant to encourage the underemployed/unemployed urban youth to set up small micro-enterprises like petty business and manufacturing for which there is a lot of potential in urban areas. Under the SUME the loans are given to urban poor with 25 per cent subsidy with a ceiling of Rs. 4,000 per beneficiary, while 75 per cent of the unit cost is provided as loan by the Scheduled Banks. For SCs/STs and women the ceiling is Rs. 5,000. It aims at assisting eligible beneficiaries to secure technical training, and providing financial assistance for setting up micro-enterprises by way of the government subsidy and credit from banks. The subsidy is shared between the Centre and the State Governments in 50:50 ratio. The SUWE seeks to provide wage employment opportunities to the urban poor through creation of socially and economically useful public assets in low income neighbourhoods within the local bodies. The schemes are applicable to all urban areas with population below one lakh. The Urban Basic Services (UBS) scheme was primarily aimed at women and child survival, immunization, nutrition, water supply, sanitation and developing community structures for articulating the felt needs of the urban poor.

THRIFT AND CREDIT SOCIETIES

As a part of the implementation of SJSRY, thrift and credit societies were formed in all the municipalities. Efforts were made to motivate and to encourage the poor women to form and to strengthen the thrift groups. Conscious efforts were made to constitute smaller groups to facilitate them to work more effectively through regular and frequent interaction in small groups.

Development of Women and Children in Urban areas (DWCUA)

DWCUA is an important urban self-employment programme under SJSRY. These groups should be constituted with 10 or more members and they should be facilitated to undertake micro-enterprise. They are provided with skill training as well as credit facilities. This involves considerable counseling to the members of the groups as most of them were habituated to work individually or run family enterprises rather than group enterprise involving members from other families. Some of these groups are still in initial stages of articulating the enterprise.

Urban Basic Services for Poor (UBSP)

This is an integrated approach to improvement of conditions in Slums. The components of the programme are health and nutrition, education for women and children, water supply and sanitation, training of community workers and development of community organizations in the slums. Under the water supply and sanitation component, hand pumps are installed and low cost pour-flush latrines are constructed. The latrines are constructed up to the plinth level only with the programme funds, while the superstructure is built by the user as per his/her affordability.

Objectives of the Study

1. To present the socio-economic profile of the study respondents.
2. To analyze the performance of the municipal authorities for development of the study respondents.
3. To examine the participation of the respondents in the welfare programmes.
4. To suggest suitable measure to improve the participation of the respondents in welfare programmes.

METHODOLOGY

Akuthota, a slum area in Nellore Municipal Corporation has been chosen for the present study. The study is based on the primary source of data collected through a well structured interview schedule. The interview schedule has been filled in with the help of the respondents through a face to face conversation by the researcher. The household data are collected on a random sampling basis. Thus, the total sample house hold comprises 25 per cent of the universe. Interview schedules have been tabulated into many tables for the purpose of analysis.

Major Finanding

- Our study reveals that 55 per cent of the respondents are illiterates. Only 2.5 per cent of the respondents are studied up to graduation. The respondents have studied up to the primary level, can read and write, and there are also respondents possessing the middle and high school education. The total figures stand at 22.50, 7.50 and 6.30 per cent respectively.

- Majority (88.00%) of the respondents depend on labour for their livelihood.
- About 40 per cent of the respondents had ketch houses and 26.30 per cent of the respondents had semi-pukka houses. The total figures stand at 17.50 and 3.80 per cent respectively.
- Majority (68.8%) of the respondents are not the members in any one organization, like Self-help Groups, Neighbourhood Committees, School committees etc.
- Sevently two per cent of the respondents expressed dissatisfaction about the environmental situation, like sanitation, drainage, roads etc.
- Majority (63.80%) of the respondents had debts. They are lending money from money lenders at a high rate of interest.
- Thirty two per cent of the respondents saved money in SHGs. They felt that SHGs are very useful for their economic needs.
- Majority (72.00%) of the respondents had the habit of taking alcohol, 80.00 per cent of the respondents had smoking habit and chewing tobacco.

SUGGESTIONS

In view of the shortcomings discussed, the following measures are suggested to strengthen the implementation of the programmes to improve the living conditions of the slum-dwellers.

- Identification of the specific needs of the slum people must be the first step in the formulation of the slum development plans. For this, a base-line survey is a pre-requisite and it is suggested that it should not be a one time affair. There should be a fresh survey at least once in two years so that changing needs or requirements of the slum people can be considered while formulating the plans. When the needs and aspirations of the target sections find expression in the actual implementation of the programmes, there will be no valid reason why these sections will not participate in the programme process. The surveys can serve two purposes: *firstly*, slum development plans can be formulated and implemented according to the felt needs of the poor and *secondly*, this can stimulate the interest of the targeted sections in the programme which will result in their asset-building, create proper sustenance.
- Since the peoples' participation, specifically, the women's participation is the corner stone of the programme, priority is to be given to cultivate in them the capacity to make decisions, to stand for benefit sharing and self-evaluatory and monitoring aspects which improves their common and individual good. The level of participation at present is not

satisfactory due to ignorance, therefore, there is an immediate need to bring about awareness and attitude changes in the slum-dwellers through traditional as well as modern means of communication. In this respect, the help of the slum elders, youth clubs and other voluntary associations can be sought. A better informed citizenry is an asset in the successful implementation of development programmes.

- The review meetings should take place regularly, so that on the basis of the feedback, necessary changes could be made in the implementation strategy.
- There is a mismatch between the need priorities of the poor and the policies and programmes as formulated by planners and decision-makers. This creates problems in optimizing the efficiency of programmes. The benefits of the housing and other programmes do not reach the poorest of the poor. Hence, the programme design requires effective participation by the poor in their formulation.
- Schemes for the provision of urban services should take into consideration affordability and the paying capacity of urban poor, which vary from person to person and from one urban situation to another depending upon the occupation, level of skills etc.
- The self-employment programmes for urban poor will undoubtedly provide financial assistance to the urban poor.
- It is not only necessary that development programme should generate employment at least at the minimum wage rate, but also these should help in the development of technical skills for their productivity and upward occupational mobility.
- Towards making the urban development programmes financially self-sustaining particularly those designed to benefit the poor, there has to be a proper employment and income-generation schemes and services.

CONCLUSION

Under the programme attempts were also made with a fair amount of success to empower the slum communities by creating community assets, by imparting skill training and by launching education and awareness campaigns. The aim was to encourage and promote self–reliant development process. A flexible, informal and user-friendly delivery system made it possible to overcome these problems. At the same time, participatory delivery system helped in minimizing the role of bureaucrats and bureaucratic processes in service administration.

REFERENCES

Government of India, (1995), *Annual Report, 1993-94*, New Delhi, Ministry of Urban Development.

Hanumantha Rao, C.H., (1998) "Agricultural Growth, Sustainability and Poverty Alleviation", *Economic and Political Weekly*, Vol. XXXIII No. 29 and 30.

Kapadia, Kundu and Kanitkar, (2002), "Primary Healthcare in Urban Slums", *Economic and Political Weekly*, December 21.

Kumar, Shikura and Harade (2003), "Living Environment and Health of Urban Poor, A Study in Mumbai", *Economic and Political Weekly*, August, 23.

Mahta P., and Pathak, (1996), "Country Report of India" Royston Brockman A.C. and Williams (eds) *Urban Infrastructure Finance, Manila*, Asian Development Bank.

Satterthwale and Tacoli, (2003), *The Urban pat of Rural Development, The Role of Small and Intermediate Urban Centers in Rural and Regional Development and Poverty Reduction*, IIEd.

Sundar and Sharma, (2002), Morbidity and Utilisation of Health Care Services: A Survey of Urban Poor in Delhi and Channai, *Economic and Political Weekly*, November, 23.

Urban Poverty

M.V. Chandini

INTRODUCTION

Population estimates indicate that at a certain point in 2007, the world's urban population will equal the world's rural population for the first time in history. The growth in the urban population will continue to rise, projected to reach almost five billion in 2030. Much of this urbanization is predicted to take place in the developing world, with Asia and Africa having the largest urban populations. The urban growth is attributed to both natural population growth, and rural to urban migration. Urbanization contributes to sustained economic growth which is critical to poverty reduction. The economies of scale and agglomeration in cities attract investors and entrepreneurs which is good for overall economic growth. Cities also provide opportunities for many, particularly the poor who are attracted by greater job prospects, the availability of services, and for some, and an escape from constraining social and cultural traditions in rural villages. Yet city life can also present conditions of overcrowded living, congestion, unemployment, lack of social and community networks, stark inequalities, and crippling social problems such as crime and violence. Many of those who migrate will benefit from the opportunities in urban areas, while others, often those with low skill levels, may be left behind and find themselves struggling with the day to day challenges of city life.

Many of the problems of urban poverty are rooted in a complexity of resource and capacity constraints, inadequate Government policies at both the central and local level, and a lack of planning for urban growth and management. Given the high growth projections for most cities in developing countries, the challenges of urban poverty and more broadly of city management will only worsen in many places if not addressed more aggressively.

Currently an estimated one-third of all urban residents are poor, which represents one quarter of the world's total poor. Many of these are in small cities and towns where the incidence of poverty tends to be higher than in big cities. While these proportions have not changed dramatically in the past ten years, with continued urbanization, the numbers of the urban poor are predicted to rise and poverty will Increasingly be an urban phenomenon. The general knowledge and understanding of poverty has increased enormously over the past decade through poverty assessments, city level studies, academic research and other analytical work. Many studies of poverty are carried out at the national level. The poverty assessments typically include a rich analysis of poverty at country level, but say little about the dynamics of urban poverty. In those where information has been disaggregated, typically the breakdown is for urban and rural or at the state level. This level of disaggregation, however, does not tell much about what is happening within cities or details on the issues for the urban poor which are necessary foundations for policy formulation. A small, but growing number of studies aimed at understanding the characteristics of urban poverty have been carried out at the regional level for Latin America and the Caribbean, Europe and Central Asia, and East Asia and the Pacific, as well as at the country or city level in Bangladesh, Brazil, Colombia, Ethiopia, Ghana, Nigeria, Yemen, and elsewhere, including a micro-level longitudinal study of slum-dwellers in Rio de Janeiro surveyed in 1969 and one Evidence from LAC: Small area estimation data are increasingly available for poverty mapping and disaggregated analysis, and has also contributed to strengthening our knowledge base on the characteristics and estimation of urban poverty.

Finally, at the global level there have been a number of recent reports addressing issues of urban poverty to coincide with the shift in demographic trends towards urban. All of these have contributed greatly to what we know about the characteristics and to a more limited extent, the dynamics of urban poverty, from which we can draw. There are still, however, major knowledge gaps on a number of key issues related to urban poverty, as well as on understanding the impacts of program and policy interventions on the urban poor. This paper attempts to provide an overview on what we have learned about urban poverty over the past decade based on an extensive literature search, with an aim to focus on what is new, and what the implications are for the World Bank. The paper also identifies some specific gaps in our knowledge base. Section II presents information on the scope of urban poverty, Section III on the key issues for the urban poor, Section IV on regional characteristics of urban poverty, Section V on what we have learned from programs and policies aimed at the urban poor, and finally, Section VI presents priorities for urban poverty reduction within the context of an overall urban strategy.

THE SCOPE OF URBAN POVERTY

Measuring urban poverty is not an easy task. There are numerous debates around the topic of poverty measurement related to the use of money metric approaches given the multidimensional nature of poverty, where to set poverty lines, and how to account for the higher cost of living in urban areas in national level poverty estimates. There are also debates on the definition of 'urban' which affects estimates of urban poverty. While addressing these debates is beyond the scope of this paper, recent analysis on poverty measures has gone well beyond any previous work and takes us much closer to a well-founded approximation of the nature and scope of urban poverty. Data for approximately 90 low-and middle-income countries, accounting for 95 per cent of the population in developing countries, with observations over time for about 80 per cent of them were analysed. This research applies country-specific adjusted poverty lines to account for cost of living differentials, providing new estimates that can more accurately estimate poverty for 4 approximate time periods (circa 1993, 1996, 1999 and 2002). On average the urban poverty lines are about 30 per cent higher than the rural lines relative to the total poor, as a result of the high urbanization rates in these regions. Overall, MENA has the lowest incidence and share of urban poverty.

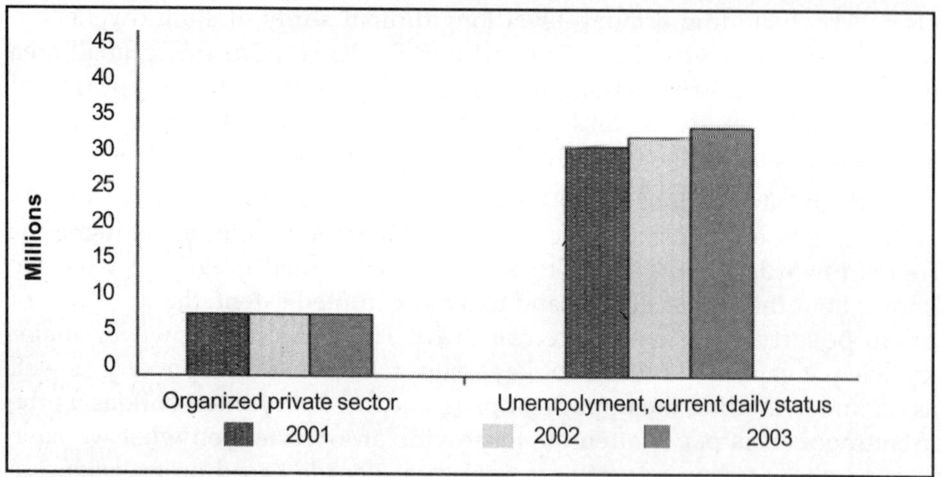

Trends Urban Poverty

During the period of 1993-2002, the incidence of urban poverty has not changed much globally using the $1/day line, and has shown a decline for the $2/day line following the trends of overall declines in poverty. Overall, the urbanization process has played an important role in poverty reduction by providing new opportunities for migrants and through the second-round impact on those who stay in rural areas. The pace in urban poverty reduction has been slower than the reductions in rural poverty reduction, reflecting an overall urbanization of poverty. Of the total decline in the poverty rate for the $2/day line (8.7%), 4.8 per cent is attributed to rural poverty reduction, 2.3 per cent to urban, and 1.6 per cent to the population shift effect (Ravallion, et.al., 2007).

KEY ISSUES FOR THE URBAN POOR

Though the urban poor are quite diverse across regions, countries and even within cities, they tend to face a number of common deprivations which affect their day to day life. The main issues raised in the literature include:

(i) Limited access to income and employment.

(ii) Inadequate and insecure living conditions.

(iii) Poor infrastructure and services.

(iv) Vulnerability to risks such as natural disasters, environmental hazards and health risks particularly associated with living in slums.

(v) Spatial issues which inhibit mobility and Urban Poverty; a Gobal View 5 transports.

(vi) Inequality closely linked to problems of exclusion.

These issues are described below.

Income and Employment

At the core of the poverty, both rural and urban, is limited access to income and employment opportunities. While the urban economy provides opportunities for many and is the basis for growth and job creation, not all those living in cities benefit from these opportunities. The urban poor face challenges of low skills, low wages, unemployment and under-employment, a lack of social insurance and unsatisfactory working conditions. In some countries, the spatial location of slums, inadequate infrastructure, and negative stigma are also constraints to employment. The heavy reliance on the cash economy means that the urban poor are particularly vulnerable to shocks. The majority of the urban poor work in the informal sector. Available estimates suggest that the size of informality ranges from 30 to 70 per cent of GDP in developing countries. While the informal sector provides employment for many that cannot enter the formal labour market and supplies goods and services typically not offered by the formal sector, it is also characterized by relatively poor working conditions, lack of social insurance, operating outside the legal system, and is more vulnerable to economic fluctuations, which particularly affects the poor who have relatively little savings. Unemployment is typically higher for the urban poor, as is underemployment. For example in Dhaka, Bangladesh unemployment rates for the poorest male workers are about 10 per cent, twice that of the wealthiest (5%). For women, about 25 per cent of the poor are unemployed compared to 12 per cent of the non-poor. Youth unemployment is a major problem in many cities, and increasingly linked to growing social problems and can create urban unrest. Average youth unemployment rates were highest in.

Living Conditions and Security of Tenure

The living conditions of the urban poor can be dismal. Poor urban residents face many of the same challenges in daily life as the rural poor, with the added burden of over crowded and often unsanitary living conditions. They tend to spend a higher proportion of total consumption on housing than the rural poor, a result of the higher land values in cites. Many, though not all of the urban poor, live in slums. The estimates are at around one third of the urban population in developing countries—nearly one billion people living in slums. In Africa, the proportion of urban residents living in slums is Urban Poverty; A Global View 6 astounding at 72 per cent. The slum estimates are calculated based on the definition agreed upon at the Expert Group Meeting which is a group of individuals living under the same roof in an urban area with at least one of the following four basic shelter deprivations: lack of access to improved water supply; lack of access to improved sanitation; overcrowding (three or more persons per room); and dwellings made of nondurable material. If a home has one or all four of these conditions, they would be classified as a slum household. Access to secure tenure is seen to be a fifth indicator, but this type of data is difficult to obtain and is thus not included. While there are some major deficiencies with this approach to measuring slums such as the lack of a spatial dimension, and inability to capture improvements of individual deficiencies over time, these estimates provide a basis for understanding the scope of shelter deprivation in urban areas globally. Beyond the debate on the measurement of slums, a general characterization of slums can be described as informal settlements with poor quality housing, limited access to services, and often on insecure land. Yet there are substantial differences mainly around the size of slum, location, and age. The location of slums is either in the center of a city near to employment opportunities, or in the peri-urban area where residents are more isolated. Older settlements tend to have more services and better quality housing as the population becomes better off. The poor often end up on insecure public or private land as it is their only option. This is a result of poorly functioning land and housing markets, and the lack of planning for urban development and growth. Insecurity of tenure puts the urban poor at constant risk of eviction, hampers them from building up assets and accessing credit, inhibits using one's home for income-generating activities and does not allow for investments in service.

Infrastructure and Services

The infrastructure needs that go along with urbanization can be enormous in terms of investments in housing, water and sanitation, transportation, power, and telecommunications. Many cities have not been able to keep up, and face daunting challenges for the future projected increases in urbanization. Providing universal coverage for water and sanitation services alone in the cities of developing countries is estimated to cost nearly five per cent of those countries' GDP . The problems of accessing infrastructure and services are particularly acute for the urban poor. While access is typically higher in urban areas than rural, it can still be extremely low for the urban poor, of inadequate quality, and unaffordable. Access rates within slums in many cases are comparable or lower to access in rural areas. Quality is a major issue, but more difficult to measure. Services may be available only for a few hours a day. The poor often rely on alternative sources of supply that may be of lower quality and are offered through self-provision or informal service providers the non-poor as they have to rely on expensive delivery given the high rates that the urban poor pay for services, it is not surprising that there is considerable evidence demonstrating that the poor are willing to pay substantial amounts for services. For example, in Panama, a willingness to pay study shows that the poor are willing to pay $0.46 per cubic metre of water, more than double the tariff of $0.21 per cubic metre.

Risks

Living in cities, particularly in high density slum settlements, can also mean exposure to a number of disaster, health, and environmental risks which particularly affect the poor. The urban poor are typically at the highest risk in the event of natural disasters due to the location of low income settlements. These settlements are often in sites vulnerable to floods and landslides, infrastructure is weak or lacking, and housing is substandard and prone to fire damage or collapse. There are numerous examples of earthquakes, landslides, and floods that have caused major destruction to the urban poor. Recovering from disasters is also particularly difficult for the poor as they do not have resources or adequate safety nets, and public policies often prioritize rebuilding in other parts of the city There are several factors related to urban living, particularly in slums, that can result in negative health outcomes. The high concentration of slum populations, inadequate water and sanitation facilities, poor drainage and solid waste management, and indoor pollution contribute to acute respiratory diseases, diarrheal disease and a wide array of other infectious diseases (e.g., tuberculosis, hepatitis, dengue fever, pneumonia, cholera and malaria) (Montgomery and Hewett, 2004). Poor quality housing conditions also contribute to poor health outcomes and increase vulnerability. HIV/AIDS prevalence rates are very high in urban areas exceeding 50 per cent in some African cities. In those cities where incidence data on morbidity and mortality for these diseases is disaggregated for slum populations, it is often higher for those living in slums than that of rural dwellers despite the better access to health care in.

Location, Mobility and Transports

The spatial location pattern of low income settlements varies considerably from city to city, though a general trend is clear—a majority of the urban poor live on lands that are undesirable to others. This is a result of urban sprawl, land and housing constraints, inefficient land markets, and poor public transport systems. While some live in poorer quality low income settlements within the city to be located near to job opportunities and markets, many others choose to live in peri-urban areas on affordable sites, where access to labour markets is much more difficult. The location and transport patterns of the urban poor illustrate a complex trade off among residential location, travel distance and travel mode. In cities where the poor live remotely in order to inhabit affordable space, they incur high travel costs and long travel times. For some in Latin American cities such as Lima, and Rio de Janeiro, the poor live some 30 or 40 kilometres out of the employment centers resulting in an average commuting time of 3 hours per day for the poorest group in Rio. In Montevideo, residents living in slums outside the city cite the lack of access to public transport as a major constraint to accessing jobs. Living in a peripheral urban location, particularly without adequate access to transport services, can mean exclusion from a range of urban facilities, services, and jobs, exacerbating problems of social exclusion which are discussed further below. There are also 'neighborhood effects' based on social composition which can affect individual behavior and peer group effects (where individual behaviors and opportunities can be influenced by others). In many areas, the issue of neighborhood stigma, which can negatively affect peoples' access to jobs and increases other types of discrimination, is also a major constraint for the poor. The stigma of living in a favela was attributed to unemployment and inequality by slum-dwellers in a study of Rio de Janeiro.

In other cities, particularly Asia and Sub-Saharan Africa, the settlement patterns are more heterogeneous with the poor and non-poor living within a short proximity. In such cases, the poor tend to have shorter commutes and often rely on walking as a main source of transport. In Mumbai close to two-thirds of the poor walk to work. A substantial number also rely on public transport, though fares can be very high. Poor households in which the main earner commutes by bus spend 19 per cent of their income on transport.

Inequality

Inequality in access to services, housing, land, education, health care, and employment opportunities can have socio-economic, environmental and political repercussions. In cities, income inequality is particularly stark where

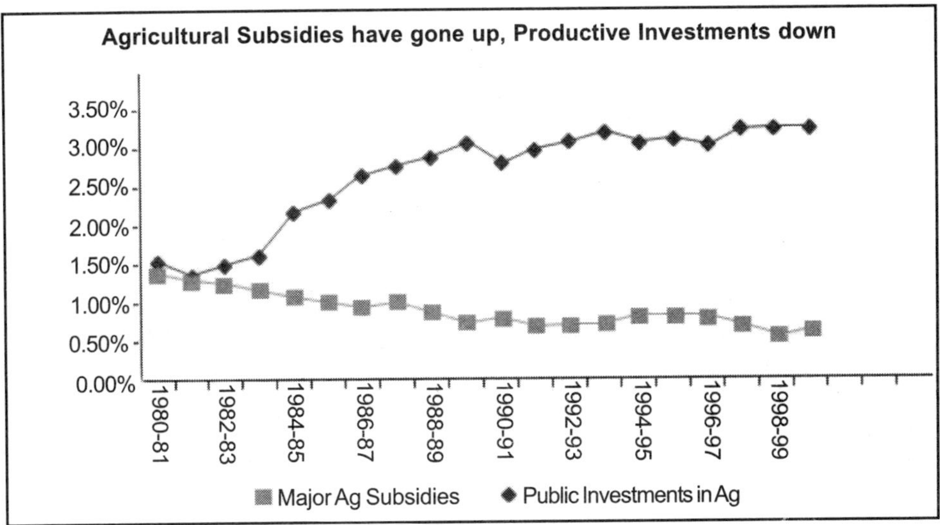

modern cosmopolitan zones can be found within a short distance from slums. In many countries, the gini coefficient within urban areas is substantially higher than in rural areas where standards of living are more homogeneous. Inequality also appears to increase with city size, though this has not been tested widely. The highly visible disparities in wealth, services and opportunities, can create frustration, tension and a sense of exclusion for the poor. The dimensions of exclusion as defined in the literature are grouped into three categories:

(i) Economic exclusion to equitable access in economic/financial, social, human and natural resource assets.

(ii) Exclusion from access to basic services.

(iii) Social exclusion restricting people from participating on fair terms in local and national social life.

For the urban poor, exclusion is extremely evident in day to day life ranging from educational inequality across schools to spatial barriers in access to jobs. While there is no direct causal relationship between inequality, exclusion, and crime and violence, there appears to be a link. Crime and violence are cited to occur more frequently in settings where there is an unequal distribution of scare resources or power coupled with weak institutional controls–highly characteristic of cities. There is evidence that crime and violence do tend to be higher in cities. Within cities in Latin America and the caribbean, disparities in violence levels are based on neighborhood income levels, with the higher income areas suffering from property-related violent crime, while severe violence is concentrated in the lower income areas, particularly in poor neighborhoods on the periphery of cities. Cities where inequalities and exclusion are strongly evident also appear to be vulnerable to insecurity. Such examples include protests in slums in South Africa, and gang warfare in Los Angeles, Nairobi, and Rio de Janeiro. Recent approaches aimed at the prevention of crime and violence have focused on improvements in the physical environment and has been applied in city planning, public transport systems, parks and recreational spaces, low-income housing, and downtown areas where people feel most vulnerable to violence and crime (Mtani, 2002).

REGIONAL CHARACTERISTICS OF URBAN POVERTY

Beyond the general characteristics facing the urban poor globally, several regional characteristics stand out. The coverage across regions is not consistent as urban poverty has been relatively well studied in Latin America, but to a lesser extent in the other regions. For example in Africa and South Asia, very few studies of the urban poor are available.

South Asia

While the proportion of the urban population (28%) and of the total poor (25%) has remained relatively stable in South Asia as a whole, the region still has the highest number of urban poor in the world (135 million $1/day and 296 million $2/day, 2002). Five of the world's mega cities are located in South Asia and are home to large concentrations of urban poor. The cities of Mumbai (18.8 million), Delhi (16 million), Calcutta (14.5 million), Dhaka (13 million), and Karachi (12.2 million) have sprawling slums and major challenges of city management which make addressing urban poverty one of many difficult challenges. 11 India alone accounts for 17 per cent of the world's slum-dwellers. Some of these cities continue to grow at a rapid pace. Dhaka is expected to reach 20 million in 2020 making it the world's third largest city. While urbanization has generated much economic growth and opportunity for many, there are however, concerns that this growth has not generated much demand for unskilled labour, particularly affecting the poor some of whom are new rural to urban migrants. In India, an estimated one million workers move out of agriculture every year, yet the organized service sector generated only 76,000 new jobs annually over the past decade. Child labor is also of concern, "children, mainly girls, are trafficked for commercial sexual exploitation in urban centers such as Mumbai, Calcutta and New Delhi".

POLICIES AND PROGRAMS FOR URBAN POVERTY REDUCTION IS TO BE TAKEN

There has been a shift in poverty reduction approaches since 2000 towards a focus on achieving the Millennium Development Goals set for 2020 led by a country driven approach. More than 50 low-income countries have prepared Poverty Reduction Strategies. The World Bank and other development agencies have aligned their activities to these national plans. Within this agenda, shared growth is widely recognized as the main driver of poverty reduction through policies that promote higher growth and an equitable distribution of its benefits across the population and specifically for the poor. This is entirely conducive to urban poverty reduction. Furthermore, much of this growth is sustained by urbanization.

Economic Growth

Economic activity in urban areas, typically industrial and commercial, accounts for one half to four fifths of GDP in most countries. A study of 14 countries globally shows that those which did well in reducing poverty during the 1990s had sustained and rapid economic growth through policies promoting macro-economic stability, defined property rights, a good investment climate, an attractive incentive framework, well functioning factor markets, and broad access to infrastructure and education. Another study from Eastern Europe and the Former Soviet Union finds that during the 1998-2003 period countries that experienced sustained growth also experienced substantial declines in poverty, with urban poverty responding more strongly than rural poverty. The reductions in poverty were to differing degrees in different countries related to the differences in growth rates, as well as differences in initial conditions, and to changes in the distribution of income during the period. In countries where there were shifts in the distribution of income towards the poor (e.g., CIS), poverty declined more rapidly than might have been expected. Vietnam is an example that stands out for its success in growth and poverty reduction, in both urban and rural areas. This is attributed to trade liberalization, export promotion in labour-intensive manufacturing, and substantial investments in infrastructure and education. Between 1992 and 2003, urban poverty in Vietnam was lowered by an impressive 11 per cent per year (not with standing the reductions in rural poverty of 4.2% per year). The strong growth of the 1990s was accompanied by greater domestic demand for labour intensive goods, and a rise in informality in the labor market with a many moving into informal industry and services to meet the demand for non-agricultural goods and services. The country invested heavily in infrastructure, prioritizing large infrastructure investments over rural infrastructure, targeted to regions with high numbers of poor people and high growth potential. The idea was to promote urban centers where capital and skills were more plentiful and to redistribute returns through public transfers to rural areas. The growth and poverty impact of this strategy has proven to be very successful. Beyond promoting policies to foster economic growth, countries have approached the challenges of urban poverty in different ways. Typically, programs and policies are part of broader national poverty reductions strategies. A review of urban issues in poverty.

Public Programmes for Urban Poverty Alleviation in India

Dr. K. Rajasekhar

INTRODUCTION

The cities in India are projecting immense development with sky scrapers, fancy flyovers, massive shopping malls and multiplexes. But what are co-existing are urban poverty, poverty of employment, poverty of shelter, poverty of basic necessities and poverty of access to basic infrastructure like electricity, water, drainage and sanitation. Housing for the poor is so scarce and consequently slums are mushrooming everywhere, with little action on the part of the authorities to ensure cheap housing for the poor. According to the 2001 Census approximately 28 per cent of the total population in India lives in urban areas. As per the future population projection that the urban population in the country which is 28 per cent in 2001 is expected to increase to 38 per cent by 2026. The urban growth would account for over two-thirds (67%) of total population increase by 2026. In absolute terms, out of the total Population increase of 371 million during 2001-2026 in the country, the share of increase in urban population is expected to be 249 million. A significant proportion of the urban population, which is poor, (around 24%) of the urban population lives below the poverty line), is economically active, working in the informal sector like vending, home based economic activities or manual labour services. Since most of the cities are unable to meet the growing needs for basic facilities such as clean drinking water, sanitation facilities, garbage disposal, electricity and transportation facilities, these poor end up living in slums where their living and working conditions lack basic infrastructure facilities making their life vulnerable.

With the increase in the urbanization, the rural population comes to the city and occupies the urban space and strains the limited resources available here. The resources, opportunities and facilities meant for the city dwellers are taken over by someone else which, then gives rise to the urban poverty. There is ample place in the city, particularly the downtown areas, where every next house suffers due to unemployment, underemployment and lack of resources. Most of these families live jointly to share their income which on an average would not be over two USD per day and on this meager income are over four to five dependants in a family. The need of the hour is not only to create opportunities for the city dwellers but also to augment their income; financial assistance through soft and hassle free loans need to be provided to them. In urban areas, several programmes have been launched to address urban poverty, which includes the Scheme of Urban Micro-Enterprises, Nehru Rozgar Yojana and Prime Minister's Integrated Urban Poverty Alleviation Programme and Urban Basic Services for the Poor [UBSP], etc. But most of them have failed, due to three important reasons.

(i) Leakages at various stages.

(ii) Lack of commitment on the part of the implementing agencies financial agencies.

(iii) Lack of follow-up by the promotional and financial agencies.

With the view to rectifying the loopholes in the earlier urban programmes mentioned above, Government of India recently in 1999 combined all the programmes under a single head called Swarna Jayanthi Shahari Rozgar Yojana [SYSY] in urban areas. The present paper aims to study the urban poverty and public policies for urban poverty alleviation in India based on secondary sources (data).

Definition of Poverty

In general, poverty can be defined as a situation when people are unable to satisfy the basic needs of life. The definition and methods of measuring poverty differs from country to country. According to the definition by Planning Commission of India, poverty line is drawn with an intake of 2400 calories in rural areas and 2100 calories in urban areas. If a person is unable to get that much minimum level of calories, then he/she is considered as being below poverty line.

In Indian context, poverty can be defined as "a situation where a person/family are living below the minimum acceptable standard of life". Thus, the definition of poverty is related to food, clothes, shelter, health, education and other basic needs which are essential for a quality of life.

Eestimation of Urban Poverty

The Planning Commission has been estimating the incidence of poverty at national and state level using the methodology contained in the report of the Expert Group on Estimation of Proportion and Number of Poor

(Lakdawala Committee) and applying it to consumption expenditure data from the large sample surveys on consumer expenditure, conducted periodically by the National Sample Survey Organization (NSSO). The latest available data is from the 55th Round of NSSO survey (1999-2000) covering the period July 1999 to June 2000. In the earlier large scale surveys, the NSSO estimated monthly per capita consumption expenditure on the basis of responses using a 30-day recall period though data were collected for some of the non-food items using reference periods of both 30 days and 365 days from the same household. In the 55th round, consumption expenditure on clothing, footwear, medical (institutional) and durable goods were collected by using a 365-day recall period. In the case of all other non-food items, the 30-days recall period was used as earlier. The data regarding consumption of food items were collected by using two different reference periods of last 30 days and last 7 days from the same household in that order. Thus, the Planning Commission has estimated poverty from both distributions reported by the NSSO, using the accepted methodology. State specific poverty lines have Lakdawala Committee and updating them to 1999-2000 prices using the Consumer Price Index for Agricultural Labourers (CPIAL) for rural households and the Consumer Price Index of Industrial Workers (CPIIW) for urban households.

Problems of Urban Poverty

- Restricted access to employment opportunities and income.
- Lack of proper housing facilities.
- Unhygienic environments.
- No social security schemes.
- Lack of opportunity to quality health and educational services.
- Proliferation of slums and bustees.
- Fast growth of the informal sector.
- Increasing casualisation of labour.
- Increasing pressure on civic services.
- Increasing educational deprivation and health contingencies.

Urban Poverty

The main causes of urban poverty are predominantly due to impoverishment of rural peasantry that forces them to move out of villages to seek some subsistence living in the towns and cities. In this process, they even lose the open space or habitat they had in villages albeit without food and other basic amenities. When they come to the cities, they get access to some food though other sanitary facilities including clean water supply still elude them. And they have to stay in the habitats that place them under sub-human conditions. While a select few have standards of fails to get two meals a day. India has shared the growth pattern and rapid urbanization with some of the fastest growing Regions in Asia. India will have 41 per cent of its population living in cities and towns by AD 2030 from the present level of 286 million and 28 per cent. With India becoming increasingly globalized and urban, there is also an increase in the number of poor people living here. Economic development and urbanization are closely linked. In India, cities contribute over 55 per cent to country's GDP and urbanization has been recognized as an important component of economic growth. As per the latest NSSO survey reports there are over 80 million poor people living in the cities and towns of India. The Slum population is also increasing and as per TCPO estimates 2001; over 61.80 million people were living in slums. With the increase in urban population, there has been phenomenon growth in slum areas and slum population. During 2001, about one-fourth (1/4th) urban population was reported to be living in slums. There are certain states where the slum population has been reported to be significantly higher than the national average. The slum population is found to be more concentrated in the metropolitan cities and particularly in those areas where there is high Concentration of economic growth, for e.g. 11.2 million of the total slum population of the country is in Maharashtra followed by Andhra Pradesh (5.2 million), and Uttar Pradesh (4.4 million). Although the slum population has increased, the number of slums is lower (National Sample Survey Organization's 58th Round), which makes them more dense. There is higher concentration of slum population in the large urban centres (Census, 2001). As per 2001 census report the slum population of India in cities and towns with a population of 50,000 and above was 42.6 million, which is 22.6 per cent of the urban population of the states/Union Territories reporting slums. This could also roughly be the size of Spain or Columbia. India has shared the growth pattern with some of the fastest growing regions in Asia. The country has witnessed around 8 per cent growth in GDP in the last couple of years. India's urban population is increasing at a faster rate than its total population. A large number of states report poverty figures in urban areas much above that in rural areas. Poor people live in slums which are over crowded, often polluted and lack basic civic amenities like clean drinking water, sanitation and health facilities. Most of them are involved in informal sector activities where there is constant threat of eviction, removal, confiscation of goods and almost non-existent social security cover. A substantial portion of the benefits provided by public agencies are cornered by middle and upper income households. 54.71 per cent of urban slums have no toilet facility. Most free community toilets built by state government or local bodies are rendered unusable because of the lack of maintenance. As per the 2001 census, the total urban homeless population is about eight lakhs (778599 people). Urban poverty in India remains high, at over 25 per cent, rural poverty is higher than poverty in urban areas but the gap between the two has decreased over the past couple of decades. The incidence of decline of urban poverty has not accelerated with GDP growth. The poverty in cities is not an overflow of the poverty in villages but has happened because of the faulty nature of urbanization in India, and that urban workers were being increasingly pushed into informal sector, even as the space for informal economic activities was gradually shrinking. And within the informal sector, the profile of the work in urban areas has moved from casual employment (which is paid on regular basis) to self-employment, which carries its own uncertainties. So the urban poor were increasingly a street vendor, a rickshaw puller, a rag picker, a cleaner, a washer man, a load carrier or a domestic servant. While these workers contributed to the growth of cities, there was growing trend to push the poor to the urban periphery, as they were increasingly seen as threat to civic existence. Further the absence of rights to land and livelihood, and the higher cost that the poor have to incur on transportation and travel to workplace. As many 81 million or 25.7 per cent people (2004-05) subsist in urban areas on incomes that are below the poverty line. Eighty per cent of their meager income goes towards paying for food and energy, leaving very little for meeting the cost of living in an increasingly monetized society.

It is interesting to note that the ratio of urban poverty in some of the larger states is higher than that of rural poverty leading to the phenomenon of 'Urbanization of Poverty'. Urban poverty poses the problems of housing and shelter, water, sanitation, health, education, social security and livelihoods along with special needs of vulnerable groups like women, children and aged people. Poor people live in slums which are over crowded, often polluted and lack basic civic amenities like clean drinking water, sanitation and health facilities. Most of them are involved in informal sector activities where there is constant threat of eviction, removal, confiscation of goods and almost non-existent social security cover. With growing poverty and slums, Indian cities have been grappling with the challenges of making the cities sustainable i.e. inclusive, productive, efficient and manageable. The sustainability of urban development in India is seen in the context of shelter an India has entered the Eleventh Plan period with an impressive record of economic growth. However, the incidence of decline of urban poverty has not accelerated with GDP growth. In fact, urban poverty will become a major challenge for policy-makers in our country as the urban population in the country is growing, so is urban poverty. Therefore, a need has arisen to develop new poverty reduction tools and approaches to attack the multi-dimensional issues of urban poverty. For this, policy-makers at the national and local levels should have a good understanding of the nature of urban poverty as well as accurate data on various issues relating to it, in order to develop programme/policies to manage urban poverty in a systematic manner. India Urban Poverty Report using human development framework provides a good insight on various issues of urban poverty such as basic services to urban poor, migration, urban economy and livelihoods, micro finance for urban poor, education and health, unorganized sector and livelihoods.

Poverty in India (1973-2005)

Year	Urban Poverty (%)	Rural Poverty (%)	All India level (%)
1973	49.0	56.4	54.9
1978	45.2	53.1	51.3
1983	40.8	45.7	44.5
1988	38.2	39.1	38.9
1994	32.4	37.3	36.0
1999	23.6	27.1	26.1
2005	23.3	28.1	31.4

PUBLIC PROGRAMMES FOR URBAN POVERTY ALLEVIATION (UPAPs)

The issues of poverty reduction have dominated the course of economic planning in India since inception. From an historical perspective, government policies and programmes addressing urban poverty have moved from an emphasis on mechanisms to address social and economic inequities in the First Plan and distortions in income distribution in the Fourth plan, to a focus on access to productive employment, shelter and services in the Eighth and Ninth Plans. The programmes related to poverty reduction have remained an important goal of urban policy in India. Urban poverty initiatives really began in the 1950s with community development programmes. The first formal attempt to experiment with community development approach in cities was the Urban Community Development (UCD) pilot project which was started in 1958 and followed by a series of UCD pilot projects based on an area-oriented approach. Subsequently, Environmental Improvement of Urban Slums (EIUS) was identified as a basic need of slum population in the Fifth Five Year Plan and consequently, the Scheme of EIUS was started in 1972 at the Central level to provide basic physical facilities to urban poor like safe drinking water, sewerage, storm water drains, community baths and latrines, street lighting, etc. This Scheme was later on transferred to State Governments for onward implementation in 1974.

Urban poverty alleviation is the major thrust of development planning in India. However, poverty eradication is a daunting task as the problem is gradually increasing due to migration of rural poor people in urban centres. There has been paradigm shift in urban governance in India. Subsequently, in the Seventh Five year Plan (1985-90) first conscious attempt was made to directly address urban poverty issues. Thus, in the very beginning of the Seventh Plan, Government of India had decided to expand the programme of Urban Basic Services (UBS) implemented during 1981-84 with collaboration of the UNICEF in 42 towns, to 168 towns. The UBS aimed at catering to the basic physical and social needs of the Urban Poor with a view to improving their living conditions. Consequently, as a follow up of the recommendations made by the National Commission on Urbanization (NCU), the first major comprehensive intervention at addressing the issues of growing incidence of poverty in urban areas, was started in 1989, when the Government of India adopted a four pronged strategy comprising:

(i) Employment creation for low income communities through promotion of micro-enterprises and public works:.

(ii) Housing and shelter up-gradation.

(iii) social development planning with special focus on development of children and women.

(iv) Environmental up gradation of slums.

Based on the above mentioned strategy, the Government launched two schemes for the betterment of urban poor, namely:

- The Nehru Rozgar Yojana (NRY) launched in 1989; to cater to the economic needs of the urban poor by providing them employment opportunities through skill up gradation and assistance by setting up their own micro-enterprises.
- The Urban Basic Services for the Poor (UBSP) which was a modified UBS Programme, started in 1990. The UBSP programme envisaged fostering community structures comprising urban poor for ensuring their effective participation in their developmental activities.

Decentralization as envisaged by 74th Constitutional Amendment Act., 1994 has led the process of municipal reforms and ensuring urban governance, however, the task of devolution of powers, functions, and finances to local bodies is still showing unfinished agenda. The escalating demand for urban infrastructure and services has called for mobilization of resources through public private partnership initiatives and introducing municipal reforms in urban local governments. The urban infrastructure development schemes—JNNURM, UIDSSMT and IHSDP have shown the new path of infrastructure development and its maintenance since the schemes are reforms oriented and seek public private partnership, community participation, resources mobilization and focus on augmenting efficiency of urban local governments. The urban governance is also experiencing a paradigm shift. The policy on urban housing and habitat intends to promote sustainable development of human settlements with a view to ensuring equitable supply of land, shelter, and services at affordable prices to all section of society. The strategies for empowering urban poor are also changing. Present report purports to examine the status of urban poverty in India and review the poverty alleviation strategies in different states. It also aims at suggesting measures for poverty reduction through effective implementation of urban poverty alleviation programmes and schemes. Poverty reduction is an important goal of the urban policy. Therefore, it is necessary to view urban poverty as distinct from rural poverty and not as mere transfer of rural poverty into urban areas.

The Urban Poverty Alleviation Programmes (UPAPs) have three themes:

(i) Those that seek to enhance productive employment and income for the poor.

(ii) Those that are directed towards improving general health and welfare services.

(iii) Those that focus on infrastructure and the built environment of poor neighbourhoods.

Nehru Rozgar Yojana (NRY)

Nehru Rozgar Yojana was launched at the year 1989 with the objective of providing of employment to the urban unemployed and underemployed poor. The Central Government indicated its overall contribution while the essential task of identifying, earmarking and coordinating the relevant sectoral inputs was undertaken by the State Governments. The NRY consisted of three schemes namely;

- The Scheme of Urban Micro-Enterprises (SUME).
- The Scheme of Urban Wage Employment (SUWE).
- The Scheme of Housing and Shelter Up-gradation (SHASU).

Urban Basic Services for the Poor (UBSP)

The UBSP Programme was implemented as a Centrally Sponsored Scheme during the Eighth Five Year Plan with the specific objectives of effective achievement of the social sector goals; community organization, mobilization and empowerment; and convergence through sustainable support system. The expenditure on the Programme was being shared on a 60:40 basis between the Central and the State Governments and UTs (with legislatures). Further, the per capita expenditure on any slum pocket is Rs. 75 in the first year and Rs. 50 from the second year onwards after the basic infrastructure is developed.

Prime Minister's Integrated Urban Poverty Eradication Programmes (PM IUPEP)

The Prime Minister's Integrated Urban Poverty Eradication Programme (PMIUPEP) for improving the quality of life of urban poor by creating a facilitating environment for them through community based planning and implementation was launched in 1995. The objective of the scheme was effective achievement of social sector goals, community empowerment, employment generation and environmental improvement. The PMIUPEP was an Rs.800 crore schemes approved for the period up to the year 2000.The programme was applicable to 345 Class II towns' urban agglomerations with a population ranging between 50,000 and one lakh subject to the condition that elections to local bodies have been held, and 79 specifically identified district headquarters and hill areas. The programme was being implemented on a whole town/project basis extending the coverage to all the targeted groups for recurring a visible impact. It may be observed that the NRY, UBSP and the PMIUPEP were launched at different times having overlapping features. The PMIUPEP incorporated within itself, all the Components of UBSP as also the self-employment, physical infrastructure creation component and the shelter up gradation components of NRY. However, the PMIUPEP applied only to Class II urban agglomerations whereas NRY applied to all other towns and the UBSP applied to selected towns only. There was some dissimilarity between these Programmes as well. The NRY and PMIUPEP, because the latter was launched six years after the former, differed widely on vital ingredients such as, definition of "family", amount of available subsidies, amount of loan both for self-employment as well as for the Shelter up-gradation components. The abysmally low allocations for these programmes to States and Urban Local Bodies ensured that these programmes got the minimum priority both in the State Governments as well as with the Urban Local Bodies.

A high level Committee was set up in February 1997, under the chairmanship of Prof. S. R. Hashim, then Member, Planning Commission to "Review and Rationalize Programme of Poverty Alleviation and Employment Generation". Members of the Committee were Secretary to Prime Minister, Secretary (Expenditure), Secretary (SSI), Secretary (REPA) and Advisor (RD), Planning Commission. The Committee examined in detail various poverty alleviation schemes (both urban and rural) of Government of India and submitted its report to PMO in April 1997. The main recommendation of the Prof. Hashim Committee regarding these Programmes was as follows:

(i) The Self-Employment Component of NRY and PMIUPEP be combined or merged together so as to have single self-employment programme applicable to all urban areas in the country.

(ii) A separate wage employment programme to be introduced which would apply to all urban centres with a population up to five lakhs.

(iii) As regards, the shelter and housing up-gradation component, it was recommended that either a separate scheme be drafted for this purpose or this component be merged with the National Slum Development Programme (NSDP)/Basic Services Programme.

The Swarna Jayanti Shahari Rozgar Yojana (SJSRY)

As per the recommendations of the Hashim Committee Report, all the three Urban Poverty Alleviation Schemes, namely Nehru Rozgar Yojana (NRY), Urban Basic Services for the Poor (UBSP) and Prime Minister's Integrated Urban Poverty Eradication Programme (PMIUPEP) were subsumed in a new scheme namely Swarna Jayanti Shahari Rozgar Yojana (SJSRY), which was launched with effect from 1-12-1997. The programme SJSRY is primarily an employment generation programme for the urban poor and the salient features of this programme are as under:

(i) It seeks to provide gainful employment to the urban unemployed or underemployed through encouraging the setting up of self-employment ventures through the Urban Self-Employment Programme (USEP) and has a provision of wage employment through the Urban Wage Employment Programme (UWEP).

(ii) It also relies on creation of suitable community structures and delivery of inputs through the medium of urban local bodies and such community structures.

(iii) The SJSRY is funded on a 75 : 25 basis between Centre and the States.

(iv) The Programme targets urban poor, being as those living below the urban poverty line, as defined from time to time.

(v) The Programme is applicable to all urban towns in India.

(vi) The shelter up-gradation components of both NRY and PMIUPEP will be merged with the National Slum Development Programme.

(vii) The Swarna Jayanti Shahari Rozgar Yojana rests on the foundation of community empowerment.

(viii) Community organizations like Neighbourhood Groups (NHGs), Neighbourhood Committees (NHCs) and Community Development Societies (CDSs) will be set up in the target areas based on the UBSP pattern.

The CDSs will be the focal point for purposes of identification of beneficiaries, preparation of applications, monitoring of recovery and generally providing whatever other support is necessary to the programme. The CDSs will also identify viable projects suitable for that particular area. These CDSs may also set themselves up as Thrift and Credit Societies to encourage community savings, as also other group activities. A maximum expenditure at the rate of Rs.100 per member for the first year and Rs. 75 per member for each subsequent year will be allowed for activities connected with the CDSs.

SJSRY has two sub-schemes namely:

(i) Urban Self–Employment Programme.

(ii) Urban Wage-Employment Programme.

The Urban Self Employment Programme (USEP)

This programme will have three distinct components, they are;

(i) Assistance to individual urban poor beneficiaries for setting up gainful self-employment ventures.

(ii) Assistance to groups of urban poor women for setting up gainful self-employment ventures. This sub-scheme may be called "The Scheme for Development of Women and Children in the Urban Areas (DWCUA)".

(iii) Training of beneficiaries, potential beneficiaries and other persons associated with the urban employment programme for upgradation and acquisition of vocational and entrepreneurial skills.

Coverage

(i) The programme will be applicable to all urban towns in India.

(ii) The programme will be implemented on a whole town basis with special emphasis on urban poor clusters.

Target Groups

(i) The programme will target the urban poor, i.e those living below the urban poverty line, as defined from time to time.

(ii) Special attention will be given to women; persons belonging to Scheduled Castes/Tribes, disabled persons and other such categories as may be indicated by the Government from time to time. The percentage of women beneficiaries under this programme will not be less than 30 per cent. The SCs and STs must be benefited at least to the extent of their proportion in the local population. A special provision of 3 per cent will be reserved for the disabled under this programme.

(iii) There will not be any minimum educational qualification set for beneficiaries under this programme. However, to avoid an overlap with the PMRY scheme, for self-employment component, this scheme will not apply to beneficiaries educated beyond the IX standard. As regards the wage employment component, there will be no restrictions of educational qualifications what so ever.

(iv) A house-to-house survey for identification of genuine beneficiaries will be undertaken. Non-economic parameters will also be applied to identify the urban poor in addition to the economic criteria of the urban poverty line.

Components

Self-Employment through setting up Micro-Enterprises and Skill Development

To avoid duplication with the ongoing Prime Minister's Rozgar Yojana (PMRY), this component of SJSRY is confined to the below poverty line beneficiaries who have no education up to ninth standard, with emphasis on those accorded a higher priority on the basis of the non-economic criteria. The maximum unit cost will be Rs. 50,000 and the maximum allowable subsidy will be 15 per cent of the project cost, subject to a limit of Rs. 7,500. The beneficiary is required to contribute 5 per cent of the project cost as margin money. In case a number of beneficiaries decide to jointly set up a project, such project will be eligible for a subsidy which will be equal to the total of the permitted subsidy per person as per the above criteria. In this case to the provision relating to 5 per cent margin money per beneficiary will apply. The over all project cost, which can be permitted, will be the total of the individual project cost allowable per beneficiary.

Skill development through appropriate training is another element of this programme. The unit cost allowed for training will be Rs. 2000 per trainee, including material cost, trainers' fees, other miscellaneous expenses to be incurred by the training institution and the monthly stipend to be paid to the trainee. The total training period for skill upgradation may vary from two to six months, subject to a minimum of 300 hours. Infrastructural support may also be provided to the beneficiaries setting up micro-enterprises in relation to marketing of their products etc.

Development of Women and Children in Urban Areas (DWCUA)

This scheme is distinguished by the special incentive extended to urban poor women who decide to set up self-employment ventures as a group as opposed to individual effort. Groups of urban poor women will take up an economic activity suited to their skill, training, aptitude and local conditions. Besides generation of income, this group strategy will strive to empower the urban poor women by making them independent as also providing a facilitating atmosphere for self-employment. To be eligible for subsidy under this scheme, the DWCUA group should consist of at least 10 urban poor women.

Financial Pattern

The DWCUA group society will be entitled to a subsidy of Rs. 1,25,000 or 50 per cent of the cost of project whichever is less. Where the DWCUA group sets itself up as a Thrift and Credit Society, in addition to its other entrepreneurial activity, the group/Thrift and Credit society will also be entitled to a lump sum grant of Rs. 25,000 as a revolving fund at the rate of Rs. 1000 maximum per member. This revolving fund will be available to a simple Thrift and Credit Society also even if the society is not engaged in any project activity under DWCUA.

The Urban Wage Employment Programme (UWEP)

This programme seeks to provide wage employment to beneficiaries living below the poverty line within the jurisdiction of urban local bodies by utilizing their labour for construction of socially and economically useful public assets. This programme will apply to urban local bodies, the population of which is less than five lakhs as per the 1991 Census. The material labour ratio for works under this programme will be maintained at 60:40. The prevailing minimum wage rate, as notified from time to time for each area, will be paid to the beneficiaries under this programme. UWEP programme will be dovetailed with the State sector EIUS scheme as well as the National Slum Development Programme (NSDP). This programme is not designed to either replace or substitute the Environmental Improvement of Urban Slums (EIUS), the NSDP, or any other State sector schemes.

Other Urban Eradication Poverty Programmes

The specific urban poverty reduction schemes are only a small proportion of the over all activities sup-ported and funded by the Indian Government, and a number of government departments run schemes to address poverty.

These schemes can be divided into three types:

(i) Provision of basic services.

(ii) Anti-poverty programmes (APPs).

(iii) Empowerment and safety nets.

(a) Provision of Basic Services

The government provides basic services, such as education, health and environmental services, such as water, sanitation, solid waste collection, etc. The priorities of the Ninth Plan are the provision of basic minimum services, such as safe drinking water, primary health care, universal primary education and shelter. In addition, special programmes have been designed to control communicable diseases (e.g. the National Malaria Eradication Programme, the TB Eradication Programme, and non-communicable diseases (blindness).

(b) Anti-Poverty Programmes (APPs)

Alongside the above, India also invests in eight anti- poverty programmes. These focus on special employment generation programmes and the provision of free or heavily subsidized basic needs (water, sanitation, housing, food). They can be summarized as:

(i) Works programmes to provide the poor with income from employment and the community with new assets.

(ii) Self-employment programmes, which aim to provide the poor with income-generating assets.

(iii) Food subsidy/nutrition programmes aimed at providing the poor with cheap food, which are managed by the Ministry of Food and Civil Supplies. The Public Distribution System (PDS) is the most visible and important government provided safety net for the poor, especially in urban areas.

(c) Empowerment and Safety Nets

(i) Empowerment Programmes.

(ii) Insurance/social security schemes.

(iii) Social Welfare/safety nets schemes.

- Empowering those with disabilities.
- Reforming social 'deviants'-restricting the production of alcohol and distribution of drugs.
- Caring for other disadvantaged people.

Proposed Solutions to Urban Poverty

- As interstate and intercity disparity in resources/funds, need a greater equity in the provision of basic services.
- Provision for special assistance/grants to small and medium towns, particularly in backward states.
- Constitutional amendments for decentralization of powers and responsibilities and provision for proper utilization by the municipal bodies/corporations.
- Need to restructure of the subsidized programmes/schemes and to ensure that these subside is meant for only targeted vulnerable section.
- Encourage/Establish potential slum communities, through which authorities can organize awareness programmes on various issues/aspects.
- To improve sanitation standards, need to construct community management toilets and to extend sewerage networks to slum areas.
- Wherever possible and feasible solar, bio-gas and non-conventional energy needs to be promoted for slum-dwellers.

SUMMARY

Urban poverty is a major challenge before the urban managers and administrators of the present time. Though the anti-poverty strategy comprising of a wide range of poverty alleviation and employment generating programmes has been implemented but results show that the situation is grim. Importantly, poverty in urban India gets exacerbated by substantial rate of population growth, high rate of migration from the rural areas and mushrooming of slum pockets. Migration alone accounts for about 40 per cent of the growth in urban population, converting the rural poverty into urban one. Moreover, poverty has become synonymous with slums and about one-fourth urban people in India lives below poverty line. The relationship is bilateral i.e. slums also breed poverty. This vicious circle never ends. Housing conditions in large cities and towns are depicting sub human lives of slum-dwellers. With the reconstruction of poverty alleviation programmes in urban India, it is expected that social and economic benefits will percolate to the population below the poverty line. However, eradication of poverty and improving the quality of life of the poor remain one of the daunting tasks.

The 74th Constitutional Amendment Act. of India envisages that the functions of urban poverty alleviation and improvement of slums and their up-gradation including the provisioning of urban basic amenities to the poor are among the key functions of the local bodies (Municipalities/Corporations). Therefore, Urban Local Bodies (ULBs) have to compulsorily provide appropriate provisions in their Budget to cater to the needs of the urban poor and develop separate" Budget for the Poor". Urban Local Bodies (ULBs) have to follow a convergence approach in formulating the service delivery to the urban poor by optimum utilization of both financial and manpower resources available in various Central and State sector schemes and programmes.

REFERENCES

Chandra Shekhar, S. and A. Mukhopadhya, (2007), *Multidimensions of Urban Poverty: Evidence from India*, Indira Gandhi Institute for Development Research, Mumbai.

Dhar, V.K. et.al. (2006), *Urban Poverty Alleviation Initiatives and the JNNURM, National Institute of Urban Affairs*, New Delhi.

DFID (2001), *Urban Poverty and Vulnerability in India*, DFID, New Delhi.

Government of India (2009), *India Urban Poverty Report*, Ministry of Housing and Urban Poverty Alleviation, Goverment of India, OUP, New Delhi.

Hashim, S.R. (2009), Economic Development and Urban Poverty, in *India Urban Poverty Report*, Ministry of Housing and Urban Poverty Alleviation, Government of India, OUP, New Delhi.

Palnitkar, Sneha (2009), *The Millennium Development Goals and The Role of Cities in India Urban Poverty Report*, Ministry of Housing and Urban Poverty Alleviation, Goverment of India, OUP, New Delhi.

Planning Commission (2001), *Report of the Steering Committee on Urban Development for Tenth Plan*, Planning Commission, Government of India, Delhi.

Yesudian (2007), Poverty Alleviation Programmes in India: A Social Audit, *Indian Journal of Medical Research*, 126, October.

Child Labour is a Consequence of Urban Poverty

Need of Social Work Intervention

Dr. V. Sunitha, Dr. K.Suneetha and
Prof. K. Surekha Rao

Child labour is one of the consequences of urbanization and urban poverty. Rapid increase of industrialization and urbanization there is a lot of demand for child workers as they are having less bargaining power and less litigant nature. Children used to work for fewer wage, for long hours till morning to late nights. Due to this the children forego basic education, good health, recreation etc which makes them to live at the bottom of social ladder. The number of child labour is increasing due to improper implementation of laws and welfare services. The prevalence of child labour is high through out the world.

In the light of above facts a study on "Child labour a Consequence of Urban Poverty: Need of Social Work Intervention" has been planned to know the causes and consequences of child labour and suggest measures to curb the menace of child labour through social group work. A sample of 12 child labours was purposively selected in an urban slum of Tirupati where a prevalence of child labour is high. By using interview schedule and focus group discussion, the information pertaining objectives was gathered. Later the collected data were analysed and planned some interventions and provided for them. The outcome of social work intervention is that the now the child labour was aware about importance of education and health etc. The follow up visits revealed that at present many of the group members are attending child labour school regularly.

Child labour is one of the consequences of urbanization and urban poverty. In the past children were working in their fields mostly which was their family occupation. However the prevalence rate is less. But industrialization brought changes in the life of the people, which made them migrate to urban and semi-urban areas from rural areas in search of jobs, education etc., this ultimately led to urbanization. Patil (1997) opined that "Industrialization everywhere had a negative outcome in the form of employment of women and children of the twin problems it is the child labour that is quite undesirable as the future of a society is intertwined and enmeshed with the future of the children". Due to rapid increase of industrialization and urbanization there is a lot of demand for child workers as they are having less bargaining power and less litigant nature.

Adult unemployment, illiteracy, large family size etc., causes increase of poverty in the urban families. Due to this, they are unable to educate, provide good nutrition, immunization as children at young age has to take good nutrition, immunization, health care otherwise it shows effect on their future. Agarwal and Aradhana (2009) in their study found that only 40 per cent of urban poor children received complete immunization and also found that children whose fathers are salaried/professional workers are associated with better health status than others. So, the urban poor children are facing many problems due to poverty.

Mohanti (1997) listed out the poverty into five categories based on several South-East Asian Studies finalized as Economic poverty, Geographical poverty, social poverty, cultural poverty and political poverty. Economic poverty is one of the poverty that existed in any society which makes child labour. Children in the urban areas are mostly involved in the sectors like restaurants, dhabas, tea stalls, mechanic shops, industries, rag picking, house hold, domestic chores etc. Raju (2003) in his study on child labour in mechanical workshops in the urban areas of West Godavari district found the reason for employing the children in the workforce as economic need of the family.

Children employed in the workforce at an early age and used to work for less wages and long hours since morning to late nights. They are also ill-treated; harassed by the employers as there is less resistance from the children. Due to work they forego basic education, good health and food, recreation etc., which makes them to live at the bottom of social ladder. To abolish child labour government has enacted laws like Factories Act, minimum Wages Act, Motor and Transport Workers Act, 1961, Child Labour (Prohibition and regulation) Act, 1986 etc. Due to less commitment and improper implementation loopholes in the Acts enhances the prevalence of Child labour. The prevalence of child labour is high through out the world. According to ILO and other official agencies there are 73 million children between 10 to 14 years of age are employed all over the world. In India 14.4 Per cent children between 10 and 14 years of age are employed in labour (www.childlabour.in). According to 2001 census there are 13, 63, 339 children in the age group of 5-14 years as child labour.

Government realized that legislations will not be sufficient to eradicate child labour and adopted a National Child Labour Policy in 1987, for elimination of child labour in hazardous industries in a time bound manner, and the emphasis on a constitutional right to primary education. Education is a weapon to eradicate child labour. Based on this Government initiated National child labour projects with an objective to withdraw children working in hazardous occupations and suitably rehabilitate them through education in special schools; where they are provided with non-formal education, vocational training, stipend, nutrition etc. (Report on National Child Labour Project, Sambalpur, 2006). To fulfill this, NCLP Schools were started in 1994 in some districts with the support of NGO's. Though NCLPs are providing education, nutrition, vocational training etc., to children their continuation of studies is not at an expected level as counselling and guidance is not available to these children. To mainstream these children into formal schools professional intervention is essential. Here social work can play an important role.

Expansion of urbanization and growth of industrialization created problems within the families. To assist these families social work attempts to resolve social and economic situations which lead to ill health, psychological and social problems. According to Joshi (2004) there are six methods of social work; those are social case work, social group work, community organization, social welfare administration, social action and social research. Social case work is used to intervene at individual level, group work with a group of people and community organization is used to intervene at community level. Social research, social action and social welfare administration methods are used to formulate policies, programmes and their implementation to intervene with problems of child labour. Social group work is an apt method to work with child labour issues.

Social group work aims to strengthen the group life. In social group work, the worker from outside the group with skills and techniques interact and deals with the group members to solve the problems. Trecker (1955) defines "Social group work as a method through which individuals in groups in social agency settings are helped by a worker who guides their interaction in programme activities so that they may relate themselves to others and experience growth opportunities in accordance with their needs and capacities to the end of the individual, group and community development".

MODELS AND PRINCIPLES

Different models of group work like Social Goals Model, Remedial Model, Reciprocal Model etc. which guided with a body of knowledge and principles such as principle of planned group formation, specific objectives, purposeful worker group relationship, continuous individualization, guided group interaction, democratic self-determination, flexible functional organization, progressive programme experience, resource utilization and principle of evaluation.

The group worker has to equip himself with a set of skills to deal with problems of child labour, at various stages of group work process. During the process the worker focuses on both at individual development and group as a whole. In group work, a group worker does an intervention with group members (children) where they share, interact, and learn with each other. As quoted by Zastrow (1982), "Research has also shown that it is generally easier to change the attitudes of an individual while in a group than to change a person's attitudes individually". Child labour is one of the major social problems where group work helps in main streaming the children into school rather than to go for work. So, the researcher conducted group work with children who were irregular to National Child Labour Project School, MASS in Tirupati with few objectives.

Objectives

1. To know the respondent's socio-economic profile.
2. To study the consequences of child labour on respondents and their families.
3. To educate them about how to overcome the consequences of child labour.
4. To motivate them to adopt the suggested measures to mitigate the problem of child labour.

Universe and the Sample

The universe of the study comprised the children who are attending National child labour school, MASS, Tirupati. The researcher purposively selected 12 children who were irregular for school on the reference of NCLP school teachers to form group and provide social work interventions.

Group Dimensions

- Twelve children were selected from the school (MASS) for the purpose of the study.
- Thirteen sessions were conducted with the respondents, their parents and staff of NCLP School.
- Group work was held twice in a week and continued for two months, the duration of each session is about 90 minutes.
- The type of group is short term education group. Urania Glassman and Len kates (1990) explained about the short term groups are those that will meet from three to a dozen sessions, more or less. This type of group is usually developed by the agencies around a particular theme, or to deal with a special issue. Many of these groups are education or growth oriented rather than for remediation purposes.

METHODS AND TOOLS OF DATA COLLECTION

Primary and secondary data were used. Primary data were the data collected from the respondents directly by using the interview schedule and secondary data from the existing literature about child labour, urban poverty, group work etc. Interview and observation methods were used to collect the data before and after intervention. During the intervention process, the tools like role play, flip charts, lecture, competitions, story telling, paper cuttings, pamphlets, games, anthakshari, black board demonstration etc., were used to create awareness on health, nutrition, education, welfare programmes, legislations enacted for child labour etc.,

Group Work Design

The researchers used one group pre-test, post-test design for the purpose of the study. It is one of the pre-experimental research designs which is undertaken to assess the effectiveness of social work intervention with groups [Lal Das (2005), Raymond Mark (1996].

$E \rightarrow y_1 \rightarrow x \rightarrow y_2$

X: Independent variable (intervention)

Y_1: Dependent variable before introduction of X (pre-test)

Y_2: Dependent variable after introduction of X (post-test)

E: Experimental group.

Groups Work Process

Group work intervention with the children was done in a process/stages, whole intervention process was written according to the stages of Siddiqui (2008).

Beginning Stage

In the initial stage group worker met the staff of NCLP School and collected all the details of irregular students and formed a group with those children. After formation of the group, a few objectives were framed like to know the group members' socio-economic profile, consequences of child labour on group members and their families, to educate them about how to over come the consequences and to motivate to adopt the suggested measures to overcome the problem. Slowly, a rapport was established with the group member by conducting a small game and interacting individually. As most of the group members belonged to same community they are having good contacts and there was less relationship with the school children. To over come this situation a game was conducted which makes them to move closer, so that the group members can come to school to play with friends and to share each other. The group worker explained to the members about the programme details which are going to be carried out for two months. Majority of the members not showed interest because their parents send them to work. After convincing their parents by the researcher contacted them directly, members were happy to attend the sessions regularly.

Middle Stage

In this stage the relationship within the group members, other children and worker was well established. The group worker collected the data from the group members initially by using the interview schedule which were prepared based on the objectives like socio-economic background, consequences of child labour, welfare and legal measures etc. After collecting the details from the members the data were collected from the parents of the members by using separate interview schedule. The two schedules were analyzed and found out that members and their parents were not aware of health, nutrition, education, welfare measures etc. while collecting the data the researcher spent 15-20 minutes for each respondent. Based on the analysis group worker planned the programme with the help of resource persons. Group worker collected the resources such as materials, games, lectures, demonstrations, group discussions etc., Initially it was difficult to the worker with members to motivate all the group members to participate actively in the sessions. Hence, individual counseling was taken to those members who did not participate and made them involve in the sessions.

According to the pre-plan, the group worker implemented the activities planned programme to meet the objectives of health and nutritional care. First group worker planned to implement with the group members. With relation to the health all the members were not taking bath regularly and not wearing washed clothes etc., worker explained to them about the consequence of being like that and asked them to take bath daily, washed their hands neatly before taking food etc. When coming to the nutrition as all the members were not taking lunch in the school they are foregoing nutritious food given in the school and they are not aware of use of taking leafy vegetables, milk, egg and other vegetables. For this with the help of school teacher and charts it was explained to the members that if they are not taking these vegetables they are proned to health problems and sickness. To create awareness on education group discussion was held within the two groups after discussing the importance of education, welfare and legal measures enacted for them were explained to the group members. After giving all the information essay writing and eloctution were conducted to the group members and all the group members participated actively. For the purpose of recreation, games, *anthakshyari,* dance etc. was conducted.

To create awareness to the parents of the group members i.e. (only mothers) home visits was planned. In the home visit the worker explained to them about the importance of taking good food, keeping premises clean, taking treatment from the hospitals, taking immunization, vaccination, health check ups regularly to the pregnant women and their children in time. With the help of paper cuttings, charts importance of nutrition was explained to them. Some of the cases were explained to them about the consequence of not taking good food, referring hospitals when they were sick and effect of not taking regular vaccines, health check ups and immunizations. Legal measures related to children and backward classes like Child Labour (prohibition and regulation) Act, 1986, Untouchability Act, etc. and welfare measures like NCLP schools, mid-day meals, welfare hostels, reservation, fee reimbursement, Aarogyasree etc., and other Non government programmes which were helpful to them like family counseling centres, de-addiction centres, special schools for disabled children, distribution of hearing aids, tricycles were explained to them.

During the group sessions all the members were participated actively. Finally the data was collected by the group members and their parents by using the same schedule which was used initially and it was analyzed. The results revealed that majority of the group members and parents were aware of education, health, nutrition, legal and welfare measures needed/available for main streaming of child labour (Table 17.1).

Table 17.1: Pre- and Post-intervention Scores of Members and their Mothers

Response	Pre- intervention		Post- intervention	
	Group members	Mothers	Group members	Mothers
	score	score	score	score
Awareness on Nutrition				
Yes	3	5	11	12
No	9	7	1	0
Total	**12**	**12**	**12**	**12**
Awareness on Health				
Yes	4	4	12	12
No	8	8	8	0
Total	**12**	**12**	**12**	**12**
Awareness on Education				
Yes	6	5	12	11
No	6	7	0	1
Total	**12**	**12**	**12**	**12**
Awareness on Legal and Welfare Measures				
Yes	2	3	10	11
No	10	9	2	1
Total	**12**	**12**	**12**	**12**

Termination Stage

The change within the group members was observed by the worker after creating awareness in them through some energizers. Termination stage is the last stage where the group members have to leave from the group. All the members got awareness and stated that they will continue education as their parents accepted. Lastly all the group members terminated from the group.

Follow up

Follow up was done to the group members after two months, among 12 members 10 members were coming to school and 2 dropped out. Later home visits were done to dropout student's houses to know the reason, and they said that due to financial problem they were unable to send them to school. They were suggested by the worker to join them in the vocational training like tailoring, technical work which will be helpful to them for self-employment.

ANALYSIS

Profile of the Group Members

Profile of the group members showed that 67 per cent were in the age group of 13 to 14 years followed by 33 per cent in 11-12 years. Gender distribution of the respondents showed that nearly three fifths i.e., 58 per cent were boys and remaining 42 per cent were girls. Coming to the caste wise distribution a majority i.e., 83 per cent belonged to scheduled caste and 17 per cent were from scheduled tribe. All the members were Hindus. Regarding education a little above two fifths i.e. 42 per cent were studying 4th class followed by 33 per cent studying 5th class and 25 per cent studying 3rd class. Monthly income of the family members revealed that a half of the members i.e., 50 per cent are in the income ranging from Rs. 2,500-3,000 pm followed by 33 per cent with Rs. 2,000-2,500 pm and 17 per cent were with Rs. 3,000 and above. These earnings were seasonal and income fluctuations were common and sometimes the unplanned expenditures also influence the financial status of the group members. Regarding family type a majority of the respondents i.e. 66 per cent were from nuclear families and 34 per cent from joint families.

Table 17.2: Paired Sample Tests for Group Members (Children) Awareness Scores

Pair one group members (children)	Mean	N	Std deviation	Std error mean	correlation	't' value	df	Sig (2-tailed)
Pre-intervention scores & Post-intervention scores	3.7500 11.2500	4 4	1.7078 0.9574	.8539 .4787	.866	— 15.000		3.001

Table 17.2 shows the group members (children) awareness on health, nutrition, education, welfare and legal measures before and after intervention through Paired Sample 't' test. Table shows that the mean scores of children awareness pre-intervention is 3.7500 and the post-intervention score is 11.2500. This clearly indicated that the post intervention score is higher than pre-intervention score. So their awareness is higher than pre-intervention score. So their awareness on nutrition, health, education, legal and welfare measures is enhanced with the social group work intervention.

Table 17.3: Paired Sample Tests for Mothers Awareness Scores

Pair one Mothers Pre-intervention scores & Post-intervention scores	Mean	N	Std deviation	Std error mean	correlation	't' value	df	Sig (2- tailed)
	4.2500 11.0500	4 4	09574 .5774	.4787 .2887	.302	— 15.145		3.001

Table 17.3 shows the group members' mothers' awareness on health, nutrition, education, legal and welfare measures before and after intervention. From the table, it is clear that pre-intervention mean scores of mothers' awareness is 4.2500 and post-intervention mean score is 11.0500. It reveals that the post intervention score is higher than pre-intervention score. So it can be concluded that the social work intervention has enhanced their awareness is spheres of nutrition, health, education, legal and welfare measures.

CONCLUSION

Children are the assets of any nation, most of the time children were neglected and abused. If the families failed to play their crucial role in upbringing the children may lead the children to face so many difficult circumstances. Even though several acts have been formulated from time to time for the welfare of the children they do not reach those in need and the problem of child labour are increasing alarmingly. So the researcher made an effort to study the problems of child labour and provided intervention through group work to curb exploitation of children. By doing group work with child labour (the group members) and their mothers enhanced their awareness regarding health, nutrition, education, legal and welfare measures. Due to this the people living in the urban slums can overcome the poverty by educating their children and utilizing the government and non-government services.

Recommendations

- Learning by doing, play oriented innovative and participatory teaching methodologies has to be adopted in lower primary classes to create interest on education among children and reduce-dropout rate.
- Measures should be taken for strict enforcement of child laws like compulsory education, child labour etc. is essential.

- Appointment of school social workers at schools is necessary, as they solve the problems of students at individual, group with co-operation of parents and teachers and they also deal with the educational, social and psychological problems.
- In schools (NCLP schools also) formation of parents association is essential to monitor the development of child and motivate/provide guidance about importance of education and necessary available services for the children now a days.
- "Community action teams" has to be constituted and work effectively to reduce dropout, child labour and promote continuation of education and developmental activities for children as there 'community action team approach is one where local body members, NGO, parents etc., become members and it serve as a basic tool for inclusive development of all marginalized people.

REFERENCES

Agarwal, S. and Aradhana.S, (2009), "Social Determinants of Children's Health in Urban Areas in India", *Journal of Health care for the Poor and Underserved*, 20, pp. 68-69.

Glass man, Urania and Len kates, (1990), *Group Work: A Humanistic Approach*, New Delhi, Sage Publications, pp. 257-262.

Joshi, C.S., (2004), *Hand Book of Social Work*, New Delhi, Akanksha Publishing House, pp. 9-10.

Lal Das, D.K., (2005), *Designs of Social Research*, New Delhi, Rawat Publications, pp. 128-129.

Mohanti, N., (1997), "Gender Perspectives in Child Labour", *Journal of Social Welfare*, Vol. 44, No. 1, pp. 9-12.

Patil, B.R., (1997), "Eliminating Child Labour, Some National and International Initiatives", *The Journal of Social Change*, Vol. 27, No. 3-4, pp. 169-185.

Raju, A.V.N., (2003), "Child Labour in Mechanical Workshops", *Journal of Extension and Research*, Vol. V, No. 2, pp. 34-36.

Raymond Mark, (1996), *"Research made Simple" –A Handbook for Social Workers*, New Delhi, Sage Publications, pp. 148-150.

Report on National Child Labour Project, Sambalpur, 2006, (Unpublished).

Siddiqui, H.Y., (2008), *Group work–Theories and Practices*, New Delhi, Rawat Publications, pp. 97-111.

Trecker, H.B., (1955), *Social Group Work and Principles*, New Delhi, Association Press.

Zastrow, Charles (1982), *Introduction to Social Work*, New Delhi, Atmaram and Sons.

Street Children

Problems and Need for Social Work Intervention

Dr. D. Sai Sujatha and
D. Mahammad Rafi

INTRODUCTION

Children constitute an important resource of a nation. Any country that satisfies the provisions of the convention on rights of the children (CRC) is a successful country. The situation is worst in the developing countries where one of the problem are street children, which hade taken some serious proportions. India is suffering with the problem of street children.

According to some estimate, there are about 100 million street children in the world and out of them 40 million are in Latin America, 20 to 30 million in Asia and 10 million in Africa. The expected street children in India are 10 to 15 million. The major metropolitan cities like New Delhi, Mumbai and Calcutta etc., has around one lakh street children each.

In 2001, UNESCO defined, street children as, "those who are of the street and on the street", of the street refers to those who live in the street and on the street refers to those who spend significant part of the day on the street either for vocational reasons or on a wide range of other activities such as begging, rag picking, car washing etc., The street children are also known as 'high risk children', 'Children in need of care and protection', abandoned children etc.

Classification/Categorization of Street Children

Street children are broadly categorized in three types:

- Children with continuous family contact: children who have their family contacts but are forced to spend most of their time on the pavements and streets only to return home for spending night.

- Children with occasional family contact—children whose parents have no commitment towards them so they stay on the street not only during day but also often during the nights and only occasionally meet their parents.
- Children with no family contact the abandoned and neglected children who work, sleep and live fully on the streets or pavements of the big cities.

Street Children may also be Classified into Categories such as:

(i) 'of the street' children — Those who live on the streets.

(ii) 'on the street' children — Those who spend a considerable part of the day in the streets for earning their livelihoods.

Children with no Family Contact can be Classified into:

(i) Orphans

(ii) Abandoned children

(iii) Maladjusted children, hence run way children.

CHARACTERSTICS OF STREET CHILDREN

The phenomenon of street children is an off shoot of complex interplay of various factors in India. A large scale presence of street children is a symptom of social disease, which is due to exploitative structure, lopsided development, large scale unemployment, rapid urbanization, rapid population growth, extreme poverty, increasing disparities in wealth and income, cut backs in government social and educational budgets, high level of child abuse by the parents and society and a break down of traditional family and community structures contribute to a problem. Migration from rural to urban areas has also contributed significantly to a substantial increase in the number of street children.

Street children have specific characteristics. They live on streets. Many have no contacts with their families. Some have work and others do not have work. Work is street based and confined to informal sectors. Majority of them work as rag-pickers. As compared to boys, the girls are highly vulnerable and subjected to sexual abuse. Hardly they have any social status.

Street children are the worst sufferers in the society. They suffer from the worst kind of deprivation and denial of basic necessities such as education, health, food, shelter, psychical protection, security and recreation.

Street children include rag-pickers, beggars, street vendors, etc. They move from place to place during the seasons and earn their livelihood. Most of them stay on the roads and market places.

Street children constitute a deprived group suffering with insecurity, delinquency and criminal behaviour as compared to children working in factories. The fate of these children is miserable and pathetic. Most of them do not have proper shelter and they live only on platforms, on pavements, bus stands, making tents on road side, markets, temples, squatter colonies etc.

PROBLEMS FACED BY STREET CHILDREN

Life on the street is without any protection. This status brings several problems for the street children. They are subjected to violence, harassment and physical abuse. In order to survive, they may fall prey to nefarious activities like, smuggling, stealing, peddling of drugs, pimping and prostitution etc. They face several problems such as forced labour and exploitation, sexual harassment, various forms of abuse and neglect and abandonment. They fall prey to drug abuse. The girl child on the street is the most vulnerable to sexual abuse and harassment. Often a girl child ends up as a commercial sex worker, because it is used as tool to survive on the streets.

The Sexual Behaviour of Girls on the Street can be Explained in Terms of Three Categories:

1. Survival sex which is very common and they are not necessarily paid for it.
2. Protection sex, here the girls offer sexual service in exchange of protection or money.
3. The last category is of commercial sex where girls render sexual service in exchange of money.

Some of the Special Problems of Street children are:

- Deprived of adult protection, guidance, love and support.
- Soft targets for police excesses, psychical and sexual assault and child prostitution.
- Lack of shelter, forced to sleep on pavements, railway stations.
- Forced to earn livelihood, usually in unhygienic occupations like rag-picking.
- Deprived of even minimal access to school and health facilities.
- Irregular, unhygienic and in adequate in take of food.
- Vulnerable to a 'here and now' existence centered, around films, gambling, smoking and drugs.

The street children can be found in jobs like begging, collection of edibles from garbage, washing cars, selling newspapers, rag-picking, cleaning of trains and platforms etc.

CAUSES

Marital disharmony, separations or divorces, family tensions, death of parents, ill-treatment by step parents, bonded labour are some of the conditions that have brought a large number of children on the street.

Felt Needs of Street Children

- *Food and health needs:* Food takes a priority over other needs. Street children find it difficult to get one square meal a day and they do not get quality of food. The greatest need for their health is nutritious food.
- *Shelter:* Shelter is another priority area. These children spend their nights on pavement and railway platforms. They are vulnerable to HIV/AIDS.
- *Education:* Most of street children have very little or no eduction at all. There is high rate of illiteracy in this group of children. Education can help these children worthy citizens of the future.
- *Psychological and emotional needs:* Psychological and emotional needs of these children are equally important in terms of giving them satiability and security. These children suffer from low self esteem and in security which lead to behaviour problems. They have uncertainty about their future. They live life on a day to day basis.
- *Gender specific needs:* Girls on the streets are most vulnerable to sexual harassment and abuse. They have to carry out their daily tasks on the roads without any privacy. With the adolescent girls, this is a major problem.

STRATEGIES

The strategy for muting the needs of these street children in the context of child rights convention comprises four broad areas of child rights.

1. Basic needs for survival.
2. Protection and care.
3. Development.
4. Participation.

1. **Basic Needs for Survival**

- Food.
- Shelter.
- Clothes.

The basic needs include food and shelter as priority areas. Street children lack access to nutritious diet and proper shelter. There is a need for clothes to wear, and bedding material.

2. **Protection and Care**

The right to protection and care is the next area of child rights. It is necessary to protect the child against different forms of exploitation. This protection can be given at the legal level and at the NGO level, by providing shelter with certain services.

- *Night shelters:* This shelter would give a child protection from sexual and physical abuse. The following major facilities should be organized in the night shelter.

  (i) Locker facilities

  (ii) Bathing facilities

  (iii) Recreation

  (vi) Basic needs

  (v) Counseling

  (vi) Emergency assistance.

- *Legal aid centers:* Street children work and live in difficult situations. There may be harassment by law enforcing agencies i.e., police, since they have no acess to legal support, they end up in jails. Hence they need legal support.

(i) *Awareness programmes about child rights:* The street children should be made aware of their rights and the legal weapons, they should have access to there in times of arrest, harassment etc., The peer educators could be trained from amongst the children to educate about child rights.

(ii) *Legal counseling:* Counseling could help provide them with needed information about legal procedures.

(iii) *Legal support:* Children need legal support in the form of lawyers representing them in courts of law.

- Family relinks.
- Mobile health clinics.
- First aid.
- Health checks-up.
- Free medicines to be made available.
- Dispensary.
- Shelter during illness.
- Adequate nutrition during illness.
- Medical care given by doctor and trained nurses.

3. **Development**

Children should be given a chance to unfold their capacities and develop in a positive way, without development opportunities, there cannot be betterment in the conditions of street children.

Development can be ensured through:

- Half way house.
- A house mother.
- Regulated life
- Four meals a day.
- Emotional support.
- Counselling, education, health care and recreation.
- *Drop-in-centers:* It is necessary to provide the children a place of their own. This place acts as a recreation centre and the first place the child goes to. The activities of the centre are planned in such a way so as to enhance the child's development.
  - *(i)* Nutrition facilities.
  - *(ii)* Basic education and recreation facilities.
  - *(iii)* Emotional support.
  - *(iv)* Medical support.
- *Preparatory centers:* These centers prepare the children and main stream them into formal schools.
  - *(i)* Education provided by trained teachers.
  - *(ii)* Preparing the child to enter formal school.
- *Vocational training centers:* They are to be given an opportunity to make a better future by equipping them to become independent earners. i.e., by skill development and vocational training. Girls want training in sewing, knitting, beautician courses etc.
  - Providing will skill training.
  - Literacy and numeracy.
  - Placement services.
  - Retailing outlet for finished products.
  - Recreation and creativity centres.
  - Play grounds, cultural activities like music, dance, drama etc.,
  - Out door and in door games.

4. **Participation**

- Participation is another important area of child rights. Participation would ensure progress.
- Peer educators training.
- Assess to information on health related issues.
- Holding of focus group discussions to asses their needs and failures.
- Referral services.
- *Community mobilization:* The community should be mobilized to secure a better deal for these street children.

MODE

- *Involving the media:* Media should be involved for highlighting the street children issues, since otherwise is often overlooked by the people.
- *Sensitizing the influencing members of the community:* Law-makers, police, railway authorities, municipal bodies etc., should be sensitized to ensure a greater success in the implementation of the NGO's programmes.
- *Networking among NGO's working with street children:* If the NGO's are to work in a concerted way then they will have to pool in their efforts and know how by the sharing of experiences and expertise.
- *Creation of forums and pressure group:* Creation of forum and pressure groups would make for advocacy at the policy making levels, that is the highest level and help to sensitize the law makers to the problems of the street children and thus making the laws more child friendly.

The above strategies throw light on some of the possibilities that can be employed to achieve the goals of child rights convention (CRC).

Need for Social Work Intervention

Social workers provide interventions to individuals, families and groups in order to assist them with their needs and issues. Interventions are intended to aid clients in alleviating problems impending their well-being. The interventions used by social workers are those that are identified as potentially helpful on the basis of the social worker's ongoing assessment of the client.

Social workers work in many different types of settings, including hospitals, mental health facilities, child welfare centers, guidance clinics, schools, substance abuse programs and prisonscorrectional facilities. These program and service areas vary on the type of problems that clients bring to a particular setting, representing specializations in social work.

Social work interventions are selected on the basis of the issues, needs and strengths of the clients, group and community.

The problem of street children is a global one, it exists in developed as well as developing countries, with difference notice in terms of size and magnitude. Hence, there is a need for social work interventions to eradicate or prevent such situations of street children and to develop the life of the street children.

Social Work Interventions

- Giving street children a future, make a difference to their life.
- *Child line:* a help line for children needing assistance on information.
- To create a comprehensive system of services to fulfil children's long-term needs for education, skills and emotional support, as well as their short term needs for nutrition, health and shelter.
- To assist children with their immediate challenges, such as homelessness, malnutrition and illness, while also develop their attitudes and skills.
- To rehabilitate the children from exploitation, begging child labour by giving them protection, love and development.
- Maximize the impact of this system through integrated programs, monitoring, improve the quality of service, and seize opportunities to expand.
- Focusing attention on issues, problems and polices related to the welfare of the street children.
- To provide institutional and non-institutional services.
- To enable their in born talents and capabilities to unfold naturally.
- Street child rescue projects, multitudes of deprived.
- Street education.
- Residential rehabilitation programmes.
- Preventive programmes.
- Sustainable motivation.
- To conduct and promote sports development activities.
- To organize various enjoyable and creative activities.
- Mainly focus on the ways needed for their upliftment.
- To provide free education, educational materials, uniform and other.
- *Vocational training centers:* Vocational training skills for girls in making of jewellery and handicrafts.
- To provide a safe environment.
- To change the attitudes of families and communities.
- To develop social skills and self esteem.

- To organize *'child awareness day'.*
- Conduct seminars, awareness camps, group meetings to the people.
- Conduct research.
- Workshops for employers, government officers and volunteers of the NGO's.
- The NGO's initiatives are very much needed.

CONCLUSION

Children constitute an important resource of a nation and any country that satisfies the provisions of the CRC is a successful country. CRC speaks about four broad areas of child rights, viz:

(i) Basic needs for survival, such as food, shelters and clothing.

(ii) Protection and care, i.e., night shelter, counseling

(iii) Development such as regulated life, nutrition.

(iv) Participation, i.e., their involvement in social and economic development.

Street children are worst sufferers and toiling themselves for the sake of the family survival in unorganized nature of work in their early ages. This is really a social crime and it is attributed to the state's irresponsibility and in ability, several schemes are in implementation for the welfare of these children including the latest child labour elimination project. The juvenile justice act came into effect from 1986 to safeguard the interests of the children. But what has been done so for remains to be questioned.

The increase in the number of street children is a matter of concern to the ministry of social justice and empowerment. The basic objective is to promote wholesome development of children without homes and families and prevent destitution. The essential components of the programme include the provision of shelter, nutrition, health care, sanitation and hygiene, safe drinking water, education, recreation, protection against abuse and neglect of street children. The government is expected to play a crucial role since the task is gigantic. There is need for shelter homes to be provided to the street children. They are to be integrated with the mainstream of social development and provided with opportunities to grow.

Social worker's interventions are needed to give street children a future, to develop social skills and self esteem. Social work intervention can also create a comprehensive system of services to fulfill children's long-term needs for education, skills and emotional support, as well as their short term needs for nutrition, health and shelter and focuses attention on issues, problems and polices and social work interventions related to the welfare of the street children.

REFERENCES

Chattarji Amitha, The Forgotten Children of Cities, India.

"Social Work Interventions"–www.socialworkinterventions.com.

UNESCO (2001) *A Hand book for India*, New Delhi.

UN Convention on the Rights of the Child, *The Right to be a Child UNICEF* (1994).

Urban Poverty and Micro-finance in India

A Study

Dr. K. Rajasekhar

INTRODUCTION

In India, at present poverty is one of the main problems which have attracted attention of sociologists and economists. It indicates a condition in which a person fails to maintain a living standard adequate for his physical and mental efficiency. It is a situation people want to escape. It gives rise to a feeling of a discrepancy between what one has and what one should have. The term poverty is a relative concept. It is very difficult to draw a demarcation line between affluence and poverty. According to Adam Smith- Man is rich or poor according to the degree in which he can afford to enjoy the necessaries, the conveniences and the amusements of human life. India is stepping forward for becoming a country with more urbanized. The recent experiences tell that the urban areas are facing the same problem of poverty as of the rural areas. Poverty in India can be defined as a situation when a certain section of people are unable to fulfil their basic needs. India has the world's largest number of poor people living in a single country. Out of its total population of more than one billion, 350 to 400 million people are living below the poverty line.

The Indian state has undoubtedly failed in its responsibilities towards its citizens over the last 60 odd years. There is a need for the state to move out of many areas and the process has been started with economic liberalization. The process of decentralization should devaluate lot more powers, both functional and financial, to panchayats. The lack of transparency and accountability has hampered our economic development at all levels. The problem of poverty persists because of a number of leakages in the system. New laws have to be evolved to ensure more accountability. Bodies like the Planning Commission should be modified into new constitutional bodies that can hold governments accountable for their failure to implement development programmes. A strong system of incentives and disincentives also needs to be introduced. The encouragement of non-governmental organizations and private sector individuals in tackling poverty is imperative, as the state cannot do everything. The need of the hour is not only to create opportunities for the city dwellers but also to augment their income; financial assistance through soft and hassle free loans need to be provided to them. In urban areas, several programmes have been launched to address urban poverty, which includes the Scheme of Urban Micro Enterprises, Nehru Rozgar Yojana and Prime Minister's Integrated Urban Poverty Alleviation Programme and Urban Basic Services for the Poor [UBSP], etc. As the number of migrants increase, so does the index of poverty. The poor do manage to find some work, but it is either not regular or in the unregulated sector with no guarantee of minimum wages and number of working hours. Unsecured employment or no employment force the urban poor to eke out a living some how. Some of them take to crimes, but a majority of them work in factories or homes or do some petty trading The skilled ones manage to get employed somehow, but the large majority of unskilled people forces work in the unorganized sector. Some are even forced to driven to begging, prostitution or peddling drugs in the hope of getting easy money. Poverty is an accepted situation. Today urban poverty has been globally recognized as a problem area and the Millennium Development Goals adopted by the UN and accepted by India includes the alleviation of urban poverty as one of the primary goals. To tackle urban poverty there is a dire need of setting of a micro finance institution, which would focus on the urban poor and would identify the needy persons who have a positive bent of mind to work for them self and for the society at large. In the above context, micro finance becomes important as a tool of poverty alleviation. Most of the financial institutions, being commercial institutions, do not find it commercially feasible to lend to the poor. The poor are generally illiterate, they have no fixed address and they cannot offer anything as collateral security. Moreover, the cost of lending becomes unprofitable since the number is large but the quantum of loan is insignificant. So in spite of the availability of huge funds, bigger financial institutions do not finance the poor. The present paper aims to study the urban poverty and role of micro-finance in reduction of urban poverty in India based on secondary sources (data).

MICRO-FINANCE CONCEPT, MEANING AND DEFINITION

The concept of micro-finance is actually the brain product of Prof. Muhammad Yunus, an eminent economist from Bangladesh who set up the Grameen Bank in 1976 to provide easy and cheap loan to the socio-economically vulnerable sections of the society. Since then the role of micro-credit in tackling the problem of the disadvantaged masses has been getting a huge response in almost every part of the globe. Most of the micro-finance programmes in the world are based on group system for delivering various financial services to their poor clients. The concept is to provide very small loans to poor families to help them engage in productive activities or grow their tiny businesses. Over time, micro-finance has come to include a broader range of services like credit, savings, insurance etc.

Meaning and Definition of Micro-finance

Micro-finance refers to small savings, credit and insurance services extended to socially and economically disadvantage segments of society. In the Indian context terms like "small and marginal farmers", " rural artisans" and "economically weaker sections" have been used to broadly define micro-finance customers.

The Declaration of Micro-Credit Summit, (1997), defined Micro-credit programmes as those, "extending small amount of credit to poor people for self-employment projects of that generates income allowing them to cure for themselves and their families."

In India the Task force on Supportive and Regulatory framework for Micro Finance (NABARD, 2000) defined Micro finance as, "Provision of thrift, credit and other financial services and products of very small amounts to the poor in rural, semi urban and urban areas enabling them to raise their income levels and improve living standards." This definition is also accepted by the Reserve Bank of India (RBI).

Need of Microfinance Services in India

Due to its large size and population of around 121crores, India's GDP ranks among the top 15 economies of the world. However, around 300 million people or about 60 million households, are living below the poverty line, and further it is estimated that among these households, only about 20 per cent have access to credit from the formal sector. According to micro-financers estimation the annualized credit usage of all poor families (rural and urban) at over Rs. 45,000 crores, of which some 80 per cent is met by informal sources. Generally, credit on reasonable terms to the poor can bring about a significant reduction in poverty and with this hypothesis; micro-finance/credit assume significance in the Indian context. With globalization and liberalization of the economy, opportunities for the unskilled and the illiterate are not increasing fast enough, as compared to the rest of the economy. This is leading to a lopsided growth in the economy thus increasing the gap between the haves and have-nots. It is in this context, the institutions involved in micro finance have a significant role to play to reduce this disparity and lead to more equitable growth. In terms of demand for micro-finance/credit, there are three segments of people: they are:

1. Those who are landless and are engaged in work on a seasonal basis, and manual labourers in forestry, mining, household industries, construction and transport.
2. Weavers and those self-employed in the urban informal sector as hawkers, vendors, and workers in household micro-enterprises.
3. Those engaged in dairying, poultry, fishery, etc.

MICRO-FINANCE AND URBAN POOR IN INDIA

Micro-finance programmes have been promoted since the mid-1990s as a key strategy for poverty reduction. Micro-finance services for the poor have rapidly expanded in many countries, and many Micro-finance programmes have increasingly targeted women in response to experience of excellent repayment rates. Although emphasis has varied between the different agencies, it is now generally accepted that poor women and men have a right to financial services and that these can be established on a sustainable basis. More recently attention has also focused on the potential contribution of microfinance to other related development goals like women's empowerment, health, education, democratisation and environmental improvement.

Access to micro-finance services can initiate or strengthen a series of interlinked and mutually reinforcing 'virtuous spirals' of poverty reduction and social and political empowerment:

(i) Savings and credit can contribute to the livelihoods of poor households, increasing incomes and assets and/or decreasing vulnerability to crises and market fluctuations. More recent products like insurance and pensions can further contribute to these goals.

(ii) Increasing women's access to microfinance services can contribute to positive changes in gender relations and women's empowerment.

(iii) Microfinance products can be used to fund service providers of health, education and environmental services and/or purchase of such services.

Many programmes are group based. Group formation can reinforce the development contribution of access to micro-finance services through:

- Providing an organizational base for delivery of non-financial services and dissemination of information in areas like enterprise development, health, nutrition, literacy, gender equality and environmental management
- Providing an organizational base for collective community action, networking and advocacy as part of participatory local planning and strengthening of civil society and democracy.

The micro-finance that is popular at present is not new in India. The micro credit and lending had been in practice since man started trade. The idea of micro-finance was mooted sometime in 1992, when attention was focused on the experience of other developing countries, where such micro-finance was already introduced. National Bank for Agriculture Reconstruction, and Development (NABARD) took the lead in this direction. Micro-finance works through the operation of Self-help Groups (SHG), which are a group of fifteen odd women living in the same neighbourhood. These women work and generate small savings, which are invested in the common pool from which loans can be availed of and all the members agree on the rate of interest and the number of instalments. Where savings generated are substantial, they are invested in a bank deposit, against which banks advance loan to the SHG, which in turn can advance it to the members.

At initial stage, the financial services to the poor and low income households in India has revolved around the rural population only, and the flow of financial resources to urban populations was never a matter of serious issue in India. The tendency among micro-finance intermediaries to move towards urban centres came only after it found that the rural markets coming to a saturation point. Credit flow from formal financial institutions to the urban population groups steadily increased in India since the 1970s, but the actual first targeted credit programme in urban areas was launched in 1989. The 74th Constitutional Amendment has given a significant role to urban local bodies in terms of empowerment and expanding their normal functions to include poverty alleviation. In this regard, all the urban local bodies have to focus on micro-finance at the grass root level. The present quantum of micro finance can be enhanced by sustained efforts on the part of financial institutions, SHGs and interested NGOs. Once it is accepted that micro finance can be enhanced to fund profit generating activity, the SHGs should be suitably educated and trained to take on more activities. Later on, various urban poverty alleviation schemes with a credit focus introduced on a top-down approach. The Swarna Jayanti Shahari Rozgar Yojana (SJSRY) is the first such urban scheme launched by Government of India where community based organizations, especially poor urban women, were recognized as the critical points of delivery of benefits Indian Bank has started Micro state branches that are exclusive satellite branches for servicing micro loans (Business Line, 2007). Later State Bank of India has promoted about 7000 SHGs in the city of Mumbai of which nearly 2000 are bank linked. It is in effect doing SHG-bank linkage in an urban area, with the assistance of about 51 registered NGOs it is currently lending to about 4000 active groups out of an estimated 14,000 spread over about 140 slums in Chennai. Average group size is 17, and the main member activities are retailing, trading and handicrafts. Though the social banking efforts of the central bank and the government financial intermediation in rural areas too have gone through a phase of expansion but the low income asset holding segments of urban areas have largely been bypassed by such overall expansion in financial intermediation. While the state's poverty alleviation approach has steadily expanded from mere provision of basic amenities and services to facilitating creation of income earning opportunities, it has failed to make any significant impact on the urban poor. The pioneers of urban microfinance such as SEWA, WWF, and SPMS, whose experience over the years is being reexamined by the new comers for the valuable lessons they offer.

However, micro-finance in India is largely centred on rural and semi-urban settlements. The foray into urban areas and the subsequent strong growth has only taken place in the past couple of years. The reason for this kind of clientele distribution also happens to be conscious approach adopted by Micro-finance institutions (MFIs) owing largely to the "fragile" nature of their urban clients. Studies and research have time and again indicated the complexity and persistent nature of problems of the poor in urban settlements. This automatically translates into the complex nature of financial services both demanded for and offered to the poor in those areas. It may be interesting to note that micro finance in urban areas is synonymous with the emergence of the Institutional form of micro-finance pioneered by Grameen Bank, Bangladesh. As a matter of fact micro-finance in Bangladesh spread from the urban areas to the rural areas and if one closely observes the nature of financial services offered namely credit, the various business models at the retail level overwhelmingly supported the productive use of credit as against maintaining an open case for its end use:

Urban poor mostly reside in rental houses and though *prima facie* their residence is near permanent, it cannot be naturally assumed as in the case of their rural counterparts. This aspect is an immense business risk for the MFIs as repayments for loans are very frequent and in the form of tiny installments the urban poor find it extremely difficult to finance their small businesses as compared to their rural counterparts. Government sponsored schemes are largely implemented in rural areas and development of urban areas fall under the purview of their respective Urban Development Authorities. However, due to the unpredictable financial systems they face, the urban poor are adept in managing their finances and use highly innovative arrangements to meet their ends. MFI's also need to adopt a very innovative approach towards designing their products and systems that are both market responsive in addition to being client friendly. Micro-credit to the urban poor is strongly evincing interest from all quarters of the sector; this is an excellent opportunity to help improve the livelihoods of a vast majority requiring these services. At the same time, it is also an opportunity to build strong and sustainable MFIs specializing in catering to the financial needs of the urban poor.

A World Bank report (2000) suggests that 95 per cent of the members do not default in repayment and the efforts of these SHGs need to be lauded. In small ways these groups have mobilized savings and employed it on economic activities, which are earning steady rate of returns. The sustainability of these micro finance institutions depends upon the zeal of the members to save more and employ the funds in profit generation. While micro-finance is growing as an institution it has not yet been able to fill the huge gap between poverty and sustainable economic activity. Urban poverty, in absolute terms, is far too huge for micro finance to make a sizeable dent.

Limitations

Even though microfinance services for the poor are now widely promoted as a key strategy for poverty reduction, but it is not magic bullet, because of badly designed micro-finance programmes (even if financially sustainable and female-targeted) may have very limited impact on poverty.

- Credit programmes may not enable people to increase incomes but may accelerate a downward spiral of indebtedness.
- Female targeting may not benefit women but merely shift the burden of household debt and/or household thrift onto women.
- The poorest are the most difficult and costly to reach with financial services and also the least able to pay the costs of such service delivery. They are often excluded from micro-finance programmes without being offered any other form of assistance
- Women may not control their own incomes and/or men may divert more of their incomes to their own personal expenditure.
- Where women actively press for change in gender relations this may increase tensions in the household and domestic violence.
- The funds obtained from micro-credit are often employed on domestic necessities, such as marriage or cost of hospitalization and not on profit generating activity.

TASK FORCE ON MICRO-CREDIT/FINANCE

Ministry of Housing and Urban Poverty Alleviation set up a Task Force under the chairmanship of Secretary (Housing and Urban Poverty Alleviation), with the objective to evolve formulations for a viable micro-credit mechanism for the urban poor/informal sector. The Task Force comprised members from the various Government organizations including Reserve bank of India (RBI), representatives from nationalized banks, NABARD, SIDBI, other financial institutions/rating agencies such as HDFC, ICICI, ICRA and Non-Governmental organizations such as SEWA, DHAN Foundation, Dr. Reddy's Foundation and Sa-Dhan. The Task Force has since submitted its Report to the Ministry and it is under consideration. It is expected that this report will be a major milestone in setting up of a viable mechanism for delivery of micro-credit/micro-finance to the urban poor in the country.

CONCLUSION

To tackle urban poverty there is a dire need of setting of a micro finance institutions, which would focus on the urban poor and would identify the needy persons who have a positive bent of mind to work for them self and for the society at large. In the above context, micro-finance becomes important as a tool of poverty alleviation.

The urban poor form part of the informal sector and the access to micro-finance in the formal system is not easily available to them. There is, therefore, a need to formulate a viable micro-finance mechanism for them so that they do not fall prey to the money lenders who charge exorbitant rates of interest from them to fulfill their consumer and housing needs.

REFERENCES

CARE, MSDF and ICICI Bank, 2006, "A Promise to Pay the Bearer: An Exploration of the Potential for Urban Microfiinance in India", *Report Presented at Microfinance India Conference.*

Centre for Micro-Finance (CMF), 2006, "Reaching the Other 100 Million Poor in India"Microfinance India Conference, *Report Presented at Microfinance India Conference.*

DHAN Foundation, 2005, "Impacting Urban Poverty Through Microfinance: The SPMS Experience", DHAN Foundation, Madurai.

Mankar, Veena, and Lara Gidwani, 2007, "Metro Microfinance: Opportunities and Challenges in Mumbai", in *Intellecap* 2007.

Mukheree, RK, 2004, "*Study of the Demand for Micro Financial Services and Livelihood Promotion Services in Delhi*", Conducted for Indian Grameen Services, New Delhi, Mimeo Pasheva, Vanya and Manasee Desai 2006, in CMF 2006.

University of Manchester, Also Published in Journal of International Development.

Ujjivan, 2006. "A Study of Economically Active Poor Women in Bangalore—2005", *Report done for Ujjivan by Delphi Research Services, Bangalore.*

Urban Poverty

A Need for Confiscate for Urban Growth

Dr. P. Subramanyachary

"Poverty is the Parent of Revolution and Crime."— Aristotle

INTRODUCTION

Urbanization and urban growth have accelerated in many developing countries for the last few years. In the world by 1970 urban population was 37 per cent, by 2005 it increased to 50 per cent. 20th century witnessed a rapid growth in urban population. Definition of urban areas are based on national criteria such as, population thresholds, density of residential buildings, level of public services provided, proportion of population engaged in non- agricultural work and officially designated territories. At present of urban population is 28 per cent. It is estimated that there will be 46 per cent of population in urban areas by 2030.

There is no consensus definition on urban poverty, but two broad complementary approach are prevalent namely, one is conventional economic definition which uses income and second is Anthropological interpretation i.e. variation in social differences. As per latest report of NSSO over 80 million poor people are living in cities and towns of India. Over 61.80 million people were living in slums. It is interesting note that in some larger states urban poverty is higher than that of rural poverty to the phenomenon of urbanization of poverty. Indian cities have been grappling with challenges of making the cities sustainable i.e. inclusive, productive, efficient and manageriable with growing poverty and slums. As per estimates of the planning commission urban poor is 80 million by 2004-05. Poverty is pernicious and distressing feature of an economy. Urban poverty is an acute and chronic as rural poverty in India. Urban India has a high incidence of poverty despite being hailed as an engine of growth and instrument of globalization. There is urgent need for a mission mode approach to combat urban poverty.

URBANIZATION TRENDS IN INDIA

The census authorities in India defined urban areas as follows:

- All places with Municipality, Corporation, Cantonment Board or notified town
- All other places which satisfy the following criteria:
  - *(i)* Minimum population of 5000.
  - *(iii)* At least 75 per cent male workers population engaged in nonagricultural pursuit.
  - *(iv)* A density of population at least 400 per km^2.

In 2001, about 285 million people, or 27.8 per cent of India's 1.02 billion populations, lived in 5,161 cities. About 37 per cent lived in 35 million-plus metros, the rest being equally divided between 388 large towns (0.1 up to a million) and 4,738 small towns (less than 0.1 million). Over the last five decades, annual rates of growth of urban population ranged between 2.7 to 3.8 per cent - 2.7 per cent being the growth rate during 1991-2001. Projections estimate that 331 million people would be living in Urban India by 2007, growing in the Eleventh Plan period to 368 million by 2012 (Office of Registrar General and Census Commissioner, Government of India, 2006). According to 2001 population census 285 million populations exists in urban areas and 742 million population is living in rural areas. The most urban population Union Territory is Chandigarh and States are Tamilnadu with 43.9 per cent, Maharashtra with 42.4 per cent population.

Table 20.1: Classification of Urban areas Based on Population size

Cities	Population Size	No. of Towns
1.	1 lakh above	393
2.	50,000 to 99999	401
3.	20,000 to 49,999	1,151
4.	10,000 to 19,999	1344
5.	5000 to 9999	888
6.	Less than 5000	191
unclassified		10
All classes		4378

The above table shows there are 393 class-I areas with above 1 lakh population. Like those class-II urban areas are 401, class-III urban areas are 1,151, class- IV urban areas 1344, class-V urban areas are 888 and class-VI urban areas with 5000 are 191, finally unclassified town are 10. There are 4378 town areas in total. The Government of India population census report said there are 13 cities with one million populations. The major metropolitan cities are Bombay with 16.4 million populations, Kolkata with 10.9 million, Delhi with 8.4 million Chennai with 5.4 million, Hyderabad with 4.3 million and Bangalore with 4.1 million populations.

Table 20.2: Shows that Pattern of Urbanization and Growth of Urban Population across Major States in India 1971 to 2001.

S. No.	Name of the State	Percentage of Urban Population				Annual Exponential Growth Rate		
		1971	1981	1991	2001	1971-1981	1981-1991	1991-2001
1.	AndhraPradesh	19.31	28.25	26.84	27.08	3.94	3.55	1.37
2.	Bihar	07.97	09.84	10.40	10.47	4.27	2.66	2.57
3.	Gujarat	28.08	31.06	34.40	37.35	3.42	2.90	2.50
4.	Haryana	17.06	21.96	24.79	29.00	4.65	3.56	4.11
5.	Himachal Pradesh	06.99	7.72	8.70	9.79	3.02	3.11	2.01
6.	Karnataka	24.31	28.91	30.91	33.98	4.08	2.55	2.53
7.	Kreala	16.24	18.78	26.44	25.97	3.19	4.76	0.74
8.	Madhya Pradesh	18.58	22.34	25.27	26.67	4.25	3.63	2.71
9.	Maharashtra	31.17	36.03	38.73	42.40	3.35	3.27	2.95
10.	Manipur	13.17	26.44	27.69	23.88	9.70	2.98	1.21
11.	Meghalaya	14.55	18.03	18.69	19.63	4.87	3.10	3.16
12.	Orissa	8.41	11.82	13.43	14.97	5.21	3.08	2.61
13.	Punjab	23.73	27.72	29.72	33.95	3.62	2.55	3.19
14.	Rajasthan	17.63	20.93	22.88	23.38	4.52	3.31	2.71
15.	Tamilnadu	30.25	32.98	34.20	43.86	2.45	1.76	3.56
16.	Tripura	10.43	10.98	15.26	17.02	3.26	6.19	2.53
17.	Uttar Pradesh	14.02	18.01	19.89	20.78	4.78	3.27	2.84
18.	West Bengal	24.75	26.49	27.39	28.03	2.75	2.54	1.84
India		**19.91**	**23.33**	**25.72**	**27.78**	**3.79**	**3.09**	**2.73**

Source: Census of India 1981, 1991 and 2001 Reports.

DIMENSIONS OF URBAN POVERTY

Urban poverty and growth of slum population are founded by migration. Slums are visual manifestations of urban poverty. The U.N Habitual defines a slum hold as a group of individuals living under the same roof in an urban lacking one or more of the following: durable housing, sufficient living space, easy to access to adequate sanitation and security of tenure that forced evictions. India urban poverty report using human development frame work provides a good right on various of urban poverty such as basic services to urban poor, migration, urban economy and livelihoods, micro finance for urban poor, education health, unorganized sectors and livelihood. Incidence of poverty is more for rural-urban migrations. There is 25 per cent urban poverty in India. Poverty levels are higher in small towns than big cities. Between 1983, 2004-05 rural poor declined by 12.31 per cent while the urban poor increased by 89 per cent. Micro-finance to urban poor is 23 per cent only. Above 12 per cent total Indian towns have slum population 42.6 millions. It is projected that 40 per cent population would be urban in India by 2025. According to 2005 World Bank estimates 41.6 per cent of Indian population falls below international poverty line of us $ 1.25 a day. Planning commission accepted Tendulkar Committee report that 37 per cent living urban poverty line. 20 per cent people receiving 25 per cent of government expenditure on healthy 20 per cent receiving 15 per cent only the poor people.

Causes for Urban Poverty

As urbanization increases urban poverty is also growing Urban growth is result of the following factors:

- National increase in population.
- Net migration from rural areas to urban areas.
- Re classification of towns.
- Drought.
- Water laggings.
- population pressure and land fragmentation.
- Poor mountains and forest regions.
- Globalization.
- Other factors like life style, security etc attract people from rural areas.

In addition to this, different major factors caused for urbanization in different decades, which are given as follows:

Factors affecting urbanization in India

1901-11 – famine and plague

1911-21 – influence epidemic

1921-31 – agriculture depression

1931-41 – world war

1941-51 – partition and after effects

1951-61 – planned development

1961-71 – urbanization growth in backward areas

1971-81 – decentralized urban growth

1991-2001 – metropolitization

It is necessary to view urban poverty as distinct from rural poverty and not as more transfer of rural poverty into urban areas. NSSO 62nd reports also have shown that urban is growing than rural poverty.

CONSEQUENCES OF URBAN POVERTY

Urban poverty is hindrance to economic growth. Urbanization involves concerns with poor health and poor environment facility, high living densities, over crowded housing, hazardous and inadequate supply of clean water, sanitation, solid waste disposable, urban violence have grown by 3 to 5 per cent past decades. Urban poverty leads also proliferation of slum and busters, fast growth of informal sector, increasing casual labor, increasing pressure on civic services, increasing educational deprivation and health contingencies. Urban slums are characterized by high density of population, lack of protected water supply, lack of drainage and sanitation, low per capita income, low levels of literacy, malnutrition, high incidence of respiratory and gastoentic diseases. Due to the economic, social and psychological stresses in slum life are degraded, creates law and order problems, as well as political unrest.

PROGRAMMES TO ELIMINATE URBAN POVERTY

Urban Poverty Alleviation is a challenging task before the nation which calls for imaginative new approaches. The goal is to adequately feed, educate, house and employ the large and rapidly growing number of impoverished city dwellers. According to 2001 census the urban population has increased to 285 millions, which is nearly 28 per cent in the population The bulk of the urban poor are living in extremely deprived conditions with insufficient physical amenities like low-cost water supply, sanitation, sewerage, drainage, community centres and social services relating to health care, nutrition, pre-school and non formal education. A significant portion of the urban poor belongs to Scheduled Castes, Scheduled Tribes and minorities. The need of the hour is to improve the skills of the urban poor and to assist them to set up micro-enterprises thereby providing them avenues for enhancement of their incomes. Another major area for assistance to this target group is provision of funds for housing or shelter up gradation. The Dept. of Urban Employment and Poverty Alleviation is monitoring the implementation of four significant urban poverty alleviation programmes.

(i) The Nehru Rozgar Yojana.

(ii) The Urban Basic Services for the Poor.

(iii) The Environmental Improvement of Urban Slums.

(iv) Prime Minister's Integrated Urban Poverty Eradication Programme. A brief account of these schemes is given in the following paragraphs.

Nehru Rozgar Yojana

In response to the challenge posed by urban poverty, the Nehru Rozgar Yojana was launched by the Ministry in October, 1989. It was recast in March, 1990 and accordingly the guidelines were suitably revised. The entire expenditure on the Yojana is to be shared on a 60:40 basis by the Central and the State Government w.e.f. eight Plan.

The Yojana consists of three schemes:

- Scheme of Urban Micro Enterprises (SUME).
- Scheme of Housing and Shelter Up gradation (SHASU).
- Scheme of Urban Wage Employment (SUWE).

The Scheme of Urban Micro-Enterpriese (SUME)

The Scheme of Urban Micro-Enterprises (SUME) assists the urban poor in upgrading their skills and Setting-up self employment ventures. At present, the criterion of urban poverty is an annual household income less than Rs. 11,850. A subsidy is provided towards setting up the micro enterprises up to 25 per cent of the project cost with a ceiling of Rs. 5,000 for SC/ST/ Women beneficiaries and Rs. 4,000 for general beneficiaries. The remaining amount of the project cost is available from banks as a loan up to a maximum of Rs. 15,000 for SC/ST and Women beneficiaries and Rs. 12,000 for general category beneficiaries. This Scheme is applicable to all urban settlements. A large number of States have set up State Urban Development Agencies/ District Urban Development Agencies for streamlining the administrative mechanism for implementing the Nehru Rozgar Yojana.

The Scheme of Housing and Shelter up Gradation (SHASU)

The Scheme of Housing and Shelter Up gradation (SHASU) seeks to provide assistance for Housing and Shelter up gradation to economically weaker sections of the urban population as well as to provide opportunities for wage employment and up gradation of construction skills. A loan up to a ceiling of Rs. 9,950 and a subsidy up to a ceiling of Rs. 1,000 is provided under this scheme to entitled beneficiaries for housing/shelter up gradation. In case of enhanced financial requirement beyond Rs. 10,950 an additional loan up to Rs. 19,500 can be taken from HUDCO under its scheme for EWS Housing. This scheme is applicable to urban settlements having a population up to twenty lakhs. Requirements for institutional finance for the scheme are met by the Housing and Urban Development Corporation (HUDCO). The targets could not be achieved as the States are not coming forward with schemes to HUDCO due to post-sanction formalities like furnishing of State Guarantee etc. Urban Local Bodies are playing a significant role in the implementation of the Nehru Rozgar Yojana. They are involved in providing work places and selling-out lets to the beneficiaries, maintaining liaison with banks and ensuring provision of backward and forward linkages so that the micro-enterprises set up under the Scheme record stable growth. Non-Governmental Organizations (NGOs) are also expected to play a significant role in the implementation of the Nehru Rozgar Yojana especially in relation to training and strengthening backward-forward linkages under SUME, setting up Municipal Service Centres and craftsmen's guides under SUWE and Housing Corporation/Associations under SHASU. Thus, the Nehru Rozgar Yojana through activities aimed at skill up gradation, assistance for setting up micro-enterprises, wage opportunity through construction of public assets and assistance for shelter up gradation seeks to usher in a brighter future for the urban poor in India.*

The Scheme up Urban Wage Employment (SUWE)

The Scheme of Urban Wage Employment (SUWE) provides wage opportunities to the urban poor by utilizing their labour for construction of socially and economically useful public assets in the jurisdiction of Urban Local Bodies. A material-labour ratio of 60:40 is to be maintained under the Scheme for various public works aggregating at the district level. The minimum wages prevalent in each urban 'area are to be paid to the unskilled labour. This scheme is applicable to all urban areas with a population below one lakh.

Urban Basic Services for the Poor (UBSP)

The Urban Basic Service (UBS) Programme in India was initiated during the VIIth Five year Plan period for urban poverty alleviation. Based on the experience of implementing the UBS Programme and the Urbanisation, the Government revised it as Urban Basic Services for the Poor (UBSP) (1991) and integrated it with other urban poverty alleviation programme, namely, Environmental Improvement of Urban Slums (EIUS), Nehru Rozgar Yojana (NRY) and Low Cost Sanitation (LCS).The objective of UBSP is to create participatory community based structures through which community participate in identifying normative/felt needs, prioritize them and play a major role in planning, implementing, maintaining services and monitoring progress. One of the important features is to provide social services and physical amenities through convergence of various ongoing schemes of Ministry of Urban Affairs and Employment and various specialist departments like Health, Family Welfare, Women and Child Development, Education, Welfare Labour, Small Scale Industry, Non-conventional Energy Resources and Science and Technology. Such a convergent approach will lead to optimum utilization of scarce resources and help in successful implementation of various sectoral programme there by providing socials and vices and physical amenities to the urban poor. The urban poor residing in low income Neighbour hoods are the target groups for Provision of social services under the Scheme and physical amenities to be provided under the Environmental Improvement of Urban Slums (EIUS) Scheme. Urban poor residing contiguous to low income neighbor hoods slums would also be able to avail of the social services provided under the Scheme. Special emphasis is given to women and child beneficiaries.

NGO:-NGOs are increasingly becoming critical element in the UBSP programme. Within the UBS Pprogramme, NGOs are involved as Field Training Institute for city level training. At city level, NGOs conduct collaborative activities including community mobilisation, basic education, women's income generating and thrift societies and community nutrition etc., 344 Community Development Societies have been formed in 3455 slum pockets selected for coverage with 69228 Resident Community Volunteers.

The Scheme of Environmental Impovement of Urban Slums (EIUS)

The EIVS was formulated as a response to the growing problem of slums during the Fifth Five Year Plan. The scheme was made an internal part of the Minimum Needs Programme (MNP) in 1974 and was transferred to the State Sector. The scheme aims at ameliorating the living conditions of urban slums dwellers and envisages provision of drinking water, drainage, community baths, community latrines, widening and paving of existing lanes, street lighting and other community facilities.

Prime Minister's Integrated Urban Eradication Programme (PMI UDEP)

Recognizing the seriousness and complexity of urban poverty problems, especially in the small towns where the situation is more grave due to lack of resources for planning their environment and development, the Prime Minister had announced on 15th August, 1994 an integrated scheme for eradication of poverty known as Prime Minister's Integrated Urban Poverty Eradication Programme (PMI UPEP), which seeks to address the problems of urban poverty with a multi-pronged and long term strategy. The new strategy is to put the community structures in the centre with direct participation and control by the very groups who are envisaged to benefit from this programme. The programme launched in November 1995 is applicable to all Class II Urban Agglomerations (345Nos.) with a population ranging between 50,000 and one lakh as per 1991 Census, subject to the condition that election* to urban local bodies have been held there. The specific objectives under the new programme are:

(i) Effective achievement of social sector goals.

(ii) Community empowerment.

(iii) Convergence through sustainable support system.

(iv) Improvement of hygiene and sanitation.

(v) Employment generation and shelter up-gradation.

(vi) Environmental improvement.

The programme will be implemented on whole town/project basis extending the coverage to all the targeted groups for having visible impact and facilitating overall development of the towns to be covered. While the target group of the programme is urban poor, specially women beneficiaries and beneficiaries belonging to Scheduled Castes and Scheduled Tribes will constitute special target groups among the urban poor.

Beside the above programmes the Ministry of urban development has the following objectives.

Vision

An equitable and inclusive sustainable growth of towns and cities free from slum which provides dignity and a decent quality of life to all inhabitants in the urban areas.

Mission

The provision of affordable housing for all livelihood, shelter and basic civil services to all slum bevellers and poor in the urban areas.

Objectives

1. Implementation of national urban housing and habitat policy.
2. Slum development.
3. Slum free city programme for inclusive urban growth.
4. Promoting cost effective building technologies.
5. Eradication of dry latrines in the country.
6. Facilitating generation of employment and import skill training to urban poor.
7. Sharing information with public.

Functions

- Formulation of housing policy and programme and review of implementation of plan schemes.
- Human settlements include the UNHABITAT and intermation cooperation and technical assistance in the field of housing and human settlement.
- Urban development includes slum clearance schemes and jhuggi and *jhopri* removal schemes.
- Implementation of specific programmes of urban employment and urban poverty allivation including other programmes evolved from time to time.
- All matters relatives to the housing and urban development corporation other than those relating to urban infrastructure.

Jawaharlal Nehru National Urban Renovation Mission (JNNURM) was started on 3rd December 2005 for the development of urban areas. The mission adopted strategies which include formulation of prefecture day 20 25 years city development plan (CDP). This programmes has two sub missions *(i)* Urban infrastructure *(ii)* Basic service for urban poor (BSUP).

FACTORS RESPONSIBLE FOR FAILUREOF PROPER IMPLEMENTATION

For the elimination of urban poverty the governments have been implementing different programmes. Though there are some loopholes and defects in the implementation due to the following reasons:

1. Shortage of funds became an important factor.
2. Lack of trained and skilled staff for implementation.
3. Lack of coordination with different department in urban local bodies.
4. Lack of awareness about policies and programmes among urban poor.
5. Limited power to the urban local bodies.
6. Misuse of funds for other purposes.
7. Lack of cooperation among Local bodies and Urban development Authority.
8. Problems related to identification of urban poor and records related to slums.
9. Improper monitoring on implementation of programmes.
10. Lack of people's participation in the implementation of programmes.

ROLE OF NGOs AND VOLUNTARY ORGANISATIONS

For the elimination of poverty especially in urban areas the cooperation and coordination of Non-Government Organization and voluntary organizations is needed. In the following way they can help to eliminate poverty:

- They have to bring awareness among urban poor about government policies and programmes for poverty alleviation.
- By using Right to Information Act, the implementation progress of the policies will be opened to the public.
- They have to give proper report to government on urban slums and benefits for smooth implementation of programmes.
- They have to move to the court, if necessary, wherever implementation violates rule and regulations and involving illegal activities.
- Mobilization of public opinion to be done by the NGOs and Voluntary organizations regarding implementation of programmes.

- Monitoring has to be done by them and they have to encourage the people to participation in the implementation of the programmes.
- They have to participate in the review of the implementation and have to give appropriate suggestions to the government and local bodies.

MEASURES SUGGESTED FOR PROPER IMPLEMENTATION

The following measures are useful to reduce urban poverty:

- Proper implementation of land-use planning.
- Strict Implementation of Government regulations namely right to housing and land to urban poor.
- Proper drainage system and Construction of community toilets for the protection of public health.
- Public transport should be adopted to avoid form exploitation.
- Solar and bio-gas, and non-conventional energy need to be promoted for street lights as well as household needs for the protection of environment in urban areas.
- Economic reforms have observed the following are useful Market based solutions for slums, Increase in land and property prices, Urban land diverted to real estate projects and townships, Permits FDI to real estates, De regulation of land use zone conversion and Introduction of land management tools.
- Development a provision of water supply, sanitation, solid wastage management, road network connectivity, electricity, drainage system etc. in slum and system new initiates for improving the amenities.
- Public policy instruments are divided into two parts
  - *(i)* *Indirect instrument:-* those which use resources to accurate growth and there by impact on the incomes of the poor i.e. trickle down.
  - *(ii)* *Direct instrument:-* those roles on public provision of shelter, services and subsidies and other form of transfers.
- Decentralization of the following also helps in the given way
  - *(i)* ULB'S finance system strengths.
  - *(ii)* Fiscal relation with central and state.
  - *(iii)* Civil society local people enrolment in decision strategies.
  - *(iv)* System of accountability.

CONCLUSION

Urban growth is possible when poverty is reduced in urban areas. For the government the removal of urban poverty becomes major task. The programmes to be implemented very strictly. There is necessary to encourage the people to stay in the rural areas by developing rural areas. There should be review and revision of implementation of programmes always and has to take new steps for elimination of poverty in urban areas.

REFERENCES

Chandra Sekhar, S., Indira Gandhi Institute of Development Research, Mumbai June 2007).

Census of India 1981, 1991 and 2001 Reports.

Glaeser, Edward (Spring, 1998), "Are Cities Dying?", *The Journal of Economic Perspectives* 12 (2): 139–160.

Indian Urban Poverty Report, 2009.

Pathak, P. and Mehta, D., (1995), Recent Trend in Urbanisation and Rural-Urban Migration in India: Some Explanations and Projections, *Urban India,* Vol. 15, No.1, pp.1-11.

Premi, M. K., (1991): "India's Urban Scene and Its Future Implications", *Demography India.*

Registrar General, 2001, Census of India, 2001.

World Development Report, 2007.

Integrated Novel Development in Rural Areas and Model Municipal Areas

Housing for Poor—An Appraisal

Dr. C.Sheela Reddy and
Dr. V. Satish Reddy

INTRODUCTION

Housing is one of the basic necessities of human life, besides food and clothing. It is an important constituent of the quality of life. Lack of proper housing is considered an indication of social poverty. Majority of families in Afro-Asian countries live in semi-*pucca* or *kutcha* houses and India is no exception. The demand for housing has been tremendously increasing due to alarming rise in the population on one side and collapse of kutcha houses due to lack of proper maintenance and natural hazards on the other. Keeping in view the serious implications of the social poverty on the overall human development, the United Nation declared 1978 as the "International Year of Shelter for the Homeless". As a result many countries have considered housing as one of the prime concerns in their national agenda.

India being a welfare state has been making concerted planned efforts towards alleviation of economic and social poverty since the starting of the First Five year Plan. However, the commitment of both Central and State government to provide shelter for shelterless families has not been consistent due to lack of political commitment, seriousness over a period of time. Despite 63 years of Independence and over four decades of programmes for providing housing to poor, vast majority of the population live in substandard housing, exposed to the elements of nature. The interventions of the Government by providing housing unfortunately has not kept pace with the demand resulting in supply/demand imbalance. The absence of adequate surpluses in the rural economy for investment in the housing programme has not helped the matters much. With a view to resolve this issue, Government of Andhra Pradesh has mounted a major initiative named Integrated Novel Development in Rural areas and Model Municipal Areas (INDIRAMMA) starting in 2006-07. INDIRAMMA is aimed at achieving a slum-free and hut-free state of Andhra Pradesh in three year period. The underlining principle is to sanction a pucca house to all the rural households who are living in kutcha houses currently, irrespective of the caste, religion or political affiliation. There is no waiting list since everyone is covered. The programme aims at recognizing 'housing' as a basic right.

Housing is also an index of the socio–economic progress of a country. It is recognized as a productive activity, which stimulates employment and growth. It also provides the base for increased access to health, education, water supply and sanitation, especially for the poor and the vulnerable groups. Shelter is one of the fundamental needs of man. It is a geographical truth, which displays the intricate relation between man and his environment. This fundamental element not only protects its occupants from the vagaries of climate but also provides them a place where they reside, rest, educate and store the things. Further, the housing activity creates additional employment opportunities and also induces voluntary savings. In spite of the fact that it has multiplier effects on the improvement of quality of life, it is most neglected aspect in our country and perhaps the weakest link in our 60 years of planned development.

Government has been implementing many programmes over the years for development of infrastructure and on individual welfare. Since there is always a universal aspiration of all the people to be part of this developmental process, the impact of the programmes implemented so far is not quite visible due to the scattered nature of the distribution of the resources. Till the conceptualization of INDIRAMMA there was hardly any objective, equitable and verifiable criteria in selection of towns and villages while implementing the programmes. An *adhoc* allocation of money for various programmes was done instead of using village as a unit for integrated planning. Even while sanctioning programmes and welfare measures all the genuine requirements of the villages/towns were not being considered, resulting in dissatisfaction among the public. Thus the approach was open ended and not focused.

Keeping the above in view, Andhra Pradesh Government has taken a decision to take up development of model villages and towns with an intention to saturate certain identified basic needs of the people and the village/town infrastructure in an integrated and focused manner.

This new model of development is named as "INDIRAMMA" (Integrated Novel Development in Rural Areas and Model Municipal Areas) to fulfil the dreams of our former Prime Minister, Smt. Indira Gandhi. It was envisaged that such development model will ensure overall development of the Villages/Towns in a transparent manner covering additional areas every year. This process aimed to remove the uncertainty and skepticism in certain quarters with regard to coverage of all eligible beneficiaries and the infrastructure needs since all the villages/towns are covered over a period of three years.

This programme is being taken up in all the mandals simultaneously. It was decided that by taking up Gram Panchayats covering one third of the population in the mandal every year, all the Gram Panchayats will be covered over a period of three years. 8026 Gram Panchayat were selected for the first phase of the programme which started on 1st April 2006 and the remaining Gram Panchayat were be intended to covered during subsequent two years.

The tiny village in East Godavari district was named 'Indiramma Gramam' to mark the launching of the State Government's prestigious scheme 'Indiramma Pathakam' by the Chief Minister Y.S. Rajasekhara Reddy on 1st April 2006. Addressing a public meeting after the launching the scheme, Dr. Reddy said: "We are ready to beg or borrow to provide housing with all basic amenities for the people living below the poverty line in the next three years. We have decided to spend Rs. 9,000 crores every year on this scheme. Making a special mention about Rajahmundry M.P. Vundavalli Aruna Kumar, the Ex-Chief Minister said that the name of this scheme was coined by Mr. Aruna Kumar and they thought it was appropriate to name the scheme after great leader Indira Gandhi, who dreamt about a Welfare State.

INDIRAMMA is the flagship programme of Government of Andhra Pradesh to deliver a package of nine services like housing, pensions, drinking water, roads, elementary education, electricity, Integrated Child Development Scheme, health and sanitation to the rural and urban poor. The programme is implemented in $1/3^{rd}$ area of the State each year so as to achieve complete coverage of the State within 3 years. Housing is the most important component of INDIRAMMA, since it is a permanent, life-long asset. As per the census data, there were 47 lakh rural households and 13 lakh urban households without a permanent house in the State in 2006. The aim of Government is to ensure that all these households should be given a permanent house within 3 years. For this purpose, 1/3rd area of the State was taken up for coverage each year. Allotment of houses was done for all eligible poor households irrespective of the political affiliations. In case, a house site is needed, the same would be acquired and given at the cost of Government.

The programme called for increasing the annual physical targets almost 10 times from the average levels. The budgetary allocations in the State annual budget have been raised to Rs. 5,000 Cr each year during the programme implementation period. Even with these allocations, it was difficult to meet the demands imposed by the programme and therefore linkages were established with the financial institutions and the self-help groups to supplement the efforts of the government in implementing the programme.

IDENTIFIED ACTIVITIES UNDER INDIRAMMA

Housing For all

Every eligible houseless family shall be provided with house. BPL families living in thatched, semi permanent and rented houses will be covered. Incomplete and unoccupied houses of previous year programmes to be completed and brought under occupancy.

Beneficiaries will have to pay Rs. 220 per month towards loan repayment to make the programme sustainable, Gram Panchayats will educate the people to pay property tax and water tax on a regular basis to enable panchayats to provide better services on a sustainable manner.

Roads

Connectivity will be provided to all the Gram Panchayats through blacktop roads to ensure proper Bus facility.

Sanitation—Individual Sanitary Latrines (ISLs)

The Government aims at having individual sanitary latrines in all the houses of the villages Government will provide financial assistance in accordance with scheme guidelines to all the eligible people below the poverty line. For the others, the Gram Panchayats would undertake responsibility to encourage them to construct individual latrines. Massive awareness campaign would be taken up in each Gram Panchayats. Gram Panchayat will make every effort to encourage the entire village to achieve the open defecation free status. Permanent and *pucca* drainage system will be provided in all the selected villages.

Drinking Water

Government has formulated plans to provide drinking water to the villages where there is no potable water and where there is insufficient water. Quality affected (Fluoride) habitations will be taken up on priority. Government will take up schemes to provide 40 liters of potable water per head per day in all the habitations.

Electricity to Every Household

Government is giving top priority to the power sector which is key to the Rural Development and is committed to provide electricity to every house in every village.

Primary Education

Steps would be taken to ensure that all the children between 6 to 10 years of age go to School with special focus on girl child. It would be government's endeavor to completely eradicate the problem of drop outs. There would be one teacher for every 40 children ensuring their attendance compulsorily. Wherever necessary, additional class rooms will be constructed. Drinking water facilities and toilets will be provided in all the primary schools, child labour system will be totally eliminated.

Integrated Child Development Scheme

For every 1000 population (in the tribal areas for every 500 population) one Anganwadi Centre will be provided. *Pucca* buildings will be constructed in respect of all the Aanganwadi Centres. Additional nutrition will be given to all the pregnant and lactating women and to the children below 6 years for below poverty line families. Iron and folic acid tablets will be given to the teenage girls in such families. All the children between the ages of 3 to 6 years will be admitted in the pre primary school.

Health for All

Ensuring hundred per cent deliveries in the health care centres. All the deliveries will be registered. Creating awareness for prevention of diseases like malaria, diarrhoea and much dreaded HIV/AIDS. Strengthening of institutional setup to ensure better health care for the people is also part of the programme.

LIST OF DIFFERENT SCHEMES BEING IMPLEMENTED

All eligible BPL families are being provided with a house under INDIRAMMA Housing Scheme. The schemes that are covered under INDIRAMMA are Rural Permanent Housing including IAY and Housing for occupational groups like Beedi Workers, Weavers, Fishermen and Urban Permanent Housing including IHSDP, JNNURM and RGK.

Types of House

- *Rural Areas:* 200 sq ft area house to be constructed with a total assistance of Rs. 54,250 (Rs. 34,250 unit cost (Rs. 13,200 subsidy + Rs. 17,500 loan + Rs. 500 beneficiary contribution+Rs. 3,050 under ISL for latrine) Rs. 20,000 as bridge loan through Self-help groups.
- *Urban Areas*: 250 sq ft area to be constructed with a total assistance of Rs. 73, 000 (Rs. 43,000 unit cost (Rs. 6,000 subsidy + Rs. 35,000 loan + Rs. 2, 000 beneficiary contribution) Rs. 30,000 individual loan from the Banks.

Eligibility Criteria

Houses are being sanctioned in rural and urban areas in the state under INDIRAMMA housing programme only if the beneficiary falls in any of the following categories:

- Beneficiary living in *kutcha* houses as a single family.
- Beneficiary living in *kutcha* houses as a member of joint family.

- Beneficiary living as a single family in fully dilapidated semi permanent house constructed with government assistance before 1993-94.
- Beneficiary living as a member of joint family in fully dilapidated semi permanent house constructed with government assistance before 1993-94.
- Beneficiary living as a single family in fully dilapidated, own semi-permanent house constructed without any government assistance.
- Beneficiary living as a member of joint family in fully dilapidated, own semi- permanent house constructed without any government assistance.
- BPL families living in rented accommodation in urban areas.
- Beneficiary living as a member of joint family in Rural Permanent Housing or urban Permanent housing colonies constructed with government assistance during the earlier years.

WORKS TO BE UNDERTAKEN BY GRAM PANCHAYATS

Panchayats are also required to own responsibility to ensure effective maintenance of the roads and other infrastructure facilities going to be created under the scheme. There is a need to mobilize necessary resources to maintain these assets. Each gram Panchayat has to work efficiently to ensure this. They have to create awareness among the people to repay the loans taken under various schemes.

The following measures for creating infrastructural facilities in the village and its proper maintenance are taken up by gram Panchayat.

- Taking up sanitation works.
- Registration of births.
- Eradication of child labour system.
- Proper collection of house taxes, Water tax and other taxes to ensure sustainable development of the village.
- Identification of the beneficiaries by multi-departmental teams, which visited each and every household in March 2006.
- Sanctions were made in the name of the woman of the household Implementation by the beneficiary herself.
- No middlemen/no contractor.
- Transparency in selection.
- Names read out in Gram Sabha.
- List of beneficiaries placed on the web site.
- Systems for execution.
- Mandal level technical teams constituted with 5 members–(one Assistant Engineer, 4 outsourced work inspectors) 3 senior officers kept in charge of the programme in each.

- Weekly payment system to avoid delays.
- Village Information Agencies for close association with the village level functionaries.
- Disbursements through Banks or Village Organisation of Self-help Groups.
- Supply of nearly 35 lakh MTs of cement at subsidised prices by the cement companies (responding to an appeal issued by the State Government).
- Training of 38,000 rural youth in masonry.
- Establishment of 700 building centres to produce Fal-G bricks and eco-friendly building material required for the houses.

Overall Physical Progress

Twenty two lakh houses have been sanctioned at a cost of Rs. 5,444 Cr. As on 23rd January 2009, 13.50 lakh houses have been completed.

Indiramma Phase I (2006-07)

The Phase I of INDIRAMMA programme was started in 2006 (the actual construction has begun only by December 2006) in 8,026 Gram Panchayats and 1,317 municipal wards.

Indiramma Phase I (2007-08)

8,037 Gram Panchayat and 1,487 Municipal wards have been taken up for coverage under the Phase II programme. Under the Phase II programme, sanction has been given for 22.92 lakh houses at a total cost of Rs. 6418 crores in rural areas and 2.79 lakh houses have been sanctioned in the urban areas with a project cost of Rs. 1,117.31 crores till 23rd January 2009, 6.97 lakh houses have been completed.

Indiramma Phase III

The last phase of wards is being covered under the Phase III programme. The identification process has been completed. The improvements made under this phase are sanction of the house at the doorstep of the beneficiary by completing the entire documentation process in the village itself. The programme named Intinta INDIRAMMA has cut down the delays in sanction and the related ills. Till 2nd January 2009, 20.61 lakh beneficiaries are found eligible during Intinti INDIRAMMA and the online data entry is in progress. As on 23rd January 2009, 2.83 lakh houses are at basement level.

Implementation Arrangement Including Disbursement System

- Assistant Engineer visits all villages himself once a fortnight as per a pre-drawn Programme.

- Assistant Engineer calls for a Beneficiaries' Meeting after completing verification of houses. Announces the list/amount payable in the open.
- Pasted in the Gram Panchayat and one other public place. (Totally open system, public scrutiny).
- Deputy Executive Engineer proposes payment only after verification of the Beneficiary Meeting minutes.
- Disbursement only through individual accounts, Transition period of 45 days.
- Beneficiaries' pass books maintained and updated during his village/ward visits.
- Pay slips distributed in the village by AE (No middlemen in disbursement).
- All transfers using counseling system based on performance.
- Online payment system linked with internet banking system.
- Generation of payment orders at Sub-division level.

Financial Mechanism

The programme called for increasing the annual physical targets almost 10 times from the average levels. The budgetary allocations in the State annual budget have been raised to Rs. 5,000 crores each year during the programme implementation period in 2007 and 2008. However, the proposed unit cost being inadequate to enable completion of houses, linkages were established with the financial institutions and the self-help groups to supplement the efforts of the Government by providing Rs. 20,000 towards SHG bridge loan in rural areas and Rs 30,000 in urban areas in implementing the programme. Further, the Government have sanctioned additional loan of Rs. 20,000 in rural areas and Rs. 30,000 in urban areas to the SC/ST beneficiaries to support them in the endeavour to own their pucca house. Government of India has introduced a scheme, Interest Subsidy Scheme for Housing the Urban Poor (ISHUP) for providing five per cent interest subsidy on the bank loans up to Rs. 1.00 lakh for urban beneficiaries. The National Housing Bank (NHB) and Housing and Urban Development Corporation (HUDCO) will act as Nodal agencies. Government of Andhra Pradesh has appointed Andhra Pradesh State Housing Corporation Limited (APSHCL) as Nodal agency for implementation, motivation and organizing the beneficiaries under ISHUP. Service providers have been appointed to assist the banks and beneficiaries in completing the documentation for sanction of loans by banks.

Status of Urban Indiramma Housing

As on 30-04-2010, total houses registered under Indiramma scheme was 64.55 lakks. Out of them 30.49 lakh houses' construction were completed, 15.36 lakh houses were under progress and 18.69 lakhs houses are yet to be started.

CONCLUSION

INDIRAMMA is the innovative programme in the history of Government of Andhra Pradesh for providing basic amenities to urban and rural poor. The main objective of the programme to provide shelter to shelterless is by and large successful. The objective of the Government to empower women has become a reality by this programme by sanctioning houses in favour of them. In spite of some lacunae in implementation the objective of the State government to provide shelter is laudable and this programme has become role model to other states and it has become a land mark not only in the history of Andhra Pradesh but also in the country.

22

Impact of Urbanization on Housing

S. Vidyalatha and
K. Sujatha

INTRODUCTION

The twentieth century witnessed a rapid shift of population from rural to urban areas in most of the countries of the world. The growing concentration of the people in the urban areas is an obvious thing, which is visible in the urbanization trend throughout the world. Within the 50 years of development, the world has seen the manifold increase of urban population. A merely 13 per cent of the global population lived in urban areas in 1900, which increased to 29 per cent in 1950 and to about 50 per cent by the close of twentieth century (U.N. 2006). However, the pattern of urbanization is to be seen very unequal between the developed and developing countries. Majority of the population of developed countries lives in urban areas compared to the majority living in rural areas in the developing countries. On the other hand, most of the urban population of developing countries is concentrated in Asian and African countries. In Asia, most of the south Asia is more rural with lower levels of per capita income than others. Not surprisingly, therefore, the pace of urban change in the south Asian region has been relatively modest, yet urbanization presents enormous challenges due to extreme poverty and lack of urban services (Cohen 2004).

Urbanization is one of the greatest phenomena in the latter half of the 20th century. The current phase of development in India shows that the rate of urbanization will be much higher in the coming decades. With growing urbanization, there is immense pressure on existing civic amenities. Housing problem in India is very chronic, particularly among the low income and such other marginalized groups who are beyond the reach of the formal institutional agencies for hosing. According to the latest estimates, there will be a shortage of nearly 25 million houses in urban areas in the beginning of the Eleventh Plan. 97 per cent of this shortage is Low Income Group (LIG) and economically weaker sections of the society. Hence, there is need for a sustainable, equitable, humane and socially inclusive development plan which will involve and caller to housing and basic services to the economically weaker sections, urban poor and slum-dwellers in the country.

Lack of housing and civic facilities have led to the creation of slums and squatter settlements. Economic liberalization and the current growth rate have raised the expectations of the people in terms of better quality housing and improved services. The National Housing Policy as advocated by the Global shelter strategy seeks to facilitate provision of affordable shelter for all by creating an enabling environment for housing by the State public agencies. Food, clothing and housing are required in that order for fulfilling the aspirations of the people. The demand for housing increases due to growth of population, rapid pace of industrialization and urbanization.

In the big cities problem of housing has become a serious concern. The authorities are always failing in their efforts to meet the housing demands of the people. The shortage of houses leads to overcrowding; insanitary conditions and it result in slums. Problem regarding the drinking water, sanitation, living environment, transport and electricity remained the main issue for increased urbanization. The problem of quality living is vital among those. Specially, in the developing countries the housing problem are manifold and key factor in influencing quality living. In India, there are huge numbers of houseless. Besides, a great portion of population lives in non-livable houses. A major portion cannot even afford a formal house. Economic condition forces them to live in an inferior housing environment. The mainstream formal housing needs a faster production system of housing maintaining quality of houses and economy to overcome the huge shortage. Appropriate solution to provide affordable, socio-culturally acceptable and environment friendly faster housing continues to be a serious challenge to public as well as private housing providers.

Low-and middle-income countries are continuing to urbanize, but in only a few of these countries are the changing demographic realities being reflected in national poverty reduction strategies (Baker and Reichardt, 2007, Baker, 2008). India is one of the forward looking examples, and its experience may well prove to be instructive. Over the past five years, two sizable initiatives have been mounted in India to improve living conditions among poor city-dwellers. The Jawaharlal Nehru National Urban Renewal Mission (JNNURM) was launched in 2005 with the aim of ensuring that the poor benefit from basic services. A complementary programmes, termed the Urban Infrastructure Development Scheme for Small and Medium Towns, focuses on the often-neglected needs of secondary cities (Kundu, 2006). As these initiatives take shape and move to the intervention stage, their success will depend in no small part on the methods that are used to measure urban living standards, identify the urban poor, and monitor their progress.

In order to address the issue of housing shortage, the first urban area–specific housing policy titled the National Urban Housing and Habitat Policy (NUHHP) 2007 has been formulated, which was laid on both the Houses of Parliament on 07-12-2007. The Policy seeks to set in motion a process for providing "Affordable Housing for All", particularly for Economically Weaker Section (EWS) and the Low Income Group (LIG) through various types of public-private partnerships.

In India as in many other countries, the urban poverty line is the principal mechanism through which poverty is quantified. In this paper, we ask whether the official poverty definition in India gives sufficient attention to basic needs in urban housing. When the Indian poverty lines were worked into their current form in 1979, the procedure that was used was based on a nutritional norm, and it provided some assurance that households living at the poverty line would have the means to consume a minimally adequate level of calories (Government of India, 1979, 1993). But the definition left unresolved whether households officially classified as non-poor would have adequate resources on hand to meet their nonfood needs, whether in housing or in other dimensions of need.

METHODOLOGY

The present chapter is based on the secondary data pertaining to 10th five year plan documents, annual reports of Ministry of housing and urban poverty alleviation, Government of India and articles on urbanization impacts.

RESULTS AND DISCUSSIONS

Urban Housing Shortage in India

According to the latest estimates, there will be a shortage of nearly 25 million houses in urban areas in the beginning of the Eleventh Plan. 97 per cent of this shortage is in Low Income Group (LIG) and Economically Weaker Sections (EWS) of the society. Hence, there is need for a sustainable, equitable, humane and socially inclusive development plan which will involve and cater to housing and basic services to the Economically Weaker Sections, Urban Poor and Slum-Dwellers in the country.

Table 22.1 shows the urban housing shortage in India during 1961-2001. In the year 1961 only 3.6 million houses were in shortage, it has tremendously increased and doubled in 1981 and rippled in 2001. A major proportion, 10.6 million people are affected by housing shortage in India in the year 2001.

Table 22.1: Urban Housing Shortage in India During 1961-2001

Year	Housing Shortage in Millions
1961	3.6
1971	3.0
1981	7.0
1991	8.2
2001	10.6

Source: 10th Plan Document

Urban Housing Shortage by States

The State-wise picture shows that Maharashtra was having highest shortage (3.72 million, followed by Tamilnadu (2.82 millions) Uttar Pradesh (2.38 millions) and Andhra Pradesh (2.38 millions).

Table 22.2: Urban Housing Shortage in India by States 2007

States	Urban (in millions)
Andhra Pradesh	1.95
Arunachal Pradesh	0.02
Assam	0.31
Bihar	0.59
Chhattisgarh	0.36
Goa	0.07
Gujarat	1.66
Haryana	0.52
Himachal Pradesh	0.06
Jammu and Kashmir	0.18
Jharkhand	0.47
Karnataka	1.63
Kerala	0.76
Madhya Pradesh	1.29
Maharashtra	3.72
Manipur	0.05
Meghalaya	0.04
Mizoram	0.04
Nagaland	0.03
Orissa	0.50
Punjab	0.69

Contd..

States	Urban (in millions)
Rajasthan	1.00
Sikkim	0.01
Tamil Nadu	2.82
Tripura	0.06
Uttar Pradesh	2.38
Uttarakhand	0.18
West Bengal	2.04
A& N Islands	0.01
Chandigarh	0.08
Dadra & Nagar Haveli	0.01
Daman & Diu	0.01
Delhi	1.13
Lakshawdeep	0.00
Pondicherry	0.06
All India	**24.71**

Source: National Building Organization, Annual Report 2008-09.

Typology-wise Housing Shortage by 2007

The total shortage at the beginning of the XIth Plan has been estimated to be 24.71 million units, as can be seen from Table 22.3 and the quantum of *kutcha* houses that needed up-gradation is estimated to be 2.18 million.

Table 22.3: Typology-wise Housing Shortage by 2007

Housing shortage	As on 2007
Households (Mn)	66.30
Housing Stock (Mn)	58.83
Pucca	47.49
Semi-Pucca	09.16
Kutcha	02.18
Excess of HHs over Housing Stock (Mn) (1 – 2)	07.47
Congestion factor (%)	19.11
Congestion in Hhs. (Mn)	12.67
Obsolescence factor (%)	3.60
Obsolescence in Hhs. (Mn)	02.39
Up-gradation of Kutcha (Mn) (2.3)	02.18
Total Housing Shortage (3+8+10+11)	24.71

Housing Programmes for the Urban Poor

A number of specific programmes for the poor have included: slum up-gradation and redevelopment, land reservation for poor in new projects; sites and services; night shelters; Environmental Improvement of Urban Slums, EWS-LIG housing programmes, VAMBAY, Million Housing Programmes etc. Various states have their own housing specific programmes targeted towards the poor. To facilitate operationalisation of these programmes, institutional mechanisms were set up including Housing Boards and Development Authorities at state/city level. Housing and Urban Development Corporation (HUDCO) was setup in 1970 to make finance available at subsidized rates for housing programmes targeted towards the poor.

Subsidised Housing Programmes for the Poor

In the initial years of independence, ambitious housing programmes for the poor were launched. Under the Rental Housing Scheme, it was proposed to provide two-room houses to the poor on subsidized rent. Huge difference between the market price and rent payable by the allotted acted as an inducement to 'sell' the occupancy rights. Most such housing changed hands in the first few years itself. The programmes was not successful due to the high quantum of subsidy involved. Maintenance cost, which were to be borne by the Government were much higher than the rent. Many allottees defaulted even on the low rent payments. Unable to bear the heavy subsidy burden, the program was shelved and existing units were 'sold' to the occupants. Same was the fate of housing provided on ownership basis. It was realized that given the magnitude of housing problem, it will not be possible for the government is to provide subsidized housing to all the poor. The next set of programs hit upon cross-subsidization as the solution wherein the burden of subsidized housing for the poorer sections was to be borne by the middle and high income groups. The state governments initiated composite housing programs including housing for all income groups.

The Government of India has launched a variety of schemes like Million Housing Programmes, programmes linking poverty eradication with provision of housing situations would have been much worse in the absence of all these schemes. The situation however, is far from satisfactory as can be seen from the report of Housing Conditions in various government reports. The policy makers are still in search of a viable solution to provide Affordable Housing for all.

National Urban Housing and Habitat Policy, 2007

Housing being a State subject the NUHHP plays only an advisory role. Concrete steps to operationalize the policy are to be taken by the State governments. For the same reason the NUHHP does not put a time-frame to achieve the aims of Housing Policy. Setting the goal of Affordable Housing for all, the NUHHP, as noted above adopts dual policy. For the MIG-HIGs the suggestions include, among others, fiscal incentives (even though these fall in the domain of Central Government, no concrete suggestions have been made); development of innovative financial instruments like Mortgage based securities to increase flow of finance to the housing market; reform of rent control act, rationalization of stamp duties and promotion of rental housing. The section on Legal and Regulatory reforms lists sixteen reform areas to be taken up by the state governments.

Features of Policy

- Focus of the policy is on affordable urban housing with special emphasis on the urban poor.
- Role of housing and provision of basic services to the urban poor has been integrated into the objectives of the Jawaharlal Nehru Urban Renewal Mission (JNNURM).
- Special emphasis has been laid on Scheduled Castes/Tribes/Backward Classes/Minorities and empowerment of Women within the ambit of the urban poor.
- The policy focuses on a symbiotic development of rural and urban areas in line with the objectives of the 74th Constitution Amendment Act.
- Within the overarching goal of Affordable Housing for All, emphasis has been laid on urban planning, increase supply of land, use of spatial incentives like additional Floor Area Ratio (FAR), Transferable Development Rights, etc., increased flow of funds, healthy environment, effective solid waste management and use of renewal sources of energy.
- Encouraging integrated townships and Special Economic Zones 10-15 per cent of land in every new public/private housing projects or 20-25 per cent FAR, whichever is greater to be reserved for EWS/LIG Housing through appropriate spatial incentives?
- Private sector to be permitted land assembly within the purview of Master Plans. Action Plans for urban slum-dwellers and special package for cooperative housing, labor housing and employees housing is to be prepared.
- States to be advised to develop 10 years perspective plan for housing of EWS/LIG.
- Policy gives primacy to provision of shelter to urban poor at their present location or near their work place.
- Approach will be In-situ slum rehabilitation and Relocation will be considered only in specific cases.
- Micro-finance institutions to be promoted at state level to expedite flow of finances to urban poor.

- Use of proven cost effective technology and building materials to be encouraged to decrease the urban housing shortage.
- All States to be encouraged to develop a "Habitat Infrastructure Action Plan" for all cities with a population of over one lakh.

CONCLUSIONS

Housing cooperative societies and private sector will also be encouraged to participate in the housing activity in a big way provided a facilitating environment is created by the State Governments in the form of legal, administrative and fiscal reforms. The above study helps us to conclude that there is a need to study a fresh about the reasons for shortage of housing in India. At the same time, it focuses on the ad-hoc of the government from time-to-time. The main aspect of providing housing is acquiring the required land. The government does not have any policy to that effect as it is evident from the reports produced by its agencies and to see that the housing rights are realizable rights in India. The Government of India also needs both existing shortage as well as the new shortage arising out of development induced displacement. This paper also recognizes need for an advocacy movement in securing the right. The movement for homestead lands in AP also established the need for social audit in case of scheme where huge amount of investment is involved to see that the pilferage be minimized and to ensure the selection of genuine beneficiaries. A nationwide experience shows that all the schemes are formulated in a manner that those who already have a piece of land get the benefit of the schemes, which needs an urgent reconsideration if the country has to ensure the shelter for all.

REFERENCES

Cohen, B., (2004), "Urban Growth in Developing Countries: A Review of Current Trends and a Caution Regarding Existing Forecasts", *World Development*, Vol. 32, No. 1, pp. 23–51.

Census India, 2001.

Kothari, Janya, *Right to Housing; Constitutional Perspectives from India and South Africa*, Lawyers Collective, June, 2001.

Roy, Ar. Uttam K., Dr. Madhumita Roy, Prof. Subir Saha, *Mass-Industrialized Housing to Combat Consistent Housing Shortage in Developing Countries: Towards an Appropriate System for India.*

Satterth, Waite, (2004) for an Overview of Urban Poverty Lines and Bapat (2009) for an *Insightful Account of the Debates Surrounding these lines in India.*

United Nations, (2006) *World Urbanization Prospects*: The 2005 Revision, Population Division, UN, New York.

Veeraiah, Konduri, *Right to Housing: Context and Trends in Contemporary Debates: Struggle for Homestead land in Andhra Pradesh*, November 23, 2009.

Housing Situation in India
A Study on Policies and Programmes

Dr. M. Reddi Ramu

INTRODUCTION

Food, shelter and clothing are the basic requirement of human beings. Shelter here refers to 'a house'. Hence, a house is a fundamental need of human beings, "The type of house in the beginning was highly controlled by natural factors and materials available in the nearby areas".[1] Thus, "a house is shelter and protection and provides for many of the physical, biological, social and aesthetic processes, necessary to sustain life".[2]

IMPORTANCE OF HOUSING

Proper housing is necessary in a community, if the level of health is to remain high. Bad dwellings also lead to deterioration of health of their unfortunate inmates.[3] Rajkumari Amrit Kaur, the Hon'ble Health Minister, while referring to the general question of health, said in Parliament on 1st July, 1952, "Our problem is how to bring health. We cannot have health unless there is a food, unless there is communication and unless there is housing".[4] Living in the compared quarters results in nervous strain and is an enemy of health of family life.

Housing and health are closely linked and they have direct influence on efficiency. Dr. B.K. Mehta had rightly observed that the problem of physical health and physical fitness for national efficiency are inseparably linked with the problem of housing. Bad housing has a negative effect on education, which ultimately affects the efficiency of future working force. Because of lack of privacy and proper ventilation and lighting, it is impossible for students to study in bad houses.[5]

Far more than being a shelter, the term 'Housing' has acquired a wider connotation because of the significant role it plays in shaping the life style of the individual and molding the future of the society. Thus, it sets in motion a spiraling multiplier effect on the socio-economic condition and cultural development of a country.[6]

The housing sector is one of the key components of the urban economy, where the bulk of housing investment takes place. Combining housing investment and housing services, the share of Gross National Product originating in the sector is usually between about 6 to 15 per cent. The housing sector is thus a key economic sector and must therefore be perceived and managed as an integral part of overall economic management.

HOUSING SITUATION IN THIRD-WORLD

The Third-world countries are characterized by a large section of the population still deprived of the basic necessities of life. However, housing is a global problem. The advance made by even the advanced countries in meeting this basic necessity is far from satisfactory. Neither the capitalist U.S.A. nor the communist U.S.S.R. could solve this basic problem. As Charles Abrams succinctly puts it, "housing programme lags far behind industrial progress in every part of the world".[7] The technical progress that broke the secrets of speed, sound, space and light still cannot build a house cheap enough for the rank and file. While a Soviet Cosmonaut can orbit the world, the state that launched him cannot establish a good housing programme on the ground. A Negro labourer's family in New York and a squatter in Caracas may both have television sets, but neither can afford a decent house.[8]

Indian scenario is not different from one, prevailing in most of the developing countries in Asia, Africa and Latin America. The picture is abysmally dismal at the lower end of the economic ladders. According to UN estimates, over 33 per cent of the population in less developed countries is homeless. Unfortunately, in a great majority of developing countries, housing is too often perceived by Governments solely as a welfare issue, requiring the transfer of physical or financial resources to low income households unable to house themselves adequately. Available resources, however, are rarely inadequate. As a result, Government Housing Agencies limit their beneficiaries, ignoring the interests of most of the population. By focussing on a small and limited housing agenda, these agencies fail either to perceive or manage the housing sector as a whole.

Housing Problem

In India, housing is a necessity shading into a luxury. Its supply does not fully meet the present needs of the Indian population, whether in terms of location, size, tenure, type or facilities due to inadequate attention having been paid to this important sector.

Housing problem is a global problem. The task of achieving the goal of "Shelter for All" is a gigantic one. The housing problem in India has assumed alarming proportions. In India, the housing situation differs widely from state to state and from region to region. While the housing problem in rural areas by and large is qualitative in nature, the problem in urban areas is largely quantitative.

Therefore a multi-pronged approach along with people's participation appears to be right answer to overcome this gigantic problem. On the one hand it call for a massive reconstruction programme for repairs and renovations of millions of housing units in rural and urban areas and on the other, there is a need for undertaking people's housing programme to meet the additional requirements.

Urban Housing Problems

The fundamental changes in man's social, political and economic environment, accompanying the massive population, shift from rural-traditional to urban societies lie at the root of the urbanization problem.

The fact that urban population in developing countries is growing at more than double (in some countries as high as three or four times). The overall rate would probably be in itself enough to destroy the previous equilibrium. But the resulting problem is not merely a product of simple proportion ratio. The corollary, of course, is that since there probably never was sufficient capital available for these purposes in the existing urban centres, the pressures were greatly intensified by the double demands of large population inflow and post war industrialization.

Rural Housing Problem

According to 1991 census, nearly three-fourths of country's population lives in rural areas. It has often argued that the slum problems resulting from a shift of population from villages to cities cannot be solved without ameliorating living conditions.

Problem of rural housing is enormous in magnitude and complex in nature. It differs significantly from the housing problem in urban areas. The perception and the need of villagers regarding housing, perhaps differ significantly from the urban dwellers. Even the big spacious houses of the rich, lack these necessities and as a result, nearly 95 per cent of rural houses do not have attached toilets and latrines.

Need for Housing

Most human settlements in developing countries reflect poverty and squalor population implying that their struggle for food, shelter and clothing has not yet came to an end. To ensure dignity of individual and to preserve the living quality of the family, basic amenities and residential privacy are essential.

Today, we find millions of people living in human conditions. Indecent, unclean, and inhuman living conditions seriously affect and endanger both physical and mental health of individuals. Many social problems particularly in the third world countries, emanates possibly from poor living conditions. If the nations are to progress, it is essential that a confirming habitat in proper surroundings with minimum basic amenities like drinking water and sewage are made available to every citizen.

'Housing Need' has been defined as "the extent to which the quality and quality of the existing accommodation falls short of that, required to provide each household or person in the population, irrespective of the ability to pay, or particular personal preferences with accommodation of a specific minimum standard and above".[9] 'Housing Demand' on the other hand is an economic concept which implies the ability to pay for the house. The concept of 'Housing Shortage' is essentially linked with the concept of housing need. To bridge gap between housing need and housing demand, Government often intervenes through provision of subsidized housing solutions that would enable the housing need to be merged into effective housing demand.

The need for housing depends upon the number of households at a particular time. If one house per household is considered as a norm, the total housing need would be equal to the number of households. We would like to distinguish between a family and a household. "A family is a biological unit while is an economic unit. A family may consist of married couple, a grandfather and/or a grand child, and a grandma and a child. Thus a family is two or more persons living in the same household who are related by blood, marriage, or adoption".[10]

HOUSING SITUATION IN INDIA

1. The National Sample Survey Organisation (NSSO) in the Ministry of Statistics and Programme Implementation, Government of India, has released the first report of a nationwide household survey carried out by it during July 2002-December 2002 on housing conditions in India. A sample of 97,882 households spread over 4,769 villages and 3,538 urban blocks in the country had been surveyed to obtain information regarding the conditions of the dwellings in which the rural and urban population of the country live and the number, size, structure, cost and financing of residential constructions undertaken by the households.
2. The survey reveals that out of every 100 households in rural areas, 36 lived in *pucca* structures, 43 lived in *semi-pucca* structures, and the remaining 21 in *kutcha* structures. In urban areas 77 in every 100 households lived in *pucca* structures, 20 in *semi-pucca* structures and only 3 in *kutcha* structures. In urban slum areas, 67 per cent of the dwellings were *pucca*. Rural areas of Delhi and Haryana, urban slums in Mizoram,

Himachal Pradesh, Punjab and Haryana, and urban areas (excluding the slums and squatter settlements) of Sikkim, Delhi, Uttarakhand, Jammu and Kashmir and Gujarat reported the prevalence of more *pucca* structures than the rest of the country. The States of Tripura, Manipur and Chhattisgarh where found to be well below the national average in terms of prevalence of *pucca* structures.

3. The floor area available to the average rural household was 38 square metres while the average urban household had 37 square metres. This survey also reveals that the average household size in rural areas was 5.15 and in urban areas 4.47.
4. Nineteen out of every 100 structures in the rural areas and 11 in the urban areas were in bad condition and required immediate major repair.
5. Ninety two per cent of rural households and 60 per cent of urban households owned the dwelling units.
6. As for the facilities of drinking water, latrine and electricity for lighting, about 15 per cent of the dwellings in urban slums and squatter settlements, 63 per cent of dwelling units in other urban areas, and 11 per cent of the units in rural areas had all the three facilities within their premises. At the other extreme, none of the three facilities were available within the premises of about 30 per cent of dwelling units in rural areas, 11 per cent of dwelling units in urban slums and squatter settlements, and 4 per cent of dwelling units in other urban areas of the country.
7. About 97 per cent of rural and 99 per cent of urban dwellings had drinking water within half a kilometer of their premises.
8. Residents of around 76 per cent of rural and 18 per cent of urban dwellings did not have access to any latrine facility. Considering both rural and urban areas together, the percentage of households lacking this facility was highest in Chhattisgarh (82%), followed by Orissa (80%), Bihar (79%), Madhya Pradesh (77%), Jharkhand (76%), Rajasthan (72%), and Uttar Pradesh (72%).
9. About 25 per cent of all rural households and 1 in 7 urban households had undertaken some construction activity during the last 5 years. In rural areas, 41 million constructions had been initiated and 34 million completed, while in urban areas, 8.5 million constructions had been initiated and 7.2 million completed during this 5-year period. Eight million constructions had been initiated and completed in U.P. alone, followed by West Bengal (4.8 million), Tamil Nadu (4.7 million), Andhra Pradesh (4.1 million), Maharashtra (3.1 million) and Bihar (3.1 million). A similar NSS survey carried out 9 years earlier (1993) had collected data on constructions completed during the 5-year period 1989-1993. It is seen that the number of completed constructions during the 5-year

period 1989-93 was only about half the number initiated and completed during 1998-2002 in both rural areas (17.5 million against 34 million) and urban areas (3.6 million against 7.2 million). Comparison with the earlier survey also shows a fall in the percentage of *kutcha* constructions in rural India from 45 per cent to 40 per cent and a rise in the percentage of pucca constructions from 34 per cent to 38 per cent. In urban India, there was a fall in *kutcha* constructions from 18 per cent during 1989-93 to 12 per cent during 1998-2002 and a rise in *pucca* constructions from 64 per cent to 74 per cent.

10. On an average, a rural household spent about Rs. 1.13 lakhs to construct a new *pucca* house, which had an average floor area of 42 sq.m., and about Rs. 21,000 to alter or repair a *pucca* structure, which on an average involved 29 sq.m., of floor area. Households living in urban areas other than the slums, on an average, spent about Rs. 2.63 lakhs to build a new pucca dwelling unit, which had an average floor area of 53 sq.m. In urban slums, it cost about Rs. 80,000 to build a new pucca house and the average floor area was 24 sq.m.
11. About 72 per cent of expenditure on residential construction by households was on materials alone. Another 21 per cent was spent on labour.
12. Rural households financed around 66 per cent, and urban households, 62 per cent of their construction cost from their own sources. In urban slums and squatter settlements, moneylenders financed 15 per cent of all construction costs. However, in other urban areas, moneylenders financed only 4 per cent of the total construction costs. In the rural areas, moneylenders financed 9 per cent of all construction costs.

Future Projections of Housing

An additional 17.1 million units had to be brought into the housing market during 1997-2001, 32.3 million units during 2001 to 2011 and 90.7 million additional units during 2011 to 2021. The SDS estimates show that over the next 20 years the housing requirement in terms of new stock would be 140.1 million units, of which 63.1 million units or 45 per cent would be in the rural areas and 77 million units in the urban areas. The past production track record suggests that the projected housing need in terms of new units, can be met with appropriate policy initiatives. An annual production of 5.6 million units will be required as against the actual attainment of 3.4 million units per annum during 1981-91 when the housing development environment and delivery system was not as developed are conducive to housing activities as is likely to be over the next 25 years. The major problem is "of clearing the backlog of up-gradation and renewal of the existing housing stock". Table 23.1 shows the estimates on the projected housing needs over a period of 22 years.

Table 23.1: Housing Needs and Investment in India Over a Period of 25 Years (in millions)

Particulars	1997-2001			2001-2011			2011-2021		
	Total	Rural	Urban	Total	Rural	Urban	Total	Rural	Urban
1. Housing Need (Million numbers)									
a. Population	1022.1	703.2	318.9	1164.3	738.5	425.8	1545.4	927.2	618.2
b. Housing demand	191.2	130.0	61.2	223.5	140.5	83.0	314.2	185.4	128.8
c. Housing stock	174.1	122.3	51.8	191.2	130.0	61.2	223.5	140.5	830.0
d. New Housing	17.1	7.7	9.4	32.3	10.5	21.8	90.7	49.9	45.8
e. Inadequate Housing	11.4	8.7	2.7	—	—	—	—	—	—
f. Up gradation	16.0	11.2	4.8	—	—	—	—	—	—
2. Investment Requirement (Rs. in Billion at 1995 prices)									
a. New	803.2	181.9	621.3	1688.8	248.0	1440.8	4087.7	1060.6	3027.1
b. Inadequate	166.5	104.4	62.1	—	—	—	—	—	—
c. Upgradation	244.8	134.4	110.4	—	—	—	—	—	—

Source: SDS Estimates, Government of India 1996, Habitat II, India National Report.

The population projections for 2001 and 2011 are as given in the Eighth Five-year Plan and those for 2021 or SDS estimates are based on past trends on in population growth rates. Urbanization rate is 31.3 36.0 and 40.0 per cent during these three periods.

Housing demand represents the number of households, estimated on the basis of household size. Investment estimates at 1995 prices are based on NSSO 44th round data on the cost of construction adjusted for 1995 prices.

Inadequate housing covers the congestion demand and upgradation includes replacement. These estimates are of estimated backlog as in 1995-1996 and the activity would be taken up in the next 5-10 years.

Per unit cost at 1995 prices for new housing is Rs. 23, 621 in rural areas and Rs.66, 094 in urban areas. Inadequate the upgradation housing estimates are based on cost at 50 per cent in rural areas and 35 per cent in urban area (Rs.12, 000 and Rs. 23000).

Housing Shortage

Housing shortage, in a statistical sense, is to be calculated on the basis of number of houses and households. It can also be conceived as a measure of inadequacy or otherwise, of the existing provision in the light of a "socially acceptable norm". Hence, housing shortage is gap between the total demand and the total stock of houses. Housing shortage may arise owing to many reasons; the trend of population growth, internal and external movement of population, changes in families and household structures, lack of supply of sufficient number of residential units because of scarcity of financial and material resources etc. are the most obvious reasons. Replacement of housing is also needed because of demolition of old structures or slum clearance or disasters like floods etc. to reduce the housing mortgage. Hence, while calculating the housing shortage, the following aspects are to be considered:

- Growth of population.
- Replacement of old structures.
- Dwelling units, inclusive of shop-cum-houses and workshop-com-houses.
- Availability of pucca, kutcha serviceable kutcha and unserviceable kutcha houses, of which the last category has been excluded from the supply or residential units.

In all the estimates of housing shortage, the housing stock taken as acceptable standard for habitation is the crucial element that determines the magnitude of the shortage.

All these factors have led to the growth of housing shortage, which is basically the excess of households over useable housing stock. Defined this, the estimated shortage was 15.2 million units in 1961, of which 75.6 per cent was in the rural areas. The housing shortage including congestion is estimated to be 41 million units in 2001, of which 62 per cent fall in rural areas and 38 per cent in urban areas. 61.2 per cent by 2001 (except in the year 1971).

But the shortage in urban areas is estimated to increase from 24.4 per cent in 1961 to 38.8 per cent by 2001, whereas the rate of fall in rural areas is 14.4 per cent as shown in Table 23.2.

Table 23.2: Housing Shortage-Rural and Urban Proportions (shortage in millions)

Year	Housing Shortage	Rural (% of Col.2)	Urban (% of Col.2)
(1)	(2)	(3)	(4)
1961	15.2	75.6	24.4
1971	14.6	80.0	20.0
1981	23.3	70.0	30.0
1991	31.0	66.5	33.5
2001	41.0	61.2	38.8

Source: Assessment of Housing Need, V.D.Lall, National Housing Seminar, October 7-9, 1996, page 18.

Qualitative Dimensions of Housing Situation in India

Housing problem will not be solved by building a few million shelters, without giving due importance to qualitative aspect. Quality of housing in India is unfortunately very poor. We have already seen that the objective of the Constitution of India is "to secure social, economic, political justice to all" when about five per cent of the people live in palaces, or handsome buildings equipped with all modern amenities, and more than 55 per cent live in slums, it cannot be said that justice, social and economic prevail on the land. Slums are known as *Zavili* and *Chawla* in Bombay, *Bustees* in Calcutta, *Ahatas* in Kanpoor, *Cheries* in Maharashtra, *Dhowras* in Cole mine areas and *Jhuggy-Jhoperies* in Delhi. Because of the increasing trend of urbanization and demand for cheap accommodation by migrants, slums have come up in big cities and towns.

There has been a tendency for more *pucca* houses to be built in urban areas. In rural areas, besides growth in housing stock being inadequate, it was also adequately inferior. This brings into sharp focus, the need to remedy the condition of rural housing. However, Government programmes like Indira Awas Yojana and Rural House-Sites and Construction Assistance Schemes for rural landless workers and artisans have contributed to improved housing situation. The total number of houses recorded to be nearly 250 million by 2001 (vide Table 23.3) in India.

Table 23.3: Housing Stock Over a Period of 50 Years, 1961 to 2001

S. No.	Year	No. of Houses (in Millions)
1.	1961	79.3
2.	1971	93.0
3.	1981	116.7
4.	1991	161.4
5.	2001	249.09

Source: 1. NBH Report on Tend and Progress of Housing in India 1993, p.6.
2. Census 2001.

As per the 2001 census the total number of houses there were nearly 250 million houses; of which 91 per cent have been occupied and 9 per cent of them recorded as vacant houses.

Uses of Occupied Houses

Slightly over 77 per cent of the houses enlisted under residences followed by 12 per cent of the houses treated as "Shop, Office", while 3.7 per cent of the residences put to use under the category of "Residence-com-Other Use", (Table 23.4).

It is significant to observe nearly two per cent of the houses were put to use for "Factory, Workshop, Workshed," etc.

Table 23.4: Houses and the Uses to Which they Are put to in 2001

S. No.		Total	%	Rural	%	Urban	%
A	Number of census houses	249,095,869	100.0	177,537,513	71.3	71,558,356	28.7
A. 1	Vacant census houses	15,811,192	6.3	9,359,172	5.3	6,452,020	9.0
A. 2	Occupied census houses	233,284,677	93.7	168,178,341	94.7	65,106,336	91.0
B	Uses of occupied houses						
B. 1	Residence	179,275,605	76.8	129,052,642	76.7	50,222,963	77.1
B. 2	Residence-Com-other use	7,886,567	3.4	5,046,812	3.6	1,839,755	3.7
B. 3	Shop, Office	13,390,292	5.7	5,566,717	3.3	7,823,575	12.0
B. 4	School, College etc	1,502,353	0.6	1,229,122	0.7	273,231	0.4
B. 5	Hotel, Lodge, Guest House, etc.	521,598	0.2	266,963	0.2	254,635	0.4
B. 6	Hospital, Dispensary, etc.	603,897	0.3	340,293	0.2	263,604	0.4
B. 7	Factory, Workshop, Workshed, etc	2,210,912	0.9	986,629	0.6	1,224,283	1.9
B. 8	Place of worship	2,398,650	1.0	1,982,515	1.2	416,135	0.6
B 9	Other non-residential use	25,494,803	10.9	22,706,648	17.5	2,788,155	4.3

Source: Census of India, 2001 Office of the Registrar General, India.

It is significant to note that less than 1 per cent of the total houses have been utilized for each one of the following categories:

B.4 School, College, etc.;

B.5 Hotel, Lodge, Guest House, etc.;

B.6 Hospital, Dispensary, etc.;

B.8 Place of Worship,

More than four per cent of the total houses have been put to use for other than non-residential use.

HOUSING POLICIES IN INDIA

An attempt has been made here to briefly state and analyse the housing policy of the government of India. As the policies of the state governments are largely moulded by the policy of the central government and as most of the housing schemes implemented by the states are subsidised by the government of India, housing policy of the state government such as, A.P. is not separately discussed. And, the states are involved in the process of discussion and finalisation of the national housing policy. With this backdrop we now move to trace the origin of housing policy.

Genesis of Housing Policies

The housing policies of the developing world may be broadly categorised into three types.[11] The first group of countries tried to emulate the developed world in terms of financial intervention in the housing market. This was executed by increasing and enlarging the existing mortgage lending and by guaranteeing the loans provided by commercial banks. Specialised banks for housing finance were started in these countries. In the second group of countries, the housing policy has been skillfully integrated with the overall developmental policies of the government. These countries successfully managed to combine their housing policies with overall economic policies of their countries. The third set of countries (mostly African) adapted their housing policies in relation to their economic and fiscal capacity. The governments of these countries realised that a vast gap existed between workers income and social housing programmes.

The First National Housing Policy, 1994

The UN General Assembly proclaimed 1987 as the International Year of Shelter to Homeless. The draft National Housing Policy (NHP) after presenting to the parliament and discussions at various levels, was finally approved in 1994. After 40 years of experimentation with many price-meal individual housing programmes, India attempted to combine all these past experiences to bring out a comprehensive policy encompassing the policies of the developing and developed world. Although India has not followed the middle class based housing policy directly in the new policy, the Indian government's endeavour has been to reduce the cost of financing housing construction. This is followed by statement of objectives and priorities.

The important aims of the policy are:

- To help every family to own an affordable shelter by the year 2001.
- To motivate and help all the people, and in particular the houseless, to secure affordable shelter through access to land, materials, technology and finance. In brief, it aims at encouraging people to build and improve their own houses.
- To promote repairs, renovation, expansion and upgradation of the existing housing stock.
- To preserve India's rich and ancient heritage in the field of human settlement, planning and architecture.

New Housing and Habitat Policy, 1998

The new economic reforms of 1990s have show altogether a new policy approach to the government. The government decided to move away from its role of direct provider to enabler and facilitator of housing. The shift in the policy encourages private and cooperative sectors to play a major role in housing, modifying the existing legal and regulatory regime. Keeping this fact in mind, the government of India adopted a new Housing and Habitat Policy. It was approved by the cabinet in 1998.[12] One of its objectives, as in the 1994 policy, is to provide shelter to all, especially to the poor and the deprived. It proposes construction of two million additional houses each year. The 10th Five-year Plan admits that the goal of shelter for all could not be achieved by 2001. It says that the time has come to ensure that the goal of shelter to all is achieved by the end of 11th Five Year Plan.[13]

The state governments are required to liberalised regulations, encouraged private and cooperative sectors and assist in training of the construction workers. It suggests that banks to earmark 1.5 per cent of deposits to housing. It recommends for the creation of national children fund. Finally, it suggests the NHP and HUDCO to lead in assets securitisation.[14]

HOUSING SCHEMES AND PROGRAMMES DURING THE PLAN PERIOD

The Five-year Plans were reared to meet the housing problem in India the following housing programmes have been announced and implemented by the governments. It may be noted that actual execution of the housing programmes and construction of houses are carried by the State governments. The latter, through housing Corporations and Boards, undertake construction of houses for weaker sections and also develop plots and sell constructed houses to any class of people, irrespective of the fact whether the schemes are evolved and financed by the union or state governments. In what follows we briefly state housing schemes and programmes announced during successive Five-year Plans.

The First Five Year Plan; targeted to providing housing facility to the following:

(i) Integrated subsidised Housing Scheme for industrial workers and economically weaker sections of the community-1952.

(ii) Low Income Group Housing Scheme-1954.

The Second Plan

(i) Subsidised Housing scheme for plantation workers-1956.

(ii) Slum Clearance and Improvement scheme-1956.

(iii) Village Housing Project Scheme-1957

(iv) Rural Housing Scheme for state government employees-1959.

(v) Middle Income Group Housing Scheme-1959.

(iv) Land Acquisition and Development Scheme-1959.

The Fourth Plan

(i) House Sites and Landless Workers in Rural Areas-1971.

(ii) Rural House Sites Programme-1972-73.

The Fifth Plan; Construction of houses as part of Minimum Needs Programme, (MNP).

The Sixth Plan; Sites and Services Programme-1983.

The Seventh Plan; Indira Awas Yojana (IAY)-1985-86.

The Ninth Plan;

(i) Additional Centre Assistance (Special Action Plan) under Basic Minimum Services.

(ii) Golden Jubilee Rural Housing Finance Scheme-1997-98.

(iii) Innovative Stream for Rural Housing and Habitat Development (A Pilot scheme under IAY for Below Poverty Line households)-1998-99.

Another scheme introduced in the Ninth Plan was Credit cum Subsidy Scheme. As IAY is for Below Poverty Line households, to benefit a segment of the weaker sections with incomes up to Rs. 32,000 p.a., in the 1998-99 Union Budget, the Finance Minister announced Credit cum Subsidy Scheme was launched as a sub scheme of IAY[15] (however, from 2002-03 it is a component of IAY). It may be noted that Rs, 32,000 income p.a. represents twice the level of income of Below Poverty Line. Under the scheme, the unit cost is the same as under normal IAY. Its subsidy and loan components are 50:50.

INSTITUTIONAL SETUP FOR PROMOTION OF HOUSING TO THE WEAKER SECTIONS IN THE COUNTRY

Housing and Urban Development Corporation (HUDCO):

HUDCO was set up in April 1970 and is fully owned by government of India which initially contributed Rs. 2 crores to its equity. It is a technofinancial institution which undertakes and accelerates residential construction activity. It also aims at setting up building material centres, popularly known as Nirmith Kendras. Its other aims are to develop new townships, provide infrastructure in rural and urban areas and to extend consultancy services for housing urban development. Its share in the total institutional finance is around 15 per cent. For along time it remained a financier of urban development and housing. Recently it earmarked 15 per cent of its funds to rural housing.

It has a number of schemes to meet the needs of different income categories such as, economically weaker sections, low, middle and higher income groups. HUDCO's rural housing scheme consists of loan and grant components. It provides loans at concessional rate of interest to economically weaker sections and low income groups. A major boost to its rural housing programme was given in the 9th Five-year Plan. During 1997-2002, it sanctioned about 800 schemes to construct 51 lakh dwelling units at the total cost of nearly Rs. 4000 crores.[16] Among six states, A.P. is one of the states which took advantage of the scheme.

Two Million Housing Programme

Housing is a State subject. The National Housing and Habitat Policy 1998 focuses on Housing for All as a priority area, with particular stress on the needs of the Economically Weaker sections and Low Income Group category. This programme, envisages to facilitating construction of 20 lakh additional units every year. Out of which 7 lakh would be taken up for construction in urban areas and 13 lakh houses would be taken up for construction in rural areas. HUDCO is to meet the target of 4 lakh dwelling units in urban areas and 6 lakh dwelling units in rural areas annually. The target of 2 lakh dwelling units in urban areas is to be met by Housing Finance Institutions (HFIs) recognized by the National Housing Bank and Public Sector Banks and the balance one lakh dwelling units in urban areas by the Co-operative Sector. Loans are disbursed by these agencies for constructions of dwelling units vide Table 23.5.

Table 23.5: Statement of Financial Allocation for Housing Under Various Schemes/Programmes

Organisation	Dwelling units (urban)	Amount (Rs. in crore)	Dwelling units (rural)	Amount (Rs. in crore)
HUDCO	2650000	6860.49	33309438	3791.42
Cooperative	555610	7476.71	—	—
HFIs	1275181	39606.51	—	—
Banks	1195758	35537.77	—	—
Total	5676549	89481.48	33309438	3791.42

Source: Ministry of Urban Employment and Poverty Alleviation, Government of India, September 27-28, 2004.

The Two Million Housing Programme (2MHP) is essentially a loan based programme. The sanctions under 2 MHP since its inception (1998-1999) till 2003-2004 in Urban areas by Housing and Urban Development Corporation Ltd. (HUDCO); Co-operative Sector; Housing Finance Institutions (other than HUDCO); and Public Sector Banks is given below. The sanctions in the rural areas for construction of dwelling units financed by HUDCO are also given below:

Tentative Figures

The primary responsibility for fulfillment of the targets in physical terms rests with the State Governments, while HUDCO and other agencies make the funds available in the form of loans. Hence the successful implementation of the scheme largely depends upon the cooperation of the agencies of the State Governments responsible for launching and implementation of various houing schemes. Housing Cooperative societies and private sector are encouraged to participate in the housing activity in a big way provided a facilitating environment is created by the State Governments in the form of legal, administrative and fiscal reforms vide Tables 23.6 and 23.7.

CONCLUSION

On the basis of the above discussion it is learnt that less than 30 per cent of the houses in rural areas classified as pucca houses while slightly over 70 per cent of the houses in urban areas classified as pucca houses. It may be conclusively stated housing is a serious problem in the rural areas where more than 70 per cent of the houses categorised as *semi-pucca* and *pucca* houses which are highly susceptible for fire and floods which often occur and damage the habitats resulting in colossal loss of lives and property worth of thousands of crores. Hence there is an imperative need to provide pucca housing facility to the rural people in India through activisation of IAY scheme by pumping needed funds to meet the housing requirements in the country.

Table 23.6: State-wise Target and Achievement of HUDCO in Urban Areas under Two Million Housing Programme from 1998-99 to 2003-04.

States/Uts	Target	1998-99	1999-2000	2000-01	2001-02	2002-03	2003-04
Andhra Pradesh	29388	33063	34316	24298	24599	67791	21451
Arunachal Pradesh	483	0	0	0	1600	0	0
Assam	20513	26250	0	314	0	195	1774
A andN Islands	181	0	0	0	0	0	0
Bihar	14873	383	0	0	0	128	512
Chandigarh	619	0	0	0	0	0	0
Chhattisgarh	9509	0	0	0	10202	11015	10184
Dadra &Nagar Haveli	45	0	0	0	0	0	0
Daman & Diu	60	0	0	0	0	0	0
Delhi	7848	0	0	0	2516	0	0
Goa	951	0	0	0	0	0	0
Gujarat	27184	13976	21970	3059	6801	18136	9259
Haryana	6113	2046	664	0	264	3263	0
HUDCO NIVAS	0	0	100000	0	75283	102366	4512
Himachal Pradesh	1645	0	0	0	0	0	0
Jammu and Kashmir	5328	0	0	0	557	0	894
Jharkhand	7662	0	0	0	500	10531	20000
Karnataka	23923	133708	55900	148384	49781	95083	277364
Kerala	12090	67568	64725	74800	4477	57449	10586
Lakshdweep	60	0	0	0	0	0	0
Madhya Pradesh	22188	50000	0	0	2749	5022	2335
Maharashtra	44240	18713	343	3442	8380	7894	34142
Manipur	4573	0	0	0	80	780	1607
Meghalaya	2777	0	0	0	0	0	0
Mizoram	6218	0	0	0	0	377	280
Nagaland	2581	0	0	0	139	463	667
Orissa	12423	12000	0	10284	1359	0	377
Punjab	8935	0	0	0	10000	4050	0
Pondicherry	679	0	0	0	170	0	457
Rajsathan	25071	0	0	0	8780	0	800
Sikkim	166	0	0	0	0	0	0
Tamilnadu	33750	18142	30600	11150	54519	17810	12026
Tripura	2717	0	1700	150	522	866	1076

Contd

Uttar Pradesh	36486	44550	0	0	126225	5711	9854
Uttarakhand	4509	0	0	0	2167	890	2135
West Bengal	24210	10000	150000	195000	9416	50149	5163
Total	**400000**	**430399**	**460218**	**470881**	**401078**	**459969**	**427455**

Source: Ministry of Urban Enployment and Poverty Alleviation, Govt. of India, September 27-28, 2004.

Table 23.7: State-Wise Progress of Housing Cooperative Under Two Million Housing Programme from 1998-99 to 2003-04 (Target: 1 lakh dwelling units per annum) (figures available as on 31-7-2004)

States / Uts	Number of Housing Units Constructed / Financed					
	1998-99	1999-2000	2000-01	2001-02	2002-03	2003-04
Andhra Pradesh	1287	1039	677	654	1012	122
Assam	1316	2340	0	2306	215	46
A and N Islands	10	0	0	0	0	0
Bihar	1985	0	2329	8	1	7
Chandigarh	1070	67	0	4184	4500	0
Chhattisgarh	0	0	0	5	1	0
Delhi	8793	4388	2563	197	337	519
Goa	562	3021	3417	4906	2259	2491
Gujarat	1811	3259	2138	1816	837	1058
Haryana	167	419	366	4565	3360	2830
Himachal Pradesh	139	52	42	240	243	0
Jammu and Kashmir	350	26	91	19	0	9
Karnataka	1838	1880	1264	2192	3105	2533
Kerala	7538	10534	10575	9695	22995	21761
Madhya Pradesh	2712	224	368	731	285	302
Maharashtra	9257	1.233	12775	14773	15042	16091
Manipur	132	176	0	0	52	627
Meghalaya	78	3	0	88	36	1
Mizoram	0	0	0	0	0	0
Nagaland	0	49	7	0	0	0
Orissa	1784	680	812	185	102	2694
Pondicherry	167	177	74	83	494	768
Punjab	4093	4489	3923	6308	2877	5261
Rajasthan	1039	1191	107	756	498	881
Tamilnadu	121630	42947	37377	14956	11716	2329
Tripura	10	24	28	0	0	0

Contd

Uttar Pradesh	6744	298	1029	2100	1908	1132
Uttarakhand	0	0	0	196	593	197
West Bengal	432	702	937	2696	993	2770
Total	**174944**	**88218**	**80899**	**73659**	**73461**	**64429**

Source: Ministry of Urban Employment and Poverty Alleviation, Govt of India, September 27-28, 2004.

The purpose of this section is to understand and analyse housing policies of the government and programmes evolved and implemented by the Central and the State Governments during the five decades of planning. It serves to appreciate housing adequacy and demand in proper prospective, it traces the origin of housing policy and explains the futures of the first and recent housing policies of Government of India; housing Programmes/Schemes designed to meet the housing needs and the important institutions, such as, National Housing Bank (NHB), National Building Organisation (NBO); Housing and Urban Development Corporation (HUDCO) and Nirmithi Kendras. This apart, it also covers a brief note on progress in weaker sections rural housing up to 2002 and "Two Million Housing Programme".

NOTES

1. Mooney, D.C., 1955, *Introduction to Human Geography*, p.3.
2. Editorial, *Yojana* 15-31, December, 1976.
3. *Economic Times*, 1st September, 1986, p.9.
4. Sreedharan, N., 1988, *Housing Market Analysis and Its Implications.*
5. *P.N.B. Monthly Review*, 10 (10), 12, Government of India, 1999, 9th Five-year Plan, Vol. II, Planning Commission, New Delhi, p. 282.
6. Cherunilam, Francis, 1996, *Housing Situation in the Third World*, Southern Economist, Vol. 25 (17) 33-35, P.7.
7. Government of India, 1986, *Textile Enquiry Committee Report*, Government of India, p. 67.
8. Government of India, *9th Five-year Plan, op. cit*, p. 292.
9. Government of India, 10th *Five-year Plan*, Vol.I, *op. cit.*, p. 299.
10. Government of India, 2002, *10th Five-year Plan*, Vol. I, Planning Commission, New Delhi, p. 19.
11. *HUDCO, SHELTER* A HUDCO Publication, October 1996, HSMI, Khelgaon Marg, New Delhi, p.4.
12. N.B.O., 1996, *Hand Book of Housing Statistics Part I*, N.B.O., Nirman Bhavan, New Delhi.
13. More, S.S., *Urban Housing Problem*, p.4.
14. Agarwal, S.C., *Industrial Housing in India*, p.54.
15. Lall, V.D., October 7-9, 1996, Assessment of Housing Need, National Housing Seminar on"Adequate Shelter for all", *Vigyan Bhavan*, New Delhi, p.5.
16. Suresh, V., April 2, 1999, "Budgetary Measures for Housing and Beyond", Keynote address Presented at the National Conclave on Housing, organized by FICCI, New Delhi, p.11.

Problems of Housing and Homelessness Families in the Rural and Urban Community

P. Subramanyam,
P. Tavitamma and
K. Srilakshmi

INTRODUCTION

Housing is one of the most primary human needs. Housing problem in India is very acute, particularly among the poor and other marginalized categories, in spite of the appreciable growth in institutional finance to housing in the ongoing reforms era. This is because, majority of the shelter less population is beyond the reach of the formal institutional system for housing finance. In fact, as per the 11th Five Year Plan (2007-2012) estimates[1], as of 2007 viz. the end of the 10th Five-year Plan (2002-07), the total urban housing shortage in India has been 24.71 Million units. Further more, of this 24.71 million units as high as 99.84 per cent belongs to EWS (Economically Weaker Section) and LIG (Low Income Group) categories. The balance 0.16 per cent alone relates to MIG (Middle Income Group) and HIG (High Income Group) put together. That is, 21.78 Million for EWS (88.14%), 2.89 Million for LIG (11.70%) and the balance 0.04 Million for MIG and HIG together (0.16%).[2] Besides the huge urban housing shortage as above, there is high rural housing shortage of seven Million also.[3] Thus, alternative financing models like micro-finance is essential to address 'the real housing problem' in India.

Housing problem in India is very chronic, particularly among the low income and such other marginalized groups who are beyond the reach of the formal institutional agencies for housing finance. Nearly the whole of the housing shortage in the country, as high as 99.84 per cent, relates to the above underprivileged group.

Definitions

According to the Stewart B. McKinney (1994), a person is considered homeless who "lacks a fixed, regular, and adequate night time residence; and has a primary night time residency that is:

(i) A supervised publicly or privately operated shelter designed to provide temporary living accommodations.

(ii) An institution that provides a temporary residence for individuals intended to be institutionalized.

(iii) A public or private place not designed for, or ordinarily used as, a regular sleeping accommodation for human beings."

PROBLEMS OF HOMELESSNESS

Homelessness is a phrase in which a broad range of people and circumstances are concerned. Homelessness is a primary existential displacement where people are living on the edge of life. All around the world, homelessness is a major problem due to several causes. Reports indicate that the number of homeless families has increased radically from last decades which may be an occurrence of natural disaster, scarcity and other significant reasons.

There are many issues concerning for homelessness. People are not responsible for their condition of homelessness but there are a number of sociological factors interconnecting at the same time to make people homeless. At present, people are dealing with problems in community setting which give rise to homelessness. One of the major causes of homelessness is poverty. Homelessness and poverty are attached together. Poor people are not in a position to pay for housing, food, child care, health care, and education. It had emerged in the 1980s because of the change over from an industrial based capitalist economy to a postindustrial capitalist service economy within the framework of globally developing global relations. Second most important cause of homelessness specifically among women is familial violent behavior. Feeble poor women are compelled to live with offensive relationships. They become homeless when violence is heated up. At national level, homelessness experienced by roughly half of all women and children is due to domestic violence.

Personal difficulties, such as mental disabilities or job loss, may increase vulnerability to homelessness, but they cannot explain the high number of people who fall into homelessness every year. And housing market trends indicate that the situation is getting worse rather than better. Current levels of housing costs, coupled with low-wage jobs and economic contraction, could push even the working poor out of their homes. Although the availability of homeless services increased significantly during the past decade, meeting the needs of people once they become homeless is not enough. A concerted national strategy is needed to prevent homelessness, and to end quickly discrete episodes of homelessness if they become inevitable. That strategy must include new housing resources as well as community-building strategies that address the societal factors contributing to homelessness. Each community must work to supply affordable housing, improve schools, and provide support services for those in need. Only strategies that address systemic problems as well as provide emergency relief can eliminate homelessness in this country.

Why Homelessness here, and Why Now?

Structural, personal, and political factors influence the level of homelessness and determine where it will occur most often:

- Changing housing markets for extremely low-income families and single adults are Pricing more and more people with below-poverty incomes out of the market.
- Dwindling employment opportunities for people with a high school education or less are contributing to the widening gap between rich and poor.
- The removal of institutional supports for people with severe mental illness, epitomized by drastic reductions in the use of long-term hospitalization for the mentally ill, are leaving many individuals with few housing options.
- That exclude affordable housing alternatives, persists in many areas.

If housing were inexpensive, or people could earn enough to afford housing, very few individuals would face homelessness. But housing costs have risen steadily across the country, and they have unavoidable situations in many areas. Further, the inability to afford housing is concentrated among households with incomes below the poverty level, whose members account for the vast majority of people entering homelessness. At the same time, people with little education or job training find it increasingly difficult to earn enough money to raise their incomes above the poverty level, even if they are employed full time and work overtime. Racial, ethnic, and class discrimination in housing, along with local zoning restrictions.

HOMELESS ADULTS TODAY

On any given day, the adult population using homeless assistance programs consists mostly of men by themselves (61%). Another 15 per cent are women by themselves, 15 per cent are households with children, and 9 per cent are people with another adult but not with children because families are mostly likely to qualify for public assistance programs, they are less likely. than individuals to be homeless, or to be homeless for long.

Childhood Homelessness

The homeless population includes not only adults but also the children these adults bring with them into homelessness. One-fourth of homeless people are children in homeless families. These children are much more likely than housed children to experience serious difficulties, including physical, cognitive, emotional, and mental problems. Further, childhood homelessness translates into a greater risk of homelessness in adulthood.

COMMUNITIES AND LEGISLATIONS AND POLICIES

Virtually all federal programmes related to homelessness focus on serving people who are already homeless. When assistance is restricted to those who are homeless tonight, not much can be done to prevent homelessness tomorrow. Developing capacity to serve those who are already homeless while ignoring prevention does little to change the underlying problems among the very poor. Only policies that expand the availability of affordable housing to people with below poverty incomes will ensure stable homes for these individuals. However, policies during the past decade have moved in the opposite direction.

The National Housing and Habitat Policy (Ministry of Rural and Urban Affairs and Employment, Govt. of India, 1998 aims to solve the "varied problems of shelter for the poor and the deprived" while also "the need for conserving our resources. This will ensure sustainable development of housing and settlements." The policy, keeping with the larger privatization focus of the government, concentrates on making the government an enabler rather than a provider or housing and related services. The policy aims to involve "women at all levels of decision making and enabling them in formulation and implementation of the housing polices and programmes". "Addressing the special needs of women headed households/single and working women/women in difficult circumstances. The specific requirements of women in terms of providing necessary facilities in homes to lessen their drudgery would be given sufficient attention" is also a policy aim. The policy also directs States to "confer homestead rights in the rural areas on the landless, persons from SC/ST community, rural poor and those displaced due to execution of development projects. Such rights may be given jointly in the name of both husband and wife."

SECURITY (PHYSICAL) AND PRIVACY

Every man, woman, youth and child has the right to live and conduct her/his private life in a secure place and be protected from threats or acts that compromise their mental and/or physical well-being or integrity. The state must address the security needs of the community once determined, in particular the needs of women, the elderly, children and other vulnerable individuals and groups.

STATE OBLIGATION

A synthesis of the jurisprudence of the Committee on Economic, Social and Cultural Rights, the European Commission and Court on Human Rights, the European Committee of Independent Experts and the contents of UN resolutions and legal texts addressing housing rights issues, set within the framework of the commonly accepted methodology of the four 'layers of obligations' (e.g. to respect, to protect, to promote and to fulfil) of States in terms of the right to adequate housing reveals much of the substance and core content of this right as recognized under international law. These can be divided into 34 discernable State obligations.

THE OBLIGATION TO RESPECT HOUSING RIGHTS

1. The right to popular participation throughout the housing sphere, including the right of citizens to influence and decide upon any housing laws or policies.
2. The rights to organize, assemble and association, particularly with respect to tenants organizations, community-based organizations and housing cooperatives.
3. Legal protection from forced or threatened eviction or house demolitions.
4. The right to equality of treatment, particularly in terms of the allocation of housing resources, access to housing finance and resident permits.
5. The right to privacy, including the protection from arbitrary searches of residences.
6. The right to be free from racial discrimination, particularly in the housing allocation process.
7. Tolerance and promotion of housing-related freedoms, including the right to self-help housing initiatives.
8. Ensuring respect for cultural attributes of traditional housing construction methods, the protection of housing of historical significance.
9. Refraining from coercive measures forcing another State to violate housing rights.

Objectives of the Study

1. To study and identify the Homeless People in the Urban and Rural Community.
2. To study the socio economic background of the homeless house holds.
3. To understand the problems of homeless families at the study area.

METHODOLOGY

The comparative study of homeless families in Tirupati Urban and rural areas. The researchers studied.

- Study design is description and analytical methods of research have been adopted.
- Chittoor dixtrict was purposely selected to study the various problems of homeless people in the Tirpat riral and urban mandals. Bommagunta Tirupati Urban and C.Gollapalli village in Tirupati rural Mandal was purposively selected for this study.

Sampling Procedure

At the first phase the researcher has been followed restricted quota sampling procedure. The researchers have interviewed 294 families in Bommagunta area in Tirupati urban Mandal and 219 families in C. Gollapalli Village Tirupati rural Mandal. Out of the total 513 families the researchers identified 56 families are homeless and they are living in huts, road side and rented houses. The researcher selected those homeless families as is sampling. This sample selected in deferent section of families in the study areas. Structured interview schedule was used to gather information.

ANALYSIS AND DISCUSSION

The researchers identified 56 homeless families out of 513 households in the Bommagunta Urban and C. Gollapalli Rural. (Table 24.1)

Table 24.1: Distribution of Category-wise Homeless Families

Sl.No.	Category	Rural	Percentage	Urban	Percentages
1	S.C	6	(3%)	10	(3%)
2	S.T	3	(1%)	-	-
3	B.C	2	(1%)	12	(4%)
4	O.C	-	-	15	(5%)
5	Minorities	-	-	8	(3%)
Total		**11**	**(5%)**	**45**	**(15%)**

Source: Primary Data.

PROBLEMS OF HOMELESS FAMILIES

Homeless families of Bommagunta Urban and C.gollapalli Rural are facing the following problems.

1. In the rainee seasons, main problem is the huts are collapsing during the rain. The people facing difficult to live in the rains, because of the rain water is directly flow into their huts thus they are difficult to stay in those huts. And also they difficulty to stay and sleep in winter and summer seasons.

2. The family members are facing/living inconvenience and incomparable live that huts. Why because single room to use all daily activities like bed room, dressing, kitchen and both etc.
3. The all family members due to execution all of the daily activities in a single room. So arising many health problems like skin allergies, sever headache, Bacteria and viral fevers, vitamin deficiency and also long term diseases.

CONCLUSIONS

Today the most dangerous process at play is the emphasis upon the instrumental value of a person, not the intrinsic value. Hence the need for human rights and the right to be human is even more paramount. However, the strategy to fight for these rights gets complicated since situations are located within changing philosophies of state role in development processes. With the sweep of globalization and liberalization, the onus of development initiatives has shifted to what has been called 'people's participation'. Hence programmes are now structured around self-help groups and people management committees. While there is no harm in involving people in planning processes and programme implementation, there is always the danger of the State's abdication of its duty towards citizens from the perspective of rights. The fine line has to be balanced between the involvement of people and the role of the state in meeting the basic needs of the people. Perhaps the answer lies within a rights-based perspective, since through it, vigilance on the part of people and transparency on the part of the state become mandatory.

Very little has been done to satisfy the basic housing rights and shelter needs of the completely shelter less or homeless urban rural population. The Homeless families living the Bommagunta Urban and C.Gollapalli Rural are economically very poor and they belongs to S.C, S.T, B.C, and minority communities. They don't have any property, even house site also. Because the government Housing programmes are not reaching properly to the poor people. Why because the Government sanctioned face by face limited target Housing scheme. Such the local influenced people getting Government Housing schemes, the poor people were not getting that schemes. The Government authorities identify the not getting the genuine homeless families to provide/sanction house loan or construct the houses for home less families. And the same time people also getting awareness to constructing the houses for the better living. For Example: The Andhra Pradesh Government incorporate the slum clearance board Tamilanadu.

NOTES

1. Anderson, E., and Koblinsky, S., (1995), Homeless Policy: The Need to Speak to Families, *Family Relations, 44*, 13-18.
2. Baker, S., (1994), Gender, Ethnicity, and Homelessness: Accounting for Demographic Diversity on the Streets, *American Behavioral Scientist, 37*(4), 476-504.
3. Bassuk, E., (1990), Who are the Homeless Families? Characteristics of Sheltered Mothers and Children, *Community Mental Health Journal,* 26(5), 425-434.

Index